Language and Sexual Difference

Feminist Writing in France

Susan Sellers

MACMILLAN

First published 1991

Published by
MACMILLAN EDUCATION LTD
Houndmills, Basingstoke, Hampshire RG21 2XS
and London
Companies and representatives
throughout the world

10 9 8 7 6 5 4 3 2
03 02 01 00 99 98 97 96 95

Printed in Hong Kong

British Library Cataloguing in Publication Data
Sellers, Susan
Language and sexual difference: feminist writing in
France. — (Women in Society).
1. French literature. Feminist writers. Critical studies
I. Title II. Series
840.909287
ISBN 0–333–44943–6 (hardcover)
ISBN 0–333–44944–4 (paperback)

For my mother and father

Contents

Acknowledgements

This book, like most others, could not have been written and would never have been completed without the help and support of family, friends, teachers, publishers and colleagues.

I would like to thank Hélène Cixous for her encouragement and inspiration, without which this project would never have happened, and Marguerite Sandré and Sarah Cornell, from whom I have learned so much.

I would like to thank Luce Irigaray, Julia Kristeva and Annie Leclerc for giving freely of their time to talk to me.

Jane Aaron's detailed and supportive reading of a first draft of this project was invaluable, as were initial discussions with Elizabeth Fallaize about French women's writing. I am also grateful to Elizabeth for acting as reader on the completed typescript.

Sue Roe read more drafts of this project than she probably cares to remember, and I am indebted to her not only for her constructive criticism, but for her patient and wise ear during numerous telephone and supper conversations. Alex Bennion and Adrienne Kern also read and commented on extracts from the typescript, and I am grateful to them for their belief that I would and could finish.

I am grateful to Margaret Whitford for the opportunity to discuss aspects of the book with her, for sending me articles and references, and for her encouragement.

I would like to thank my parents for providing me with a quiet corner in which to work, and Jonathan Wrobel for having faith in me and making the move to Paris possible.

I would like to thank Steven Kennedy for commenting on early drafts of the first chapters.

Jo Campling has been a beacon of practical help and emotional support throughout this project, and I am indebted to her for guiding me through the various stages of publication.

SUSAN SELLERS

The author and publishers wish to thank the following for permission to reproduce copyright material:

Basil Blackwell and Toril Moi for extracts from *The Kristeva Reader*; and Columbia University Press and Margaret Waller for extracts from Julia Kristeva's *Revolution in Poetic Language*.

Every effort has been made to contact all the copyright-holders, but if any have been inadvertently overlooked, the necessary arrangement will be made at the first opportunity.

Preface

If I could somehow remain outside the scene ... I would risk asking the ... master a few questions. Which he would not hear.

Luce Irigaray

It is the world of words that creates the world of things.

Jacques Lacan

My aims in this book are three. First I introduce the area of theory popularly known as 'French feminism' to non-French speakers by examining, with detailed reference to their theoretical and other writings, the works of Hélène Cixous, Luce Irigaray and Julia Kristeva. Secondly, in order to give a context to their work I have included introductions to the various theories that have shaped and influenced their writings, outlining the recent post-structural, linguistic, psychoanalytic and literary debates in France and, where appropriate, referring to a wider philosophical tradition. Thirdly, I shall demonstrate that whilst the writings of Hélène Cixous, Luce Irigaray and Julia Kristeva have been taken up by Anglo–American feminist critics as an important and challenging body of theory, both the issues that preoccupy them and a number of their conclusions are paralleled in the work of other French women theorists as well as in a range of contemporary French women's writing.

Although I have chosen, in line with common English usage, to retain the word 'feminist' in my title to refer to this body of writings, the appellation is in many ways inappropriate since few of the theorists or writers discussed here would unquestioningly accept the label as applying to their work. Both Hélène Cixous and Luce Irigaray, for instance, believe that the Anglo–American feminist preoccupation with equality forces women to function like men. Hélène Cixous to some extent side-steps the issue with her own definition of 'femininity', but since her definition needs explanation, and since there is no other word which adequately conveys the concern with subjectivity, sexuality and language that links the writers grouped in this book, I have retained the Anglo–American term 'feminist' which I use in its broadest sense to mean the challenge to the subordination of the female sex by a male-dominated world order.

Transposing the English term feminist into the very different French context has not been the only translation problem I have encountered in the course of this study. Since my aim is to make French feminism accessible to non-French speakers I have, however, omitted from my commentary all but the most glaring and important translational changes. Where possible I have rooted my introductions in texts already translated into English. Since subjectivity lies at the heart of French feminist debate, it is nonetheless worth mentioning some of the difficulties involved in translating the French subject pronoun into English. Nouns in French carry either a masculine or a feminine gender – 'hand' is feminine, for example, while 'arm' is masculine – and thus the masculine French word for 'subject' (*le sujet*) theoretically incorporates both men and women within its meaning. A number of French feminists however argue that the subject, because of the way it is constituted within patriarchy, *is* masculine. The French masculine subject pronoun (*il*) therefore both includes (according to common usage grammar) and effectively excludes (according to French feminist theories of the subject) women. The equivalent English pronoun 'he' fails to convey this complexity, since it omits women in a way the French term does not: but neither does the now commonly adopted English form 's/he' seem appropriate. The occasionally used English pronoun 'they' sometimes offers a better solution, although its plural connotation does have the effect of undermining the unicity taken by some French feminists to be a characteristic feature of the (masculine) subject. At the same time, any deliberate attempt to stress the feminine – as in Hélène Cixous' use of the French feminine word for 'person' (*la personne*) – is also lost in an English translation. My answer to this linguistic minefield has been to respond according to specific instances, and to choose whichever English form seemed most appropriate in any given context.

The area of French feminist writing I have focused on has developed from different roots and in a different direction to the mainstream of Anglo–American feminism, as well as to other French feminisms. Anglo–American feminism, including its academic and critical branches, has, on the whole, evolved from a grass-roots women's movement set up in the aftermath of the Civil Rights campaign in America, concerned to value women's experience and to protest against the political, social and economic injustices women endure,[1] whereas the French feminist writing referred to here is in the main a response to a *philosophical* tradition. This writing does not represent the whole of French feminism: Simone de Beauvoir for example, a pioneering French feminist in the 1950s, wrote extensively on the importance of social conditioning in women's oppression,[2] whilst the 1970s saw an increase in the number of grass-roots women's groups and campaigns for equal rights in France.[3] There are also many influential French feminists who refute the works of the theorists and writers I have included here for their 'ahistorical' reliance on biology and psychoanalysis (Monique Plaza) and for their failure to tackle the *material* conditions of women's lives (Christine Delphy).[4]

The link between the French feminist theorists and writers grouped together in this book is their belief that the way forward for women lies not in achieving equality with men within the present system, but in challenging the system itself. For French feminists Hélène Cixous, Luce Irigaray and Julia Kristeva, our history, our philosophy, our system of government, our laws, even our religions, are the products of a specific – masculine – mode of perceiving and organising the world. To understand this structure they draw on the works of twentieth century French philosophers and cultural interpreters, and re-examine those philosophies – such as the Greek philosophy of Plato – that underpin our current system.[5] To the French feminists included in this book our present system in the West is the result of a single – male – view of the world, encoded in our language and transmitted to us across centuries of learning so that it appears both natural and inevitable. It is in this sense that language is at the heart of French feminist debate. For many French theorists and writers it is language that embodies, carries and preserves man's vision of the world. The world has no intrinsic meaning prior to the structures we impose on it, and since it is in language that these structures are symbolised, language holds the key both to their understanding and to initiating change.

This emphasis has led to a number of differences with mainstream of Anglo–American feminism as well as other French feminisms. Whilst Anglo–American feminist critics have highlighted the role of language in women's oppression, stressing the power of 'naming' and the debilitating effects on women of our masculine or negative linguistic placing,[6] their insistence has not been as marked as that of French feminist commentators. To writers like Hélène Cixous, Luce Irigaray and Julia Kristeva, language is not only intrinsic to the way we think – the way we perceive ourselves and others and construct both our public and private persona and our knowledge of the world – but its omissions and restrictions cannot be righted simply by adding women's voices to the debate, or by the type of surface changes – such as the transforming of 'chairman' into 'chairperson' – that have become such a feature of Anglo–

American feminism. For many French feminists this endeavour is not only ineffective, since it fails to take account of the way the patriarchal system embodied in our language has repressed and made use of women's difference, but is even dangerous since it encourages women to believe we can achieve our potential *within* the existing system. To these French feminists, the Anglo–American emphasis on women articulating our experience and overcoming our conditioning to become men's equals is thus the wrong insistence. Not only do many French feminists challenge the Anglo–American notion that language can communicate our experience without affecting or creating what we say, but they see the preoccupation with equality as perpetuating the status quo in its failure to tackle – or even to recognise – the patriarchal constructions on which our society depends. Language, because of the particular world-view it encodes, represses, excludes or appropriates all other constructions; and thus it is in the repressed, feminine or unconscious 'other' of language – what language does not say – that the feminist revolution must find a base.

This emphasis has also led to differences in the area of feminist criticism. Whilst Anglo–American concern to value women's experience has given rise, in literary study, to the search for a female literary tradition and the positive representation of women characters,[7] for many French feminists this search is an erroneous one, since an 'other' (woman's) meaning can only exist in the gaps and blanks of our present language system. For these French feminists, the key is not *what* has been said, since this will inevitably be the result of our patriarchal schema and language, but the *process* by which meaning has been achieved.[8]

This emphasis has also given rise to a very different tradition of women's writing. Unlike the dominant realist modes of Anglo–American feminist fiction, with their articulation of women's experience and their creation of positive role-models,[9] to many French feminists these portrayals appear naive. Language encodes our experience, and because of the particular vision on which our language system depends, the problem for women is that we can *only* express ourselves in the language that symbolises the way man has perceived the world to be. Thus for many French feminist writers, the focus is not that of tracing or developing an authentic female voice, but on the contrary, lies in de-constructing the various symbolising procedures that hold the patriarchal vision in place, and which silence, distort and appropriate any other (woman's) view. To these French feminists, it is only by focusing on the *processes* by which language creates our meaning – as well as on what it omits – that women can begin to unravel the patriarchal structure that encloses us and, by disobeying its laws, begin to change the way we are perceived and hence end the stranglehold of the patriarchal system itself.

This different development also has implications for the structure of this book. Since the writing included here has evolved largely in response to a philosophical tradition, I begin each section with a brief account of the various theories that have informed and motivated the writing. These introductions include both the immediate post-structural, linguistic and psychoanalytic debates that have had such an impact on French intellectual life in recent decades, and the broader philosophical context, ranging from the work of the influential seventeenth century French philosopher Rene Descartes to the philosophy of Plato. Since so many of the French feminist writers I refer to here have been influenced by this philosophy, I believe this context is important. I thus begin each section by citing the various debates that have informed French feminist writing on the subject, reiterating and developing, where necessary, any further contextual points. This has led to a different style in the presentation of the contextual (male) theories and the French feminist responses. Since these contextual debates are not my main interest here, I have selected from a range of texts by each writer only those points I feel are necessary to understanding the French feminist account, referring the reader in the Notes section to the relevant English translations and further introductions and commentaries. This contrasts with my presentation of French feminist theory, where I introduce each individual writer separately – where possible with detailed page references to a direct English translation – and where I have tried to keep each new reference within the confines of a single text. This has created a certain disjointedness in my overall argument, since in order to fully convey the scope of a particular text I have sometimes repeated points made earlier, or which logically belong to another section. I have also tried wherever possible to use the words and explanations of the writers themselves.

Since part of my aim is to show how the concerns of French feminist theory are reflected and worked through in a range of contemporary French women's fiction, each chapter, with the exception of the Introduction, also includes references to French women's fictional writing, selected to illustrate the theme of each chapter. One of the major challenges of French feminism is its insistence that women's oppression must be understood *linguistically*, and thus these examples are intended to show not only how the recurrent themes of language and women's difference are also the preoccupations of many French women writers, but how a strategy of disrupting the symbolising process can itself create new forms of representation which in turn alter the power-balance of patriarchy. The space I have had available to present this wealth of women's writing has however been a limited one, and since, unlike the theory, very few of these texts are available in English,[10] my introduction to the fiction has once again taken a different direction to that of the contextual and French feminist theories. Since this book is *about* the repressive effects of a 'master' discourse, I am only too aware of the dangers in attempting to paraphrase an argument or story-line; I have therefore chosen, for the presentation of the fictional examples, to quote extensively, using my own translation, from individual texts. I hope that these different styles of presentation will reinforce the French feminist thesis that there is no such thing as an objective or neutral language, and that by introducing this complex, challenging and highly stimulating body of writings in this way, I will encourage readers where possible to turn to the source-texts for themselves.

Introduction

We are now faced with a monumental requirement. We must transform the subject in his relation to language, to the symbolic, to unity and to history.

Julia Kristeva

How can women analyze their own exploitation, inscribe their own demands, within an order prescribed by the masculine?

Luce Irigaray

Language has been a major area of intellectual inquiry in the twentieth century. The impetus for this new interest has come from the realisation of the crucial role language plays in our lives. Language is intrinsic to the way we think, to the way we construct our group and self identities, to the way we perceive the world and organise our social relationships and political systems.

In this introductory section, I have outlined recent linguistic debates, as these have developed in and influenced the French-speaking world, by presenting the work of the Swiss linguist Ferdinand de Saussure and the theories of three French cultural interpreters, Claude Lévi-Strauss, Michel Foucault and Roland Barthes, so as to provide a context for the very different interpretations of French feminism. In the second half of this section, I have introduced the writings of Hélène Cixous, Luce Irigaray and Julia Kristeva to show how their work both draws on and challenges these theories.

DIFFERENCE IN LANGUAGE

Signifier versus signified: Ferdinand de Saussure

The early twentieth century Swiss linguist Ferdinand de Saussure revolutionised the study of language in a number of ways. Here I shall pick out two of his ideas which are of particular relevance to French feminism.[1]

Saussure split language into two basic categories: the word – or *signifier* – and the concept – or *signified* – for which it stands. The letters c-a-t, for instance, or the sound of these letters as they are pronounced, constitute the *signifier* of the animal 'cat'. The *signified* of this signifier is not a cat as such, but the image of a cat that comes into our minds whenever we read or hear this word. Saussure argued that the relationship between signifier and signified is an arbitrary one. There is, he suggested, no actual reason why the word cat should stand for a feline quadruped, and dog for a canine one. Language is a system of convenience we employ to structure and transmit our experience of the world. It is the consensus of agreement amongst English speakers that c-a-t should designate a feline quadruped and d-o-g a canine one which brings these categories into play.

An illustration of Saussure's theory can be found in the way different languages distinguish colours. Colours are not distinct, separate bands, but part of a continuous spectrum of light which we divide for the sake of convenience into red, orange, yellow, green, blue, indigo and violet. These arbitrary divisions enable us to organise and communicate our experience of colour, and are an integral part of our ability to perceive different shades. The existence of the words brown and maroon, for instance, help us to differentiate between these two shades. In a language like French, where the signifier *marron* (maroon) is commonly substituted for the signifier *brun* (brown), this distinction is often blurred.

Saussure also argued that meaning is a result of the *differences* between signifiers. Thus the signifier cat evokes the signified cat because it is not bat or cap or cut. Meaning is the consequence of arbitrary differences between the signifiers of a given language system, and not the result of any intrinsic connection between reality and words.

Language as symbolic system: Claude Lévi-Strauss

The French anthropologist Claude Lévi-Strauss adapted Saussure's work on language to his study of primitive cultures. Drawing on Saussure's 'structural' approach to language as a system of meaning,[2] Lévi-Strauss showed how different symbols have different meanings within different cultures, thereby endorsing Saussure's view that there are no universal signifieds common to all humankind, only symbolic systems of signifiers, each dependant for its meaning on its position within a given system of reference. Lévi-Strauss cited the Asmat headhunters of New Guinea, who claim a special relationship with fruit-eating parrots and squirrels, as an example. Although as Westerners we might perceive a similarity between the shape of the human head and certain types of fruit, he argued that we cannot hope to understand the nature of the relationship the Asmat claim until we realise that the Asmat prize human heads as trophies, cracking open the skulls of their victims and eating the brains like fruit in a ritual ceremony.

In a work entitled *Introduction to a Science of Mythology*,[3] Lévi-Strauss developed his study of primitive cultures in an attempt to uncover a structure common to all mythologies. By translating the elements of different myths into codes, he demonstrated how the power of mythology lies not in the story told, but in the way it classifies and encodes reality. Myths, he concluded, have the same structure and function as language, and like language reflect and inform human perception and our understanding of the world.

In *The Elementary Structures of Kinship*,[4] Lévi-Strauss explored the way in which women are given significance in culture as 'objects of exchange'. He showed how men's exchange of women marks the foundation of a social order, entailing man's renunciation of the one instinct that can be deferred so as to enter into a system of social and cultural 'exchange' with others.

The construction of the other: Michel Foucault

The French philosopher and historian Michel Foucault has similarly developed Saussure's theory that meaning is a product of the differences between signifiers to explore the formative role of difference in the creation of group identity.[5] Foucault showed how, in order for a group to form, I, as a potential member, must perceive a resemblance between myself and the other group members. He argued that one of the ways in which a group's identity is forged (and mine as part of it) is through its recognition of its differences from other groups. He suggested that these perceptions of sameness and difference then create new orders within the group, as some elements designate themselves more 'same' than others. He believed these distinctions underlie all social hierarchy, as well as the structure of language and logic of thought. They operate as the fundamental organising principle in the way we think, speak and define ourselves in relation to others.

The nineteenth century German philosopher Georg Hegel provided a metaphor for the way in which identity is created through the opposition and hierarchical ordering of differences in his model of a master and his slave.[6] The model refers to the way in which masters define themselves in relation to their slaves, good in the context of evil, black in terms of white. Simone de Beauvoir, in her study *The Second Sex*,[7] develops the metaphor to show how the identity of the individual subject is created in relation to an object or 'other'; and she extends the argument to demonstrate how men have made use of women in order to guarantee their position as masters:

> She is defined and differentiated with reference to man and not he with reference to her; she is the incidental, the inessential as opposed to the essential. He is the Subject, he is the Absolute – she is the Other.[8]

Foucault devoted part of his research to exploring the ways in which this hierarchy of meaning operates in language. Extending Lévi-Strauss' insistence that there is no universal symbol that confers meaning on the world, he demonstrated how certain ideologies become encoded in language through the differentiating principle of the same equals the good and true to create our system of beliefs. Foucault examined the way in which these processes of distinction, opposition and exclusion have at various times in our history defined our conception of sexuality, criminality and insanity. He argued that reference to a norm is always a construct devised for the benefit of those in power, entailing the creation of 'laws' which both determine what is true and false, good and bad, acceptable and unacceptable, and justify the punishment of those who deviate from or challenge this norm.

One of the points that comes to light in Foucault's study is the fragile nature of the boundary between the dominant discourse of the controlling power group and those it marginalises. Simone de Beauvoir's account of the master–slave model provides an illustration of Foucault's argument. For 'man' to define himself in relation to 'woman' in the way Beauvoir suggests, man must in some sense resemble woman. He might for instance recognise in woman something he believes he possesses and thus wishes to repress in her; or she may appear to him to embody an attribute or quality he does not have but would like to possess. These principles are exemplified in man's conventional definition of woman as whore – in which repressed elements are projected onto women – or as virgin, with the accompanying desire for possession.

In addition to his historical and philosophical writings, Foucault explored the antithetical or 'other' discourses of such writers as the nineteenth century schizophrenic German poet Friedrich Hölderlin, the twentieth century French surrealist writer Antonin Artaud and the eighteenth century French 'pornographer' and asylum inmate the Marquis de Sade.[9] Foucault's insistence that the divisions between same and different are never obvious, and that the very process by which a dominant power group creates its ascendancy necessarily entails the repression of those elements it uses to distinguish and assert its primacy, led him to search the texts of marginal or consistently banished writers like de Sade for traces of this repression so as to reveal the nature of the ruling ideology.

The written text: Roland Barthes

Like Michel Foucault, the French critic Roland Barthes has explored the ways in which the prevailing ideology of the dominant power group works to conceal the processes by which it has attained power through an appeal to 'truths' presented in such a way that they appear natural, logical or inevitable. Like Foucault, Barthes argued that these processes are nevertheless revealed in the discourse and other cultural activities of the ruling group. In *Mythologies*[10] he shows how the prevailing ideology infuses even such apparently neutral texts as photographs. Citing the example of a photograph of a black soldier in uniform saluting the French flag on a front cover of the magazine *Paris-Match*, Barthes demonstrated how the picture means more than a French soldier's loyal salute. Appearing as it did at the time of the Algerian war for independence, the photograph implies the justice of the French cause. Its signified, Barthes suggests, is also French Imperialism, and an appeal for the continuation of French colonial rule.

In his work on literature, this insistence prompted Barthes to focus not on *what* texts mean, but on the *processes* by which meaning is achieved. His belief that a signifier can have several signifieds led him to develop a mode of criticism that would take into account the plurality of meanings in texts. He challenged those critics who attempt to fix a single, 'correct' meaning on a text, arguing instead for a practice of reading that would explore how meanings are created. He distinguished two different types of writer – the *écrivant* – or writer who believes they have something to say and uses language to say this as unequivocally as possible – and the *écrivain* – or writer who explores the potential of language to generate (multiple) meanings. He condemned the first type of writer, who like the old-style critic holds on to an illusory belief in intrinsic meaning and whose attempt to dictate how a work should be interpreted reveals his own ideological bias and desire for power, concentrating increasingly on the second type of writer or *écrivain*.[11]

Continuing this distinction, Barthes also distinguished between two types of text. He described the text of the *écrivant* as *lisible* – or readable – since the role of the reader is reduced to passively following the words on the page. An *écrivain's* text, by contrast, he referred to as *scriptable* – or writable – since the participation of its reader is actively sought to co-produce meanings. Barthes suggested that the *scriptable* text frees the reader from the tyranny of imposed definition, offering instead the possibility of 'other' meanings.

Drawing on the psychoanalytic theories of Freud (which I discuss in detail in Chapter 2), Barthes argued that the pleasure a reader experiences in reading a *scriptable* text is linked to the primary pleasures of infancy.[12] The word Barthes uses to describe this pleasure is *jouissance*, a word which it is difficult to translate into English since it means sexual as well as other forms of pleasure, but which may be thought of as the pleasure a reader feels in embracing the multiple, richly-textured and exploding layers of meanings in a *scriptable* text. For Barthes, the relationship between reader and text is an erotic one, and he suggested that what is offered in a *scriptable* text is the intimate body of the writer 'in process' – as it moves from a concern with meaning and nomination to the creative, merging pleasures and possibilities of language – an inter-play which is in turn offered to the participating (body of the) reader.

WRITERS OF THE FEMININE

The theories of the structural linguist Ferdinand de Saussure and those of their French interpreters Claude Lévi-Strauss, Michel Foucault and Roland Barthes offer a context for the works of the French feminist theorists Hélène Cixous, Luce Irigaray and Julia Kristeva. Drawing on post-structural accounts of the vital role of difference in language, subjectivity and the way we organise the world, their writings reflect, extend and radically challenge these accounts.

The philosophical ploy: Luce Irigaray

In her study *Speculum of the Other Woman*,[13] the philosopher, linguist and psychoanalyst Luce Irigaray examines the way in which our concept of difference depends on a single, male viewpoint. She suggests our entire system of thinking in the West has been determined by men for their own benefit, creating 'a matrix of appropriation for man' in which 'woman can only come into being as the inverted other of the masculine subject'. She explores the premises that underlie the theories of the 'great' philosophers from Plato on, revealing both their masculine bias, and how this bias has become encoded in our language and culture to reduce women to silence. Outlining her project in the 'Questions' section of *This Sex Which Is Not One* she writes:

> I am trying . . . to go back through the masculine imaginary, to interpret the way it has reduced us to silence, to muteness or mimicry, and I am attempting, from that starting-point and at the same time, to (re)discover a possible space for the feminine.[14]

Plato and Aristotle

Irigaray devotes almost a third of *Speculum of the Other Woman* to the work of the third century BC Greek philosopher Plato. The following account of Irigaray's work on Plato is taken from the essay in *Speculum of the Other Woman* entitled 'Plato's *Hystera*'.[15]

Irigaray suggests that the purpose of Plato's philosophy is to create a system of differences, determined in relation to a single idea, capable of leading 'man out of the cave' of his origin to a state of order. She argues that the formless and amorphous *khora* or cave,[16] metaphor for the matrix or womb, is perceived by Plato as a place of error and non-differentiation, and that this fear initiates a desire for order which entails the repression of the origin. This 'wisdom', she writes, is then transmitted by man-the-Father, as the 'so-called virginity and muteness' of the *khora* are re-constructed as a reflective space that will henceforth mark only his law's system of divisions.

Irigaray believes it is Plato's refusal to see anything other beyond what is reflected in his speculum[17] that has given rise to the practice of woman's appropriation and exclusion that continues to the present day. Confronted by the male gaze, woman's sex apparently presents 'nothing to see', and Irigaray suggests that women have been forced to accept this exclusively masculine 'dream of sameness' without reference to our own dreams or desires. Anything which cannot be defined by man's law, she stresses, has been branded as alien, and subjected to prohibition and denial.

Irigaray believes Plato's philosophy has had devastating consequences for women and men. 'By excluding the gaze of the other', she writes, his system has organised the world into 'a paralyzed empire', with disastrous effects on both sexes. Plato's insistence on the primacy of the father – that it is the father alone who is responsible for procreation ('will alone sow the good seed and be able to give it a proper name') – has, she argues, relegated the mother's function to that of 'mere receptacle': 'the matter needed to give birth to [the father's] deeds of credit'. From Plato on, she stresses, it is the father who has held all rights to property, whilst women have been reduced to a position of muteness or mimicry. At the same time, Irigaray suggests men's fear and subsequent determination to cut themselves free from the origin have forced them to abandon whatever dreams and fantasies cannot be accounted for in their self-ordered state.

In the same way that whatever is deemed non-visible, non-propertied and non-appropriable is excluded from man's 'economy of the same', Irigaray suggests that anything which does not fit the demarcations of its language remains unidentified, undistinguished or 'strange'. Our system of language, she writes, is also determined according to 'man's desire for the same', with the result that woman has become invisible. Even those areas which have not been delineated and given a 'proper name' are, she insists, circumscribed by man's desire; and she urges women to (re-)inscribe these 'spaces' as a way of challenging the patriarchal regime.

To this day Irigaray believes women's problem remains one of achieving definition within a male-demarcated schema. She suggests that under the present system the only way women can attain access to the 'circles of sameness' and thus to the 'heights of the intelligible' is by our accepting the dominant masculine order and allowing ourselves to be 'raised' to the stature of men. At the same time, she believes the very process of relegating the feminine to the reverse or outer side of the masculine-defined system invests it with a power capable of undermining the status quo. She suggests men may work towards change by acknowledging and confronting their fear, but argues that women's close relationship to the potentially disruptive place of alterity will provide the real impetus for revolution. Since man has not achieved the perfect definition of 'Himself as Same', she writes, the feminine has not been completely 'ringed in' or negated by male desire. She believes a new order may be at hand in which truth will lose its univocal and universal character, to be doubled or divided between *two different* genders.

In a second essay in *Speculum* entitled 'How to Conceive (of) a Girl' on the philosophy of Plato's pupil Aristotle,[18] Irigaray again locates fear as the motivating factor in the attempt to create order. She outlines how in Aristotle's work the power and mystery of the elements are gradually explained as a means of bringing them under man's control. She describes the state predating Aristotle's 'scientific' definitions as one of fusion in which 'same and other . . . have yet to find their meaning'; and she perceives an analogy between this state and the period in early infancy in which a child experiences itself as continuous with the m/other. She suggests that it is man's fear of 'formlessness' that institutes the '*Logos*' – reason, language and 'The Word' – as 'Origin beyond origins'.

René Descartes

In an essay entitled 'And if, Taking the Eye of a Man Recently Dead. . .'[19] Irigaray rereads the writings of the seventeenth century French philosopher René Descartes to show how the fear that motivated the work of the early philosophers continues to shape a system of exclusively masculine definition and control. Descartes' preoccupation is with the fact of his own existence, and Irigaray details how, in order to determine what exists, Descartes begins 'by saying no to everything'. As a result, she writes, his 'I' is completely self-absorbed, since he has removed the possibility of there being anything other than himself for his 'I' to think about. He ignores, for example, the possibility that there may be an other 'doubting "I"', as well as the fact that 'the mechanisms of thinking' are 'necessarily constituted by the other' before they can be 'appropriated by the self'. His 'I', Irigaray concludes, requires anything that might threaten the precision of his 'theoretical instruments' to be 'razed to the ground'.

Once Descartes' 'I' has thus assured itself it exists, it can, Irigaray argues:

> cut the sea into any number of pieces, subject her to any number of visual angles, inscribe her in an even vaster space in order to draw a line around her: a map of the world (p. 185).

However, in order to achieve this position of mastery, Irigaray stresses that Descartes' 'I' must first render itself impervious to the 'sea's' attractions:

> he must harden his heart to the glorious assault of her colours, to the fascination of her sheer size, to the seduction of her smells and sounds (p. 185).

Above all, she writes, his 'I' must hide from itself the fact that the truth it covets is no more than the desire to be united with his own (mirror) image.

One feature of Irigaray's critique of Descartes worth mentioning here is the form her own writing takes. In order to probe the premises of Descartes' thinking, Irigaray moves in and out of his subject, inhabiting the 'spaces' in his writing and making explicit what he does not say:

> Everything can be put in doubt, (it is) I (who) doubt(s), therefore (it is) I (who) am. The relation to the universality of being of the thinking and speaking 'I' is then assured. *Undoubtedly*. But he took good care not to suppose, not to presuppose, that some other 'I' might be doubting too (p. 181).

This strategy of inscribing the 'spaces' in Descartes' writing with her own meaning both reveals the premises on which Descartes' philosophy is constructed and undermines the certainty of his conclusions.

Immanuel Kant

In the essay 'Paradox A Priori'[20] Irigaray continues her exposition of the masculine bias of Western thought in relation to the influential eighteenth century philosopher Immanuel Kant. As in her critique of the work of Plato, Aristotle and Descartes, she locates the fulcrum of Kant's philosophy in his insistence on the transition from 'sensation to understanding', as the immediacy of the relation to the mother and diversity of feeling are again set aside. The point of Kant's reason, she writes, is not the existence of objects in and for themselves, but to organise their reflection in the imaginations of men. Kant devises a 'conceptual window' from which to view the world, and this window creates the foundation from which to impose his law on everything around him. Woman, Irigaray suggests, in the context of this philosophy exists only as a mirage, the 'imaginary sub-basement' that 'shores up the mine': 'Women are only useful in part, as openings–mirages that reflect this a priori proposition needed for the mind's/his *foundation*' (p. 212).

Georg Hegel

The work of the philosopher Georg Hegel is also scrutinised in *Speculum of the Other Woman* in an essay entitled 'The Eternal Irony of the Community'.[21] In this essay, Irigaray highlights the fear of death as the motivating influence in Hegel's creation of a dialectic, the explicit aim of which is to transcend the 'turmoil of contingent life' and 'the inner world of the senses'. Irigaray suggests that Hegel's 'rule of "law"' would be impossible in a situation where one was given as much value as the other; and she demonstrates how differences, in his philosophy, are appropriated or excluded in the attempt to institute the 'same'. Women, according to this 'logic', are relegated to the role of object:

> In her case 'I' never equals 'I', and she is only that individual will that the master takes possession of, that resisting remainder of a corporeality to which his passion for sameness is still sensitive, or again his double, the lining of his coat .... she does not achieve the enunciatory process of the discourse of History, but remains its servant, deprived of self (as same), alienated in this system of discourse as in her master and finding some hint of her own self, her own ego, only in another, a You – or a He – who speaks (p. 224).

Woman, Irigaray continues, has no gaze or discourse of her own that can render her own image, and thus no means of breaking the chain of identification that continues to hold women prisoner.Her role as 'male Other' ensures that woman's desire remains without expression. Irigaray suggests that it will be by exploring our desire that women may begin to undermine the power of the masculine state. If women were to step outside the role imposed on us as 'objects of consumption', she writes, a new mode of exchange might come into being based on a different system of logic. Woman's pleasure, she argues, represents 'the greatest threat of all to masculine discourse' since it is situated beyond patriarchal control.

An important aspect of Irigaray's reading of the 'great philosophers' is the order in which the essays collected in *Speculum of the Other Woman* appear. Instead of adopting the traditional chronological view of 'his'tory, Irigaray begins her analysis of Western thought with a discussion of the theories of Sigmund Freud, then reads backwards and forwards through the writings of Plato, Aristotle, Descartes, Kant and Hegel, interspersing her critique with an essay on mysticism and her own inditement of the patriarchal ploy. This format enables her to reiterate key ideas and gradually build awareness of their full significance as they become more familiar to the reader, and to highlight the general pervasiveness of the male order which is no longer seen to be the legacy of any one historical time.

The Father's Word: Julia Kristeva

The linguist, psychoanalyst and critic Julia Kristeva has been an important figure on the French intellectual scene since her arrival in Paris from Bulgaria in 1966. She spent her first years in Paris working with such influential thinkers as Roland Barthes, until the publication of two books, and then her doctoral thesis *Revolution in Poetic Language* in 1974,[22] earned her a chair in linguistics at the University of Paris VII. Like Luce Irigaray, Kristeva has developed accounts of how Western society is founded on the recognition and appropriation, repression or destruction of difference from a feminist viewpoint. In *About Chinese Women*[23] for example, she highlights the role of sexual difference in the creation of linguistic and social order. Like Luce Irigaray, she believes the monotheism of Western society is sustained by a radical split between the sexes, since only by distinguishing an other sex can patriarchy establish 'the principle of One Law' on which its order depends. In a number of books as well as in numerous articles and essays, Kristeva demonstrates how women have come to occupy this place of other through the structural necessity of there existing a blind spot enabling those identifying as 'the Same' to construct their position. 'The idealization of woman', she writes in *Revolution in Poetic Language*, is the inevitable outcome of patriarchy's refusal to organise itself around 'the *differential* but nonhierarchizing status of opposed groups' (p. 50).

Kristeva continues her argument in *About Chinese Women* with an account of how patriarchy became the founding order in the West. She suggests that in order to survive geographical dispersion and the threat of invasion, the nomadic communities from which Western society is descended gave increasing status to the role of the word. Acting first as an agent of cohesion, she argues that language became the sole legislating principle for these communities. As feminist anthropologists and historians have pointed out,[24] it becomes an easy step, once power is no longer centred in the material conditions of human existence but transferred to the abstract code of words, for men to assume the responsibility of procreation for themselves. Language, Kristeva argues, through the jurisdiction of the (father's) word, makes patrilinear descent a possibility. Like Lévi-Strauss, she shows how women came to occupy the position of 'permutative centre' within these nomadic communities, with no intrinsic value of their own except as objects of exchange.

As an example of the patriarchal process, Kristeva rereads the biblical account of Adam and Eve in the garden of Eden. She illustrates how, within this scene, the serpent is made to symbolise not only evil, but everything that is outside the paternal code. She suggests that Eve is made to stand as the polar opposite to God-the-Father's Ward as 'the other race' – embodying transgression and jouissance, as well as their punishment in death.

Kristeva suggests in *About Chinese Women* that it is the rule of Christianity which represents the ultimate victory of patriarchal monotheism over a variety of matriarchal, fertility-oriented religions. Within Christianity, she argues, motherhood is seen as a sign of jouissance of the female body and as such is rigorously repressed. Like Luce Irigaray, she believes this repression of women's 'pleasure' to be an important component of the patriarchal state.

Although women have been denied access to the paternal rule of the word, Kristeva suggests that women must neither refuse linguistic order nor accept the model of femininity patriarchy prescribes. She urges women to look beyond the roles allocated by patriarchy and to summon our own truth – the 'echo of our lost jouissance'. Since this truth cannot be fitted into the established order of language and social symbol, it cannot, she believes, be designated as true or false by the prevailing law, and so remains silent, invisible, situated 'outside time'. Like Luce Irigaray, she stresses the present difficulty of perceiving and giving expression to this truth. Only by listening to what is unspoken, she writes, by attending to what is repressed, new, eccentric, incomprehensible and therefore threatening to the paternal code, can women hope to disrupt its order and acquire our own voice. It is in this sense that Kristeva sees language as potentially revolutionary. Only through language, she insists, in an essay entitled 'A New Type of Intellectual: The Dissident',[25] can we hope to bring about the multiple and necessary 'sublations of the unnameable, the unrepresentable, the void'; only by dismantling the very bases of patriarchy, beginning with its language and working from language to its culture and institutions, can we hope to initiate social and political change.

Woman's abasement: Hélène Cixous

Like Luce Irigaray and Julia Kristeva, Hélène Cixous, novelist, playwright, critic, professor of literature at the University of Paris VIII and director of the Centre d'Etudes Féminines (Centre for Feminine Studies) which she founded in 1974, sees women's relegation to the role of other as a result of the binary structure of masculine thought: 'everywhere', she writes in an essay entitled 'Sorties' (translated into English as 'Out and Out: Attacks/Ways Out/Forays') in *The Newly Born Woman*,[26] 'a law organizes what is thinkable by oppositions'.

Like Julia Kristeva, Cixous believes that the established pattern of perception and classification in the West is organised 'through dual, hierarchical oppositions'; like Luce Irigaray, she believes man's 'desire to be (at) the origin' has initiated a process of separation in which the 'Selfsame' – 'the ownself (– what is mine, hence what is good)' – is differentiated from whatever 'menaces my-own-good': 'is "other"' – a pattern to which 'all concepts, codes and values' have subsequently been subjected. Like Luce Irigaray and Julia Kristeva, Cixous sees this movement of opposition and oppression in a historical perspective. 'Everything throughout the centuries', she writes in 'Sorties', has been subordinated to this 'Empire of the Selfsame' in which men have decreed what is same and so defined and assigned their other. She recalls, as an example of this process, her own childhood experience as a European jew in French colonised Algeria. She describes how at the age of three or four, she was confronted by the knowledge that 'the world is divided in half' and that 'the great, noble, "advanced" countries' had constructed their position by enslaving whatever they had deemed to be 'strange'. Just as the 'master–slave dialectic' requires 'what is strange' to be 'conquered and returned to the master', so, she writes, the oppressed peoples of the world are employed by those in power to create and perpetuate their dominion.

Like Irigaray and Kristeva, Cixous believes women have been among the main victims of man's desire for power. Like Irigaray, she argues that our system of thinking in the West has been constructed 'on the premise of woman's abasement', on the 'subordination of the feminine to the masculine order'. 'Black to his white', she writes in 'Sorties', woman is the 'strangeness' man 'likes to appropriate', her function being to enable man to 'see himself seen as he wants to be'. Like Irigaray, she suggests that men 'have theorized their desires as reality', imparting their wishes to woman's 'virginal space' without taking into account the fact that women may have desires of our own. Woman, she insists, only exists as the passive condition of man's order; with the result that women's specificity has become 'unthinkable, unthought'.

In 'Sorties', Cixous stresses that the only way out of this impasse that she can foresee is to refuse to comply with the quest for mastery. She sees man's will for power as the mainstay of Western ideology, founding and perpetuating our social, political and cultural status quo. Even knowledge, she suggests, is caught in this system of binary logic, rendering it inaccessible and sacred, and thus preventing those it subjects from questioning its authority. She concludes that the only way forward is to tear down this 'vast membrane' fabricated by the masculine, overcoming its repressions through the inventive possibilities of language.

Like Julia Kristeva, Cixous believes language has played a crucial role in the creation of patriarchal order. In 'Sorties', she argues that men's cleverness has been 'in passing themselves off as father', using 'the naming trick' of laying claim to a child in order to make it their own. In this way, she writes, they have succeeded in 'repatriating' the potential threat of women's sexual specificity, assuming its power for themselves. Paralleling Kristeva's insistence on the diversity of matriarchal religions prior to the monotheistic and patriarchal order of Christian rule, Cixous rereads the Greek tragedy of *The Oresteia*[27] as an illustration of the struggle between 'blood' and 'words'. In *The Oresteia*, she suggests, the bond with the mother is loosened, as Orestes' call to his father initiates a new order of legitimation based on the supremacy of the word. The indistinctness of the boundaries between life and death – as well as the 'abundance' that characterises woman 'the life-giver' – are, Cixous argues, subsequently dispensed with in a new relation to the body, life and death. As a result of this new order, the validation for life and death derives directly from the sovereignty of the (father's) word. Like Luce Irigaray, Cixous believes it is women who will bring about change. In 'Sorties' she writes:

> we must threaten the stability of the masculine structure that has passed itself off as eternal-natural, by conjuring from femininity the reflections and hypotheses that are necessarily ruinous for the stronghold still in possession of authority (p. 65).

She suggests that this shift from masculine to feminine[28] will transform in ways which are as yet unthinkable the entire structure of our society: 'another thought which is yet unthinkable – will transform the functioning of all society'.

Cixous argues that once society is freed from the tyrannous law of masculinity, ways of relating will come into being other than those currently prescribed. She suggests that this other, feminine mode of relating will be founded on love, though not as we presently interpret this word, caught up as it is in the 'contradictions and ambivalences entailing the murder of the other' that are the characteristic of masculine rule. Unlike the current '(Hegelian) scheme of recognition', she stresses, in which there is 'no place for the other': 'for a whole and living woman', she sees the new 'feminine economy' as engendering a love relation in which 'each one would keep the other alive and different': 'each would take the risk of other, of difference, without feeling threatened by the existence of an otherness, rather, delighting to increase through the unknown that is there to discover'.

Cixous suggests that masculine appropriation of the feminine has (re)produced itself throughout the course of 'his'tory, engendering all 'relationships of production and reproduction', with the result that 'for a long time it has been impossible (and it is still very difficult) to think or even imagine an "elsewhere"'. Like Luce Irigaray and Julia Kristeva, she believes patriarchy is neither destinal or natural; and she stresses its disastrous impact on *both* sexes.

Cixous draws on Freud's theory of psychoanalysis for an account of the way patriarchy has defined and used sexual difference to found a hierarchy of the sexes in which the masculine is privileged at the expense of the feminine. In 'Sorties', she suggests that one way of viewing the difference between these two positions is in relation to the 'problematic of the gift'.[29] The masculine subject, she writes, can experience himself as such 'only when he makes his law . . . and his mastery felt'. Like Luce Irigaray, she believes 'he' only exists in relation to his property, and thus his 'gift' functions only to reinforce his own position: 'plus-value of virility, authority, power, money, or pleasure'. His gift, she stresses, is always a 'gift-that-takes', and she argues that Western society has been set up on this premise, in opposition to and at the expense of the feminine. Like men, Cixous believes women also 'give *for*': 'giving ourselves as we give others pleasure, happiness, increased value, enhanced self-image'. But, she insists, unlike man, woman doesn't try to 'recover her expenses': her gift is extravagant, free, and genuinely desiring of the other's pleasure. I shall return to the differences between these two positions of masculine and feminine in their relation to sexuality, language, and social and political transformation in the ensuing chapters.

1

Women and language

The women say it is necessary to disregard the discourses one has made them uphold against their thoughts and which have obeyed the codes and conventions of the cultures that have domesticated them... The women say there is no reality before words rules statutes have given it form... The women say that in the first place the vocabulary of every language is to be examined, modified, utterly shaken up, that each word must be screened.

Monique Wittig

Now, I-woman am going to blow up the Law ... let it happen, right now, in language.

Hélène Cixous

THE LAW OF LANGUAGE

Post-structural accounts of the role of language in the formation of social and individual reality have had a major impact on French intellectual debates in recent decades. In this first of two chapters exploring the French feminist view of language, I shall outline how French feminists have theorised the role of language in women's oppression and show how language is also a central preoccupation of a range of contemporary French women's fiction. One critic who has had an important influence on debates on language is the French philosopher Jacques Derrida, and, in keeping with my intention to present French feminism in context, I shall begin this first chapter on women and language with a brief introduction to his work.

The signifying process: Jacques Derrida

Developing Saussure's thesis that meaning is a result of the differences between signifiers, Derrida demonstrates how part of the process by which signifiers 'mean' takes place beyond linguistic formulation.[1] Cat, in a sentence like 'the cat sat on the mat', conveys the signified of a furry, four-legged animal with whiskers and a long tail, not just because it is distinguishable from the other elements in the sentence – 'the', 'sat', 'on' and 'mat' – but also because it is differentiated against elements *absent* from the linguistic structure. 'Cat' also denotes cat because it is not 'hat' or 'ham' or 'hug'. . .

This insistence that meaning is the product of a potentially infinite system of both present and absent differences led Derrida to view meaning as being the result of a ceaseless and fluctuating *movement* across an entire linguistic formulation. He argued that meaning is both *progressive* – modified and enhanced by whatever it is followed by – as well as *retroactive* – informed by meanings already introduced. Derrida's theory provides an important extension from the structural accounts of meaning as the product of a congruent relationship between signifiers and signified. For Derrida, words do not contain meaning, rather meaning is produced round and through them as they distinguish, act upon and suggest each other. In the same way that words are traced through with their differences from other words – and thus can never exactly or in themselves denote any single or consistent meaning – so, Derrida argued, the meaning of a sentence is never completely designated by the interaction of the components of which it is made.

To describe this view of meaning, Derrida coined the term *différance*, taken from the French verb *différer* meaning 'to differ' as well as 'to defer', but also marking a *différance* from both these meanings by changing the usual *-ence* ending to *-ance*. For Derrida meaning is the effect of a ceaseless process of present and absent differences that can never be halted and pinpointed to equal 'this' or 'this'. It is always differant, always referring back to other meanings or suggesting the possibility of new ones, always endlessly deferred.

Derrida suggested that as a result of this process, it is impossible for a language user to ever take full possession of what they write or say. Not only does language constantly evoke other meanings which both exceed and disrupt the language user's intentions, but it also reveals the processes by which the writer or speaker has attempted to organise and direct what they say. Derrida argues that this is particularly true of writing, since a written text can *always* be read so as to 'deconstruct' the procedures by which the writer has striven to gain control. A writer can neither guarantee that what they intend will remain unimpaired by the signifying operation of language, nor how their text will be received.

Derrida's insistence that meaning is always other and cannot be reduced to any single or fixed meaning implies a radical critique of those systems which posit a signified – such as God, Nature, Logic, Reason or Truth – as the origin of meaning. For Derrida, our knowledge of the world is a *result* of language, organised and communicated by the linguistic procedure which also imposes its own format, 'logic' and rules. He challenges the notion that there can be any transcendental truth beyond language: what meaning there is, is an effect of the signifying process.[2]

Derrida describes the various philosophies that have attempted to erect a transcendental signified which will confer meaning on the world as 'logocentric', from the Greek word *logos* or 'word'. Like Luce Irigaray, Julia Kristeva and Hélène Cixous he perceives the effort to establish an 'origin' as masking the desire to lay claim to the world by organising it in a particular way.

Derrida's theory of *différance* has prompted him to argue for a mode of writing that will not impose a (single) meaning but will consciously work to incorporate all the possibilities for meanings generated by the signifying operation. His own writing-style matches his description, abandoning notions of a 'meta' or pseudo-objective critical language to include as many of the markers and effects of *différance* as possible. Derrida has called his writing-style 'a dance of the pen', and he employs paradox, puns and even crosses words through to show how they both ~~mean~~ (and do ~~not~~ mean) what they appear to mean. His strategy highlights the disseminating potential of language, and the 'erasure marks' remind us of the intrinsic inadequacy of words – as well as our inability to do without them.

Derrida's work presents a number of concepts which are reflected in, developed and, in some cases, rejected[3] by the writings of French feminists. Derrida's insistence that language constantly evokes other meanings which exceed, contradict or disrupt the intended meaning, and that the written text, in particular, can always be read 'other'wise, as well as his argument for a type of writing that will explore rather than seek to impose meaning, all have powerful links with the work of a number of French feminist writers. To introduce French feminist writing on language, I now explore in detail a number of texts by French feminists, beginning with a collection of essays by Luce Irigaray.

The language of man: Luce Irigaray

In the essay in *This Sex Which is Not One* entitled 'Women on the Market',[4] Luce Irigaray reiterates her belief that the Law which organises Western culture is that of the masculine desire to distinguish, reproduce and exchange the 'same' image. Woman, she stresses, under this regime, only has value in relation to the masculine: her role is split between the triptych of 'mother, virgin, prostitute'; she is the *other* in an exclusively male system, with no value or attributes of her own apart from her ability to reflect (the image of) man:

> The society we know, our own culture, is based upon the exchange of women. Without the exchange of women, we are told, we would fall back into the anarchy(?) of the natural world, the randomness(?) of the animal kingdom. The passage into the social order, into the symbolic

> order, into order as such, is assured by the fact that men, or groups of men, circulate women among themselves, according to a rule known as the incest taboo (p. 170).

In a second essay 'Cosi Fan Tutti',[5] Irigaray develops her account of man's appropriation of women's 'difference' in relation to language. She writes: 'every reality is based upon and defined by a discourse', and she stresses that this *includes* sexual reality:

> the sexes are now defined only as they are determined in and through language, whose laws, it must not be forgotten, have been prescribed by male subjects for centuries (p. 87).

As a result of this prescription, Irigaray continues, women have become the 'body-matter': the 'breach', 'lack', 'fault' or 'flaw' in which man's formulation of himself as (speaking) 'subject' can take place. Woman's absence from linguistic expression, she concludes, ensures man's position as (masterful) subject.

Irigaray suggests women can, under the present system, do little more than mimic (p. 189) the language we have had no share in creating. She insists that any attempt to 'speak' within the terms of the existing schema will merely reproduce its repressive hierarchy. As long as masculine law remains in force, she argues, our own natures will remain amorphous (p. 189) and unknown to us, since even our unconscious has been assigned and demarcated by men: 'an intolerable debt', of which men acquit themselves by fantasising that what women want is 'the part of his own body . . . he most highly values'. Irigaray does not, however, believe that this means women should passively succumb to the fate mapped out for us by the masculine. Her own writing consistently strives to reveal the mechanisms of the masculine structure and to suggest other – feminine – possibilities through the signifying potential of language. In 'The Power of Discourse and the Subordination of the Feminine',[6] she stresses the power of the feminine to disrupt and transform the masculine state. She suggests that this 'revolution' will take place through language. Like Hélène Cixous and Julia Kristeva, Irigaray sees language as the mainstay and medium of the patriarchal system, and she insists that only through language can women hope to challenge its law and create new forms. In particular Irigaray believes we must pay especial attention to the language of philosophy. 'It is', she suggests, 'philosophical discourse that we have to challenge, and disrupt, inasmuch as this discourse sets forth the law for all others, inasmuch as it constitutes the discourse on discourse'. She calls for an 'interpretive rereading' – such as is undertaken in psychoanalysis – of philosophy. 'We need', she writes, 'to listen (psycho)analytically' to its 'procedures of repression', its grammar, syntactical rules and choice of images, as well as to 'what it does not articulate at the level of utterance: its silences'.

In 'Commodities Among Themselves',[7] Irigaray explores the possibility of an other – feminine – mode of exchange deriving from women's marginalised position: a position that is, at least in part, exempt from masculine law. She suggests that if women were to refuse to reproduce the masculine – 'socializing in a different way the relation to nature, matter, the body, language, and desire' – women might finally begin to create amongst ourselves a new 'schema'. In '"Frenchwomen", Stop Trying',[8] she takes this suggestion a step further, arguing that it will be by articulating our own dreams and desires that women will break down the bastions of male law. She urges women: 'don't congeal your dreams or desires in unique and definitive representations', and she stresses the need for women to explore our own natures without succumbing to masculine boundaries or constraints. Whilst Irigaray emphasises the present difficulty of expressing any new form of exchange, she believes this will mark a number of differences from the masculine, having no 'identifiable terms', no 'accounts', sequence or end, and involving 'enjoyment without a fee, well-being without pain, pleasure without possession'.

At the end of 'Cosi Fan Tutti', Irigaray looks forward to a feminine style based on a new articulation that will attend to the gaps in discourse as well as to its markers, and entailing respect for the other as well as for the self. Like Hélène Cixous, Irigaray envisages this new language as a 'language of love', since she believes the relationships between subject and object, man and woman will necessarily be transformed. Instead of a language-system dependant on the appropriation and abasement of those designated as 'un-like', she sees this new language as involving a new relation to the other and hence entailing different possibilities for the self: 'surrounding, adorning, engulfing, interpellating oneself with the Other', she suggests, will henceforth be the means 'to speak oneself'.

Blowing up the law: Hélène Cixous

Like Luce Irigaray, Hélène Cixous sees language as fundamental in women's oppression. In 'Sorties'[9] she suggests that it is through language that man has succeeded in implementing his desire for mastery, obliterating all possibility of other. 'Woman has always functioned "within" man's discourse', Cixous writes, 'a signifier referring always to the opposing signifier that annihilates its particular energy [and] puts down or stifles its very different sounds'. Language, she concludes, has become the 'Empire of the Selfsame'; and she urges women to 'break into' language, exploding the law of its discourse to make language 'fly'.

Like Irigaray, Cixous argues that it will be by writing women's 'bodies' – by inscribing our sex-specific rhythms and desires – that women will begin to topple the repressive structures of (masculine) thought. 'What happens to the subject, to the personal pronoun, to its possessives', she asks, 'when, suddenly, gaily daring her metamorphoses (because from her within – for a long time her world, she is in a pervasive relationship of desire with every being) she makes another way of knowing circulate?' She suggests that women's liberation in language will be the crucial first step towards a new form of exchange, through the inscription of woman's 'uncensored relationship' to her sexually 'other way of producing' with its potentially other model of social 'communication'.

Cixous' insistence on 'writing the body' derives both from her belief in the potential of women's sexually different relation to the other[10] and in the impetus of the body-drives as these punctuate and propel writing. Her insistence parallels that of Roland Barthes, who perceives the writing 'body's' active participation in the *pleasure* of writing as combining with the infinite possibilities of the signifying process to produce other meanings.

Like Luce Irigaray, Cixous sees women's writing as a powerful instrument for change. 'It is the invention of a new, insurgent writing', she argues, that 'will allow her to put the breaks and indispensable changes into effect in her history'. Like Irigaray, Cixous believes women's writing will create an 'elsewhere' in which 'the other will no longer be condemned to death', and in which 'that something else (what history forbids, what reality excludes or doesn't admit)' can finally manifest itself.

In the title essay of *La Venue à l'écriture* ('Her Arrival in Writing'),[11] Cixous refers to the multiplicity of languages into which she was born – German, French, Arabic, English – to demonstrate that there is no definitive language, since the meaning of one language can never be fully translated into another. There is, she insists, 'no centre of the world', and she urges men to relinquish the attempt to master language and to embrace, instead, the plurality of language*s*: 'adoring' language's differences: 'respecting its gifts, its talents, its movements'.

Cixous's novel *Angst*[12] offers a vivid illustration of the way language entraps and suppresses women. At one point in the novel, the 'he' addresses the (feminine) 'I', and the address becomes an example of the manner in which the masculine appropriates and subjects the feminine:

> He was playing chess with himself. He didn't place a word until he had measured his chances of protecting it. On the defensive. All the sentences calculated with an enemy in mind (p. 127).

Confronted by his address, the 'I/she' is 'summoned, pressed, beseeched' by the web of his words 'to join him in a quarrel whose origins I didn't know'. As she listens, she realises that the subject of the quarrel is his need to construct himself in the masterful position: 'I suspected him of wanting to fabricate a story for himself. To trap me in. I felt I was turning into his fly' (p. 127). Trapped in his story, the I/she loses all sense of her own – feminine, other – identity:

> I was crouching on the divan, in the corner with no shield .... I saw him cheerfully moving to and fro weaving, making knots .... It was a question of my whole life. He was pulling it to pieces, I wasn't living it. He separated, unwound, killed, cut, picked through, eliminated, re-made me .... And all in praise of his fictions, he was annihilating my reality (p. 131).

The novel also explores why, within the current system, it is so difficult for women to resist this masculine address:

> Recaptured. Stopped. Condemned to listen to them . . . they had absolute power over blood and mind .... Nothing could resist them. They would have captured me even if I had shut my eyes. As if it had been written that I would obey them. And each letter repeated that necessity .... They dragged me before him by force, into his story .... I felt myself summoned by the sentence that rejected me (p. 135).

As in her more theoretical writings, the novel looks towards an other language in which the pattern of relationships will be different to those dictated by the masculine. In *Angst*, Cixous suggests that this will be a language in which 'she' will also have the status of subject: 'a sentence with room for me in it' (p. 200).

Inventing new words: Marie Cardinal

In a text entitled *Autrement dit* ('Otherwise Said'),[13] based on a series of tape-recorded conversations with philosopher and writer Annie Leclerc, writer Marie Cardinal describes her experience as a young woman growing up in the French colony of Algeria. Like Hélène Cixous, she recounts how this experience brought her into direct confrontation with 'History' (p. 44), and she relates how she underwent a period of psychoanalysis in which she attempted to come to terms with the laws that had impinged on her as a woman. She argues that women must open the words that operate as laws if we are to discover our own existence (p. 53), and she urges women to 'invent the words' that will 'fill in the spaces left empty in our language' – those 'immense unexpressed and essential domains which are all, as if by chance, feminine domains' (p. 87). She argues: 'the words for telling it, the true words, the words of beginning, those of birth, are all shameful, ugly, dirty, taboo' (p. 81), and she describes how, as a writer, she constantly feels restricted by language 'either because there are no words or because French words are so invested by men that they betray me when it is I, a woman, who uses them' (p. 96). Like Luce Irigaray and Hélène Cixous, she suggests that this new 'invention' must begin from the inscription of women's sexual and unconscious experiences:

> We must write. Tracing day after day our own text in letters of blood, of light, of love. Subverting day after day the other text which prevents us. So that day after day we undermine it, we sap it, we compel it little by little to lose its force (p. 222).

She believes this (re)inscription by women of the 'essential' questions will transform the current order, to the benefit of both sexes:

> How can we say our sex, the experience of pregnancy, time, women's endurance? We must invent. Language will feminise itself, will open

> itself, will embellish itself, will grow rich. Our sorority will be fecund and welcoming for our words will serve everyone (p. 89).

Investing the spaces: Nathalie Sarraute

Writer Nathalie Sarraute, one of the older generation of French women writers, focuses in a text entitled *L'Usage de la parole* ('The Use of the Word')[14] on a typical family group to demonstrate how language provides order, definition and the possibility of social interaction by attributing to each family member their individual identity, function and place (p. 53). Language, Sarraute implies, is a social necessity, shaping our experience of the world and ourselves within it as well as our ability to communicate our experience to others. Sarraute also examines the other side to this order, revealing in an imaginary conversation how language reduces the quality of lived experience to a rigid and partial code. She cites her imaginary interlocutor: 'you know very well that nothing here below can claim existence as long as it has not received a name' (p. 75), and then illustrates the fallacy of this statement by documenting how a sentence can cut across another's curiosity and imagination to fix all the possibilities for meaning in a convenient, vague, yet totally prescriptive formulation: 'he's mad' (p. 117).

Sarraute repeatedly uses the image of language as a wall or strong-room imprisoning and destroying life (for example p. 116), and she suggests that only by inhabiting the 'shelter' afforded by the spaces in and between words can we begin to alter this situation (see pp. 67, 79, 116). Sarraute gives a vivid account of the way meaning runs through language:

> we think we see it, it must be here, in this word . . . we make an effort, we catch hold of it, we restrain it, we examine it .... But of course, it's meaning isn't, couldn't be that which at first glance we saw in it. It has another, here it is, it's this... (p. 144).

She argues that it is in this 'slippage' that we will find the space to express the missing nuances and quality of our lived experience (p. 79).

Bearing other worlds: Annie Leclerc

Annie Leclerc, in a text entitled *Parole de femme* ('Woman's Word'),[15] argues that men have had the main say in language, which they have used to express their own preoccupations and aims, with the result that women's experience has been silenced and obliterated (p. 8). She writes: 'the world is the word of man. Man is the word of the world' (p. 6). Leclerc interprets 'the whole history of man' as the attempt to institute a domain of activity that will exclude women, and which will thus take precedence over and so reduce women's sex-specific power of procreation (p. 103). She suggests that while women have been engaged with the essential but, from the male point of view, potentially threatening task of giving birth to children, men have focused their attention on 'giving birth' to 'Man' (p. 7). She believes this split between the sexes has had devastating consequences for both women and men. Woman's silence, and the triumph of man's word, she argues, has meant women's work has been stolen from us, our bodies 'raped' (p. 12). She suggests that man's preoccupation with himself as master has resulted in a terrifying obsession with 'property' and death (p. 27). Taking the heroes of the cinema as her example, she stresses that what these heroes have in common is the fact that their 'heroism' is defined either in relation to what they claim possession of (physical strength, money, a woman), or in their relation to death.

Like Marie Cardinal, Leclerc describes her project in *Parole de femme* as that of inventing a woman's word (p. 6). She suggests that the only way out of the sterility and destruction caused by the sole application of men's preoccupations and goals is for women to 'finally speak what we know' (p. 13). She believes this must come from women's sexual experience, since everything else, including every other form of 'pleasure', has been attributed by men: 'it's only from here that a new word can be born which will be womans's' (p. 12). She stresses that only by affirming 'the difference of my sex' (p. 65) – and learning to recreate the world in the light of this – can women avoid constituting a new 'master' in place of the old (p. 38).

Leclerc illustrates her project in *Parole de femme* with reference to her own experience of pregnancy. She describes how pregnancy gradually made her more attuned to her own body, and particularly to the fact that her sexuality was not the 'single sexual celebration' she had known in her relationships with men (p. 11). The difference, she suggests, is that whereas men are continually seeking to define themselves even in copulation, in pleasure, 'I am not seeking to define myself, I am seeking to abolish what makes me say I' (p. 32). This increasing attentiveness to the 'pulsations' of her body (p. 39), and to the movements of the child growing within her (see p. 11), culminate in labour. In labour, she writes, 'I lost bit by bit that which previously made me say I, limit, temporality, separation' (p. 79). She believes this sex-specific women's knowledge is what is missing from the current male order of violence and death. The essence of women's pleasure, she stresses, is not the creation of 'I' but union: and she urges women 'to prepare the coming' of this 'other world' (p. 87) 'in which each [feminine] one is whole and has care of others' (p. 69).

Modelled on her experience, Leclerc imagines a new nexus of relations no longer based solely on the faculty of sight, since it is this faculty that distances us from others. Like Luce Irigaray, she suggests that this new 'order' will be constituted in a new (woman's) language, which would 'not be oppressive' (p. 8), since it would also include those faculties which – instead of marking our limits from others – function to recreate the relation: the 'consciousness' of ears, nostrils, tongue, fingers and skin (p. 134). Countering the logos of war and death she sees at the centre of man's endeavour (see p. 7 and p. 129), Leclerc believes this new articulation will at last engender a 'new world' of life (p. 89).

Leclerc's argument in *Parole de femme* touches on one of the key issues in the debate on women and language. Whilst Leclerc is careful to emphasise the fact that our knowledge of the world is mediated by the language she suggests men have appropriated and shaped according to their own ends, there remains the question of whether the body, which Leclerc and other French feminists see as the source of a new knowledge and mode of expression, can itself be exempt from language. Is our experience of physical pleasure, for instance, a direct and unmediated one, or is our body experience already directed by the discourse on pleasure we carry in our heads?[16]

New relations: Monique Wittig

In a fictional text *Les Guérillères* ('The [feminine] Warriors'),[17] writer Monique Wittig stresses the ways in which men have utilised women's difference to constitute themselves as masters (p. 146). Like other French feminist writers, she warns of the dangers in attempting to create a new language along the lines of the old. In *Les Guérillères*, a number of the women are compiling a dictionary, and they expose the binary structure of previous thinking in which a term could be collapsed into its opposite (p. 106). The women's 'revolt' consists in their refusal to comply with this system of exchange in which naming has come to mean possession (p. 162), rather than the conquest of their masculine adversaries since this would only lead to a reversal – and hence a repetition – of the existing structure (p. 136).

Wittig's text is itself an example of this strategy, refusing to comply with conventional rules of syntax, punctuation or page layout, and incorporating other meanings as these are generated by the writing process.[18] If the old order is not to be repeated, a new relation to the origin has to be created, and the 'O' – symbol of woman's sex and the spaces left unoccupied by man's language ('the interval that the masters have not been able to fill with their words of proprietors and possessors' [p. 164]) – takes on increasing significance through the text. The new order – like that envisaged by Annie Leclerc – is seen to derive from a new pattern of relations, to the origin, and between the self and the world. Combatting the domination that has characterised man's schema, the women of *Les Guérillères* make a pledge:

> if I appropriate the world, let this be to immediately dispossess myself of it, let this be to create new relations between myself and the world (p. 154).

THE WOMEN'S REVOLT

Language, as an instrument of women's oppression, and as containing the potential to create new relations to those decreed by the patriarchal order, is a central preoccupation of contemporary French women's fiction. The following examples are drawn from a wide range of fictional texts that differ in theme, style and mode of narration.

The body in writing: Chantal Chawaf

Writer Chantal Chawaf, perhaps one of the most innovative of recent French writers, explores the role and potential of language to create change in a series of fictional texts. In *Le Soleil et la terre* ('The Sun and the Earth'),[19] perhaps the most well-known of Chawaf's novels, the central female voice is circumscribed by a series of (masculine) discourses. The setting for the novel is partly North Africa, where Arabic law teaches that 'a man equals two women' (p. 44). There is the apparently neutral, stereotyped language of the newspapers, which report the events of the war in such a way as to make the killing and destruction appear normal (p. 33). There is also the 'masters' language' (see p. 33), which not only makes the war possible, but turns the war into a heroic story (see p. 5). Against these discourses, the text offers an alternative – a 'language of the body' (see p. 66) founded in love and respect for life (p. 78). This new language is symbolised by the birth of the woman's daughter:

> And your birth and your life, my daughter, it's the other world, it's the beginning of the other world, it's the new earth, it's the new language, it's the world of flesh, it's the world of life (p. 18).

In Chawaf's most recent work *L'Intérieur des heures* ('The Interior of Hours'),[20] the mother and daughter who are the main focus of the text are confined within a restrictive masculine space: 'the space contracts even more, traps us .... They [the masculine] surround us' (p. 10). This 'space' is demarcated by language, and Chawaf plays on the gender of the word 'language' in French to draw attention to the division between the existing (masculine) language (***le** langage*), which functions to 'confine us socially, inside our reduced, unequal and conformist lives' (p. 49), and the other language dreamt of by the mother – a language 'untranslatable in ours' (p. 10) – to which Chawaf assigns the feminine form: ***la** langue*. The distinction is one made by Annie Leclerc who, in *Parole de femme*,[21] distinguishes between the feminine word of a new woman's language – ***la** parole* – and the masculine word of man (***le** mot*). This play on the masculine and feminine, with its resultant influence on the choice of subject pronoun, is unfortunately lost in an English translation.

Of all Chawaf's texts, perhaps the one which comes closest to exploring the other language that will enable rather than reduce life is *Elwina, le roman fée* ('Elwina, The Fairy-Tale Novel').[22] In this novel a young woman, Elwine, is encouraged by an apparently sympathetic publisher to write. Through Elwine Chawaf explores the complex nature of women's willingness to be 'mastered' by men. She writes: 'our mad solitude renders us so dependant . . . on the other, so dependant on a gesture, on a word that some-one can make themselves master of us, paralyse us' (p. 142).[23] That the publisher's interests are different from Elwine's is clear even at the outset: 'she disturbs him, she must not be this woman, not this particular woman, but another: an image' (p. 15), and her writing, far from being the original but ultimately marketable work the publisher had been hoping for, seeks instead an 'other writing' that will finally 'arrive at the unsayable' (p. 130). Like Nathalie Sarraute, Elwine is acutely aware of the way language censors her experience: 'all the waves of these quivering worlds which, most of the time, the word no longer expresses and which, forbidden, lie buried therefore inside us' (p. 85). It is these 'vibrations', harboured within her body: 'poor respirations which would so much like to expand, to slacken, to dictate the words of a vital, pulmonary language, to speak, to breathe air' (p. 108), that Elwine is attempting to express. Her writing[24] becomes:

> a sort of oral writing, transitory . . . coiling, curvilinear, curving in an arc of a circle, becoming a spiral, transferring itself, belonging to symbols, to names derived from sensations and pulling out of silence the forms, this syntax, this life (p. 72).

It is a writing of 'the mother tongue' (p. 99),[25] 'bound to the fluctuations of desire' (p. 108). Like the new (women's) languages envisaged by Marie Cardinal, Annie Leclerc and others, her writing entails a new matrix of relations, and hence a new world 'order' affirming life:[26]

> And from a place of separation, of death, of murder, of suffering, we pass with Elwine to this pacified, transformed place . . . where, without block, without frontier, affectivity can evolve towards the other, towards love, allowing life (p. 151).

Forms out of love: Andrée Chedid

Writer Andrée Chedid's first novel *From Sleep Unbound*[27] tells the story of a fifteen year old Egyptian girl Samya. The novel offers a number of vivid illustrations of the way men's language rules women's lives. There is Samya's forced 'yes' during her marriage to Boutros which places her under his jurisdiction: 'My "yes" had been enough for him [the priest] to hand me over to this man with words that chained me for eternity' (p. 64). There is Boutros's own language which lays down the rules according to which the married Samya must live:

> I saw him and all the Boutros's in the world in their rigid authoritarianism. They ruled over destinies; they crushed plants, songs, colours, they crushed life itself. And they reduced everything to the shrivelled proportions of their own hearts (p. 73).

Set against this oppressive regime, the text offers a number of alternatives rooted in a different relation to meaning and others. There are the mud figures sculpted by the young girl Ammal, which express both her love for Samya and a different vision of life to that of her father and her father's religion (p. 118). There is the healing 'torrent' of the words spoken by Om el Kher, the woman who befriends and tries to help Samya (p. 76). There are Samya's own mimes, in which she dances her story for Ammal and her daughter Mia (p. 117). Despite Mia's death, and despite the fact that neither Samya nor Ammal are finally able to articulate their vision of another life, the novel ends on a note of hope. Unlike the world that condemns Samya – in which 'treasures' are hidden away 'in dark boxes' rather than enjoyed in the illusory belief that they provide 'life insurance' – Ammal's flight is seen by both Ammal and Samya as the beginning of another love that will 'count' happiness differently (p. 120).

Breaking the silence: Jeanne Hyvrard

Jeanne Hyvrard, one of a new generation of French writers, explores in a fictional text entitled *Mère la mort* ('Mother Death')[28] the experience of mental breakdown in relation to language and gender. Like Monique Wittig in *Les Guérillères*,[29]

Hyvrard plays on the grammatical division of gender in French, contrasting the feminine 'I' of the narration with the masculine 'they' responsible for organising the world in which 'she' must live: 'they have believed themselves to be the masters of the world' (p. 22), 'she' writes, defining 'our sex in the image of theirs' (p. 138) and refusing to 'allow our difference' (p. 36). This appropriation, Hyvrard suggests, has taken place in language, which has been used to structure the world according to 'their [masculine] relationships of power' (p. 46), twisting and fixing words (p. 12) so that it has become impossible for 'us [feminine] to protest' (p. 15).

Hyvrard also exposes the dilemma that thus confronts women in language. Whilst the 'I' recognises that the masculine attempt to fix 'her' identity is at the expense of the fluidity and multiplicity 'she' experiences in life (p. 16), the text also reveals the dangers in 'refusing' language and remaining 'the unnameable' (p. 17) since we thus deny ourselves access to language and hence to the possibility of communication and social exchange: 'They have language. They have words. I have only a cry' (p. 33). Like a number of the writers discussed here, Hyvrard's answer is to seek liberation (p. 44) through a new written language (p. 74): 'Let us recuperate the word [***la** parole*] they have torn from us and claim our differences' (p. 124).[30]

A feminine I: Emma Santos

Emma Santos' *La Malcastrée* ('The Badly Castrated [feminine] One'),[31] like Hyvrard's *Mère la mort*, is a fictional exploration of the experience of mental breakdown. As in *Mère la mort*, the feminine 'I' of the narration questions the way man has appropriated language to classify the world according to his own ends: 'they [masculine] have judged, classed words and colours. They have given them a content, a meaning, a form' (p. 14). The text also exposes the double-edged dilemma language poses for women. On the one hand, man's language has excluded women – 'Those who have spoken in my place have lied' (p. 43) – and defines women in such a way that when the 'I' at last begins to speak in the way 'they' (*ils*) want her to and is pronounced cured, it is not her 'but the other me who speaks' (p. 55). On the other hand, language is all there is: 'We did not want their books-lies. We will write our book, us, when we have found a different system, a system other than words. But we only have this, their words' (p. 14). Like a number of the writers discussed here, Santos believes we can at present only imagine the forms this other system might take. Since language has been invested with power, it is possible that language can be used against itself and made to transform the existing order: 'We will destroy everything with words' (p. 43), 'words can everything' (p. 44). There is also the possibility of invention in the spaces left untouched by man's language: 'the blanks, the empty spaces between the words and the lines' (p. 29). Finally, there is the hope of a new 'language of the body' (p. 15) based on women's inscription of our relationships with our children (see p. 15) and other women (see p. 43). Like Jeanne Hyvrard, Santos stresses that this new invention will come through writing (see pp. 80, 123). As 'she' leaves the asylum where writing is forbidden (p. 80), the 'I' begins to 'jostle disturb invent reverse disarticulate de-atomise words, annihilate them destroy jolt demolish empty, pulverise them' (p. 124), and then, haltingly, to write 'words' of her own. The final lines of the text record the hope that through this 'writing': 'Perhaps one day there will be a language of hers, a real language' (p. 125).

The language revolution: Madeleine Chapsal

Writer Madeleine Chapsal, in a semi-autobiographical text *Une femme en exil* ('A Woman in Exile'),[32] explores the potential of writing to create change. For Chapsal, language is a pre-established structure to which we must adhere if we are to accede to social and cultural definition and exchange (see p. 205). In *Une femme en exil*, Chapsal uncovers the complex relationship between the speaking–writing 'body', lived experience, and language as a symbolic system of signs. On the one hand, language is itself a body function: 'After all what is language if not a current which "traverses" us?' (p. 204). On the other, there remains the problem of how to translate life as it is lived by the body into a system of signs (see pp. 192, 194). Writing, for the 'woman in exile', is thus both vital and absurd. Absurd because language can never fully convey the quality of lived experience, yet vital because writing provides a powerful and even revolutionary tool:

> For such is writing when we allow it to act: now the mad woman in pursuit of the dead child, now the high precision implement that bores, breaks through, opens, creates, destroys in order to reconstruct (p. 17).

Countering the fear of loss that prompts us to cling to our identities and ideas – 'I had an intuition of humanity clamped to their precious ideas like so many ramparts' (p. 105) – writing propels us to confront this fear and take risks: 'Incomparable act which *cannot* in the long run not change the world' (p. 218). It offers the opportunity to relinquish the old, egotistical constructions of self (see pp. 112–3), and envision a new nexus of relations with the world. Like a number of the writers whose work I discuss, Chapsal believes these new relations will arise from a radical revision of the dissimulation (p. 18) and power-play that have characterised relations up until this point, entailing a new connection between language and the body:[33] 'At this moment with my fingers, at others with my throat, my teeth, my tongue, to project it out of me' (p. 204).

French feminist theorists and writers thus challenge our view of language in a number of ways. Starting from the premise that language implements men's desire at women's expense, theorists and writers alike argue that only by inscribing the feminine can we hope to transform the current order of patriarchal relations. In particular writing, through its capacity to defy established meaning, and because the written text can always be read an other way, is seen to offer the potential to generate alternate meanings. This rich, varied and controversial body of writings nevertheless raises some important questions. If language is a system which precedes us and predetermines our experience of the world, how can women create a new order that will not be a reflection or inversion of the old? Is it possible that women's sexual and unconscious experiences are unmediated by language, or is the whole of our experience already the *product* of – rather than a potential origin for an other, feminine – language? And is it feasible – even if women's sexual and unconscious experiences do provide the origin for a different language – that the ensuing system will remain untainted by the present one? If language has been appropriated by men and used to structure the world according to their own ends, how can we ensure that a new woman's language will be unaffected by the existing model? Even if women can achieve a new language rooted in a different, feminine perception and mode of organisation, what will be the effects of this separatism? Will the fact of our turning our backs on the present schema merely found a new sexual tyranny, or will the creation of an other, feminine wor(l)d reposition women in the place that has always been allotted us: the place of subordination, non-communication, and silence?[34]

2

The (feminine) unconscious

Why would there be no desire for . . . a difference that would not be repeatedly and eternally co-opted and trapped within an economy of 'sameness'?

Why would it be impossible for there to be any desire for difference, any desire for the other?

Luce Irigaray

But nothing compels us to deposit our lives in these lack-banks; to think that the subject is constituted in a drama of bruising rehearsals; to endlessly bail out the father's religion.

Write yourself: your body must make itself heard. Then the huge resources of the unconscious will burst out.

Hélène Cixous

SELF REPRESENTATION

Ever since Anglo–American feminist critics first exposed the masculine bias and misogyny of the work of Sigmund Freud to a general readership,[1] it has been fashionable in Anglo–American feminist circles to reject not only Freud but the whole area of psychoanalysis. Whilst I am not suggesting that Freud and psychoanalytic theory have been universally or uncritically adopted by French feminism,[2] Freud is widely taught as part of a general philosophy course in French schools, and the insights and mode of thinking of psychoanalysis imbue the work of a number of French feminist theorists and writers. As Hélène Cixous argues in *Writing Differences*,[3] Freud's description of human development and the unconscious offers crucial insights into the way patriarchy operates to construct us as men and women. The recent French interpreter of Freud, Jacques Lacan, has re-read Freud's theory to highlight the role of language in self-identity, and his work thus also has a bearing on French feminism.

In this chapter on psychoanalysis in its relation to language and (gender) difference, I shall begin my introduction to French feminist theory with a brief outline of the work of Freud and Lacan. My aim in presenting their work is not to prioritise this at the expense of French feminism, but to offer a context for French feminist theory and writing. Beginning with masculine (self-)representations, it becomes possible to read the other – feminine – responses and challenge of French feminism to definitions of the same.

The father's law: Sigmund Freud

The work of Sigmund Freud covers a vast range of subjects. Here I focus on his account of human development as it relates to a theory of individual identity within patriarchal culture.[4]

Freud suggested that one of the ways in which human beings differ from other animals is in the length of our dependency on parents. The human baby relies on adults for food and protection for a considerable period, and Freud demonstrated how, in addition to satisfying essential biological needs, the baby's relation to its parents also involves a number of other elements. The baby sucks at the breast or bottle for food, and Freud noted that as well as satisfying the baby's hunger the action is also pleasurable to the baby. He concluded that the baby's relation to its 'mother'[5] thus includes a sexual dimension, and he argued that this dimension increases as other erotogenic organs (or organs capable of experiencing pleasure) are awakened.

The pleasure the baby experiences in suckling belongs to what Freud designated as the first – or oral – phase of human sexuality. He argued that this phase is succeeded, though not necessarily replaced, by two further stages: the anal and the phallic phases. During the anal phase, the anus becomes an erotogenic zone, and the infant's pleasure in defecation connects with its own growing development as it becomes aware of new powers. The infant is now able to participate in – even manipulate – the wishes of those it is dependant on through the granting or withholding of the faeces. In the third, phallic phase, attention focuses on the genitals.

The three phases around which Freud suggested the infant's sexual and pleasure drives organise themselves are neither exclusive nor strictly sequential. In the early years of life the infant's body is subject to libidinal and other drives, which focus momentarily and are then replaced by new desires as different stimuli present themselves.

Freud argued that the desire for pleasure is a major motivating force during infancy. He suggested that the infant has no clear perception of itself as separate from its surroundings, since the boundaries between itself and others have still to be drawn. He also stressed that during the early phases of development there is no difference in the behaviour of boy or girl children: both sexes, because of the infant's special relationship to the mother, focus their attention on the mother and do not recognise differences of gender.

The core of Freud's theory of human development is his account of the way the self-absorbed, anarchic and desiring infant becomes a socialised, gendered individual. He labelled the process by which this occurs the 'Oedipus' conflict,[6] describing how the dyadic relation between infant and mother is opened out to form the triangle necessary for social exchange through the intervention of the father.

Freud outlined how, at a certain point in the child's development, attention focuses on the genitals as a source of pleasure. He suggested that the father's newly-acknowledged presence in the previously dyadic unit of mother and child forces the boy to become aware both of his difference and his position within a patriarchal structure. Freud detailed how the boy first perceives his father as a rival competing with him for his mother's attention, but suggested that he is ultimately forced to recognise his father's prior claim. It is at this point in his discussion of the Oedipal process that Freud introduces the concept of 'castration'. Since the boy finally accepts that it is the father who 'possesses' the mother, Freud suggests that he represents to the boy the prohibition of his own (incestuous) desire, and is acknowledged as the superior power. Freud argued that the father's prohibition is given credence since, within the boy's family and social surroundings, he sees that his mother is 'castrated'.

For Freud, the threat of 'castration' is not an actual physical threat – though it gains in force as the boy realises that there are females who are literally as well as metaphorically without the organ that is now seen to embody power – but a symbolic threat that operates as law. It legislates both differences of gender and the way gender roles are defined and valued.

Freud argued that as a result of the Oedipus crisis, the boy represses his desire for the mother which thus becomes unconscious, and accepts the father's rule. Adopting the position marked out for him within the pre-established familial and social structure, the boy aligns himself with those images and modes of behaviour his culture designates as masculine, and looks forward to the day when he may enact the father's role for himself.

The account Freud gives of the girl's experience of the Oedipal triangle is more complex. He argued that as a result of the father's entry into the mother–child relation, the girl perceives her own 'castration', and switches her attention from the (similarly 'castrated') mother to the father. But here she must compete with her mother for her father's attention. Since this is a battle the girl must not win, Freud suggested she finally accepts her inferior position, and identifies with her mother as 'castrated'/feminine. Her solace, Freud believed, is that whilst she cannot herself hope to embody the penis–phallus, she may one day reproduce it through a (male) baby.

As will be obvious from even this very brief account of Freud's theory, there are a number of major objections to his model of male and female development. Even if we accept the premise on which Freud's theory is based, it is unclear from his description why the girl should agree to her subservient position and submit to the father's law given that she already perceives herself, according to this account, as 'castrated'. It is also not clear why if this is the case the girl should switch her attention from her mother to her father, or why, having failed to win the father, she should then revert to the mother. It is as result of these and other objections that Anglo–American feminists have on the whole rejected Freud. A notable exception is the British feminist critic Juliet Mitchell. In her book *Psychoanalysis and Feminism*,[7] Mitchell draws on her own research into child development to suggest that the common desire of both boy and girl infants is the desire for a baby. She argues that the reason why fear of 'castration' (with its emphasis on the father) and not the desire for a baby (with its emphasis on the mother) is given precedence is because, within a patriarchal world order, it is the father who wields power. Mitchell's interest in Freud's theory as a model of human development within patriarchal society parallels the interest of French feminists, who see in Freud's account a useful explanation of – and hence an opportunity to challenge – the current status quo.

According to Freud, the Oedipal conflict ensures the passage from the anarchic, self-absorbed and pleasure-seeking infant state centred on a relation with the mother, to that of socialised, gendered adult individual able to perceive him or herself in relation to others, and behave in accordance with those laws which structure the society in which he or she must live. The father's prohibition thus includes the laws that create the patriarchal order – the legal, moral, economic, social and cultural rules that enable patriarchy to function and perpetuate itself.

Freud termed the individual's newly-acquired sense of him or herself as a distinct and participating member of a pre-determined order the 'ego'. He suggested that the father's law of castration as well as those rules it symbolises are carried by the individual as part of their developing conscience or 'super-ego', which he believed acts as a constant check and break on the ego. He argued that those desires which no longer accord with the role the individual must now assume within the patriarchal social structure are repressed as unconscious, and he labelled the site of this repression the 'id'.

Freud suggested that the human subject is only able to adopt his or her role within the pre-established network of political, social, economic and sexual relations that create (patriarchal) society by repressing those desires which cannot be given free reign if (this) society is to continue. He realised that these desires still influence the individual subject, splitting the conscious from the unconscious self, and threatening the construction(s) of the ego. Listening to his patients, Freud suggested that this other world of the unconscious is what is revealed to us in those moments of apparent inattention when we mislay things, or experience sudden, inexplicable losses of memory, or in slips of the tongue. He argued that the workings of the unconscious are most clearly revealed to us in dreams, which he saw as symbolic (re)enactments of our (unconscious) desires. His description of the 'dream-work' as the symbolic condensation and displacement of desire parallels post-structural theories of language, and in particular the work of Roman Jakobson,[8] who saw language as the combination of metaphor (the condensing of meaning) and metonymy (the displacement of meaning). It is this account of the language of (unconscious) desire that has prompted the French psychoanalyst Jacques Lacan to draw a link between language and the unconscious.

Mirrored images: Jacques Lacan

The work of Jacques Lacan is primarily a re-reading of Freud's theory.[9] Drawing on Freud's account of human development, Lacan describes the primary relationship between child and mother as 'symbiotic', involving a close identification between the two. He suggests that within this close relationship the child is unable to locate a sense of self that is not tied to the mother, and nor is it able to perceive itself as an entity distinct from the rest of the world.

Lacan argues that the child only gradually begins to conceive itself as separate (from the m/other[s]), and he highlights a number of elements that work to create this sense of self. He describes the different identifications that take place when the child sees a reflection of itself, suggesting that the image(s) the child sees are a literal and symbolic 'mirror' for its own developing sense of self. Lacan argues that the child recognises the image of (it)self as contained and separate from others because this image has already been mirrored by others' desire. The self the child sees is, Lacan stresses, an illusion, since the reality is still the complex network of drive-energies and desires Freud describes. Lacan called this state of (mis)recognition, whereby the child identifies with the image(s) of itself as whole and separate, the 'imaginary'. He believed that this process of (mis)recognition forms the basis for all subsequent identifications, and he suggested that we can only ever conceptualise ourselves as (independent) subjects as our (self-)image is mirrored back to us from another's desire.

Lacan re-draws Freud's model of the Oedipal triangle to take account of the child's entry into language. He re-reads Freud's description of the game he had watched small children playing in which they begin to substitute words for objects. Freud had noticed his young nephew playing with a cotton-reel, pronouncing the object first *fort* ('here') then *da* ('gone') as he threw the reel away, and Lacan re-interpreted Freud's description to suggest that objects only begin to exist for the child as such – that is, as separate from the child as subject – once they are perceived as absent or lacking (gone). Lacan argued that the word the child employs to symbolise the object's loss plays a fundamental role in creating the object to the child. Freud had shown how, as a result of the father's presence, the dyad of mother and child is split apart, and he argued that the father's intervention is necessary if the child is to assume his or her adult place. For Lacan as for Freud, the father's prohibition functions as a symbolic rather than a literal threat, forcing the child's recognition that it is part of a wider framework of laws within which it must adopt a pre-determined position. Through the menace of castration, the father blocks the child's incestuous desire to be the (sole) desire of the mother, breaking the closed circuit of this relation, and introducing the possibility of exchange with others. For Lacan it is the phallus – as metaphor for the father's intervention – that symbolises the law on which the social order is founded, and according to which roles are assigned. Like Freud, Lacan believes that the child's successful resolution of the Oedipus conflict is necessary if s/he is to develop as a socialised, gendered subject, aware of his or her difference and status within the pre-established structure of adult laws.

As a result of the father's intervention in the mother–child relation, Lacan suggests that the child's desire is redirected from the mother to the phallus itself. This however proves as illusory as the desire to model our mirrored image(s), since our construction as subject necessarily entails separation from the object/(m)other.

Lacan emphasises that the 'law' which the father represents to the child is a law of language. Drawing on Freud's account of the cotton-reel game, he highlights the role language plays in the differentiation process between self and m/other. But language is also the representative of the (father's) law, since it functions as the pre-established order within which the child must take up its appointed place. Just as the mirror-image is meaningful to the child *because* it is reflected through the m/other's desire of/for the child, so, Lacan argues, the child's appellation of itself as 'I' signals its submission to the order which creates and names it (as subject). He suggested that in the same way that the father's intervention in the closed dyad of mother and child is the necessary precondition for social exchange, so a third term is necessary for linguistic exchange as the differentiating marker between 'I' and 'you'.

Lacan termed the order of language the 'symbolic', distinguishing this from the 'imaginary' sphere of the ego and the various identifications through which the ego attempts to construct and confirm its self-image. The pre-social state of the mother-child relation he called the 'real', even though he believed that once the child has entered the symbolic order this is necessarily and forever beyond the subject's reach. For Lacan, the real is thus the state of unattainable wholeness or plenitude where desire and its satisfaction come together.

This emphasis on language marks the key difference in the work of Freud and Lacan. For Lacan, the subject is a subject of (to) language. The child's recognition of its 'mirror'-image, its reference to itself as 'I', both indicate its awareness that it is located within a larger order in which it has a pre-determined place. Since this perception of self splits the child from the m/other, and since the words the child uses to substitute for the object/(m)other are imbued with this loss, so Lacan argues the subject is created in language *as* this division and loss. Lacan's account of the separation and loss at the heart of the symbolic is challenged by a number of French feminist writers.

The function of language is communication, but Lacan locates a further dimension to the division and lack at the heart of the symbolic structure. He suggests that whenever anyone addresses another, she or he constructs this other as the 'Other': the imaginary place of truth, knowledge and certainty that can contain our individual 'loss'. This however is a fantasy, since language endlessly propels the subject from one signifier to the next. Once the subject has entered the symbolic, she or he can never again possess the desired object – m/other – and Lacan argues that this desire, derived from lack, ceaselessly motivates the individual along the infinite chain of substitutions of which language is made.

The 'subject' Lacan describes is thus one whose identity is in constant flux. Not only is the 'oneness' of the mirrored-image an illusion, but even the 'I' the subject employs to refer to itself only ever coincides with the particular moment of utterance. For Lacan this fluidity extends to the area of gender. Like Freud, Lacan sees the father's law as also embodying the law of gender, but argues that the penis–phallus that acts as marker for the division legislates in such a way that the division is both arbitrary and shifting.

There are three further points arising from Lacan's work on Freud that are relevant here. The first is Lacan's definition of woman. Lacan argues that the 'object' of language functions as an illusory place of truth and wholeness, and he suggests that within the current order it is woman who represents this place for man. Designated in relation to man, woman is the (unattainable) Other: the site of man's projection where desire and its gratification can at last come together. It is this description of woman that underlies Lacan's famous statement that 'The woman does not exist'. According to Lacan, (the category of) woman only comes into being as the object/other of man. Woman, for Lacan, is the fantasised object (other) that makes it possible for man to exchange and function.

A second element of Lacan's re-reading of Freud is the link he draws between language and power. Lacan suggests that words become meaningful to the child only as they are substituted for the (lost) object/(m)other. The words the child employs nevertheless offer the child a means of control: despite the division and absence at the heart of the symbolic the act of naming is still an act of power.

The third point I would like to raise concerns the unconscious. Lacan has described the workings of the unconscious in terms of language, suggesting that the process whereby meanings are condensed into each other or displaced outwards onto new meanings parallels the operation of language. For Freud the unconscious presents a direct threat to the ego, since it continually disrupts the subject's attempts to construct itself, whilst, for Lacan, the 'truth' of the unconscious is the fundamental experience of division and loss that creates the subject (in language).

Lacan's re-reading of Freud[10] has been adopted and rejoindered by a number of French feminists. In particular Lacan's notion of desire, in its relation to (gendered) identity and language, is an important element in the attempt by French feminist theorists and writers to locate a (feminine) self that is not bound by castration or lack, as well as in the creation of an other – feminine – writing that will reject the fantasy of 'closure'[11] to offer new possibilities for relating and naming.

The speaking subject: Julia Kristeva

In the prologue to the book of her doctoral thesis *Revolution in Poetic Language*,[12] Julia Kristeva attacks what she describes as the 'scientific imperative' that has governed the study of language. She defines this imperative as the building of arguments on the basis of empirical evidence, and believes it has lain behind the attempt to control language by turning it into an 'object'.

Kristeva stresses that what this practice of studying language as object omits is the role of the 'speaking subject' in linguistic formulation. She illustrates how traditional linguistics has consistently refused to take into account the complex network of forces that organise and propel the speaker, and particularly the motivations of the unconscious and the body. She criticises Derrida's work as an example, arguing that his analysis focuses on the material components of language without reference to the heterogeneous 'drives' that influence and impel the language user. She believes the scientific imperative underlies all forms of capitalist discourse, and argues that linguistics must develop its own theory of the speaking subject if it is to challenge the cultural and political status quo.

The account Kristeva gives of the speaking subject derives from Freud's description of the human subject governed by instinctual and body-drives. She cites as an example of this Freud's theory of the role played by the drive of 'rejection' in perpetuating life (see pp. 150, 161), in which he suggests that the energy of the rejection-drive is necessary to counter-balance the 'galloping' evolution inherent in organic matter. Like both Freud and Lacan, Kristeva emphasises the incomplete nature of the Oedipal crisis to suggest, with Freud, the ongoing impact of drive-energies on the adolescent and adult subject. Her insistence that this continuing influence of the unconscious and body-drives affects not only our behaviour but our use of language leads her to view the individual's relation to language as a dynamic one. For Kristeva, language is not 'object' but *process*.

Kristeva re-draws Lacan's account of the imaginary and symbolic phases of development to include Freud's description of the pre-Oedipal child as subject to the play of drives. She outlines how, during the first phase of life, the child has no complete or lasting conception of itself as distinct from the m/other,[13] and she employs the Greek word *chora*, meaning enclosed space or womb, to describe this infant state. She suggests that in Plato the *chora* depicts a receptacle that is both maternal and nourishing, a place without a deity prior to the creation of unity and order. For Kristeva, the *chora* delineates the non-unified, dis-ordered state which precedes subjectivity and language: the pre-Oedipal plenitude in which there is as yet no articulation of absence and hence no division between the symbolic and the real.

Since the child is governed by drive-energies organised according to physical need, and since in early infancy it is the mother who fulfils this need, Kristeva argues that the heterogeneous drives connect and orient the child to the mother. She suggests that these drives are contained or enabled by the mother. Although within the *chora* there is no prohibition on drive-energy such as that which is imposed during the Oedipal conflict, she emphasises that the *chora* is nonetheless marked by the restrictions of biological sex difference and family and social custom. She argues that this 'ordering' – which is not yet that of Oedipal law – is transmitted to the child through the mother's body.

Kristeva believes drive-forces also play a vital role in the creation of independent subjectivity. She suggests that the drive of rejection initiates the process of separation which propels the child into language, through creating as 'lost' a rejected object such as the faeces or a toy.[14] She argues that the drive-energies which bond the child to the mother involve articulations and rhythms expressed through gesture and voice. She suggests that these 'semiotic' expressions are organised according to patterns of absorbtion, retention and repetition, which are the building blocks of linguistic structure,[15] and that these precede and accompany the child's construction of itself as independent (speaking) subject. For Kristeva, the child's ability to 'speak' is an amalgam of movement, sound and the capacity to distinguish objects. She suggests that a child's first 'words' are semiotic articulations attributed to objects which thus take on the function of language. She refers as an example to the way small children attribute animal noises to animals which then become identified with the sound. The sound acquires the status of signifier as the next animal the child encounters is designated by the sound.

The child's growing perception of difference – of different objects, and of itself as different from these objects – is seen by Kristeva to crystallise during two phases of human development highlighted by Freud and Lacan: the mirror stage and the discovery of the law of castration. According to Lacan, the child's recognition of its mirror-image coincides with its growing sense of itself as external to and separate from the m/other as well as its first attempts at self-expression. Kristeva draws on this description to highlight the role of semiotic expression in the child's endeavour to identify and appropriate its image. Like Lacan, she believes this expression is the only means the child has of covering – and hence living – its 'loss'.

Together with a number of French feminist writers, Kristeva sees Freud's theory of castration as a theory of origins, offering an 'imaginary construction' of the means by which the anarchic, amorphous, drive-governed human infant is brought to accept the social order. Like Freud, Kristeva regards the child's discovery of the castration law[16] as effecting the transition from dependency on the mother to the state of autonomous individual aware of his or her position within the pre-determined patriarchal structure. She suggests that as a result of the father's presence the mother–child relation is transformed to a symbolic one, since the child must needs find a way of symbolising the mother in order to maintain a relationship with her. Like both Freud and Lacan, Kristeva views the child's separation from the mother as the necessary precondition for forming relationships and communicating with others.

According to Lacan, the subject is motivated in language by the desire to regain the pre-Oedipal state of plenitude with the mother, a desire which language both negates and postpones since language only momentarily coincides with the lost object/(m)other. For Kristeva, the continuing impact of the semiotic acts as a continual threat to the construction(s) of the subject, in their attempt to establish boundaries between subject and object, (him)self and the world. She suggests that this ongoing influence of the semiotic challenges both the unity of the subject (in language), and 'the stasis of One meaning, One myth, One logic' on which patriarchy depends (p. 148). Poetic language in particular, since it incorporates the unconscious and body-rhythms in a way other forms of language do not, offers a means of subverting the symbolic function by putting the subject into *process* – with himself as well as with the law.[17]

Unlike Freud, who viewed the law of castration as emanating solely from the father, Kristeva's account of the transition from dependant infant to speaking subject highlights the role of the mother in this process. She argues that the various prohibitions which impinge on the child are administered by the mother through her close relationship with it, from the training of glottal and anal movements to the constraints of Oedipal law. For Kristeva, the foundations of subjectivity and language are given by the mother, as the rules and conventions of the family and society are transmitted to the child through modulations in the mother's body and voice. These rhythms and articulations – received, echoed and mirrored by the child's own semiotic expression – thus form the basis for the symbolic.

As an example of the way semiotic rhythms and articulations prepare and accompany the symbolic function, Kristeva explores a child's developing ability to distinguish colours. In the essay 'Giotto's Joy' in the English collection of her work *Desire in Language: A Semiotic Approach to Literature and Art*,[18] she suggests that the child's growing capacity to perceive and differentiate colours depends on two closely related factors. On the one hand there is the child's physical ability to see colour, which combines on the other with a gradual recognition of the way colours 'mean' within a pre-established order of colours. The child's relation to colour thus fluctuates between a developing physical perception and the associations different colours acquire, both for the child as an individual and from within a pre-determined colour 'code'.

Kristeva looks at paintings by the Italian Renaissance painter Giotto to demonstrate how a dynamic relation to colour can provide the impetus for new forms of perception. She writes:

> in painting color is pulled from the unconscious into a symbolic order; the unity of the 'self' clings to this symbolic order, as this is the only way it can hold itself together (p. 220).

Freud, she reminds us, has defined 'pleasure' as the removal of prohibition through experience, and she views Giotto's relation to colour in this light, suggesting that he uses colour in such a way as to subvert the usual attempt to institute 'One Meaning' which founds the (patriarchal) symbolic. Kristeva argues that by allowing other considerations – such as instinct – to dictate his choice of colour, Giotto liberates himself from the tyranny of imposed meaning – and thus from the restrictions on himself as subject of/ to this meaning. In the same way, she believes semiotic expression can be employed to shatter (linguistic) meaning, with equally 'revolutionary' effects on the speaking–writing subject.[19]

Desire for the other: Luce Irigaray

Unlike Julia Kristeva, who finds Freud's theory a helpful starting point for her own account of human development, Luce Irigaray attacks what she sees as the masculine premise underlying psychoanalytic thought. In her work on psychoanalysis,[20] she suggests that the hidden aim of Freud's theory is the 'standardization of women's sexuality according to masculine parameters'.[21] She cites Freud's insistence that the pre-Oedipal girl 'is nothing but a little boy' as an example. Paraphrasing Freud's description of the girl's discovery of her 'castration', Irigaray shows how this in turn enables him to put forward his view that the pre-Oedipal girl switches her attention from the mother to the father, rejecting, blaming and even hating her mother for not possessing the valorised male organ. Freud's belief leads him to argue that all the girl's subsequent relations with women will be governed by a rivalrous desire for the penis; even her desire for a baby, Irigaray stresses, is seen as no more than the desire to have an equivalent of the male organ. Irigaray suggests that as a result of Freud's (masculine) assumptions, the motivating force of women's lives is deemed to be 'penis envy'; and since women are also thought to have 'less capacity for sublimating her instincts' than men, woman is thus conveniently removed by Freud from participation in the (patriarchal) political and social arena.

Irigaray gives a further example of the masculine bias inherent in Freud's theory by citing his assumption that in procreation it is the male sex that is 'actively mobile', searching out the immobile female. Woman thus becomes, according to this account, a mere 'receptacle' for man's 'product', even though, by displaying what Freud perceives to be her 'passively aimed instincts', she may facilitate – even demand – that this product be placed within her. As a result, Irigaray suggests, woman – 'whose intervention in the work of engendering the child can hardly be questioned' – becomes transformed according to his theory as 'the anonymous worker', 'the machine in the service of a master-proprietor' whose 'trade-mark' will alone be inscribed on the 'finished product'.

Irigaray's attack on Freud also questions his assumption that women must choose between two types of sexual pleasure. Why, she asks, is it deemed necessary for women to 'progress' from clitoral to vaginal pleasure, thus depriving women of the erotic potential of a number of sexual zones? Irigaray believes the answer to this question lies in a general censoring of women's difference in the attempt to reduce women to those feminine characteristics regarded by Freud as acceptable, such as those associated with the socially necessary task of mothering.[22]

This refusal to consider the possibility that women might be different underlies, Irigaray suggests, *all* Freud's work on women. She argues that Freud is a prey to his own definition of 'sameness', forcing women as a sex to conform to this notion without analyzing 'the historical factors governing the data he is considering' or his own (patriarchal) point of view. He both fails to recognise the ideological basis to his assumptions and to question the universal application of his model. 'Himself a prisoner of a certain economy of Sameness', she writes, he applies the yardstick of his own desire to obliterate potential differences, thereby resubmitting women to the 'dominant discourse of the father' 'while silencing their demands'. 'Anything he cannot see directly' or 'perceive as like himself', Irigaray concludes, is systematically repressed.

Post-Freudian psychoanalysis, Irigaray suggests, has taken on board almost all Freud's 'masculinist' assumptions. She cites Lacan's theory as an example. Lacan has re-interpreted Freud's notion of the law of castration to argue that what is at stake in the Oedipal process is the child's recognition of the phallus as signifying agent. Despite Lacan's change of emphasis to stress the hiatus between desire and its satisfaction as the key factor in (re)creating the phallus as signifier of the 'lack' without which communication and exchange cannot take place, Irigaray writes that it is still the father who guarantees the symbolic order by prohibiting the desires of both mother and child and introducing – or reintroducing – them to (desire in) language. Thus, despite some alterations, Lacan's account remains dependant in its essential features on Freud's analysis.

Irigaray stresses that psychoanalysis must review the entire framework of its theoretical assumptions and question the role that has been prescribed for women if it is to challenge the patriarchal status quo. It must, she insists, investigate the 'historical determinants' of women's sexuality, and she urges women to dispute its thesis that our sexuality is governed by our lack of – and hence our longing for – the privileged male organ.

Irigaray believes Freud's theory, which she suggests derives from his own fear of castration and 'non-possession', is responsible for an overriding emphasis on 'possession' rather than enjoyment or pleasure. She believes this insistence has led to a repression of the mother–child relation, and in particular to the language and dreams shared with the mother. Instead of interpreting those effects of language which result from the mother–child bond, psychoanalysis, she writes, has evolved a theory of the unconscious which serves to confirm its own premise. The other of psychoanalysis, Irigaray concludes, is 'a faithful, polished mirror, empty of altering reflections' that endlessly (re)creates the same image.

One of the major omissions of both Freudian and post-Freudian psychoanalysis, Irigaray suggests, is its failure to take into account the specificity of women's relation to the mother or the relationship between women. From the time of the Oedipus complex, she writes, women are 'exiled from themselves' and, prevented from maintaining any continuity with 'their first pleasures and desires', are imported into another 'economy' where 'they are completely unable to find themselves'. The female Oedipus complex, Irigaray stresses, signals women's entry into an alien system in which we appear and circulate only as we are called upon to do so by the needs and desires of man.

Irigaray challenges women to utilise our marginalised position to search for a 'voice' that will cut through the 'layers of ornamental style' the masculine subject employs to 'clothe' the feminine, and to overturn the structure of traditional syntax by refusing its 'eternally teleological order'. In particular, she writes, we must pay attention to the 'blanks' in language, reinstating those 'ellipses and eclipses' that will disrupt the closed 'circle of sameness'. Language, she suggests, creates its meaning through 'paradigms and units of value' decided by men and according to which the masculine is 'constituted as "origin"'; thus reducing the remaining, other, feminine term to the position of 'marker'. Relegated to this boundary, the feminine serves as 'a sort of inverted or negative alter ego' for the masculine, and hence can only be deciphered in language as inter-dict – the space within or between the realized meanings of the signs.

The determining of sexual difference in relation to exclusively masculine parameters and desires has meant, Irigaray stresses, that women's sexuality has been appropriated by men who have decreed women's place within the cultural order as 'off-stage' – beyond representation or knowledge of selfhood. Since the girl 'shows nothing that is penis-shaped or could substitute for a penis', her 'nothing to see' is utilised to make her sex the equivalent of nothing. Unlike the pre-Oedipal boy, whose possession of the 'seeable' penis assures his ego, Irigaray believes the little girl is denied even the right to play with possible representations of her own beginning. 'No specific mimicry of origin', she argues, is made available to her. Herself a prisoner of male-determined norms, she can only borrow the signifiers of an alien language with no hope of making 'her own mark or re-marking upon them'.

This collusion, Irigaray writes, between 'one sex/organ' and the victory won by 'visual dominance', leaves women in a sexual void; according to psychoanalysis women have the option of either adopting a 'neutral' libido or of 'substaining themselves by "penis-envy"'. Even in our roles as mothers, Irigaray suggests, we continue this role of passive object without regard for our difference. She argues that as a result of the psychoanalytic premise, nothing of women's own desire or 'the special nature of desire between women' has been 'unveiled or stated':

> That a woman might desire a woman 'like' herself, someone of the 'same' sex, that she might also have auto- and homo- sexual appetites, is simply incomprehensible to Freud, and indeed inadmissible' (*Speculum of the Other Woman*, p. 101).

Forced into the 'specular' economy of male representation, women have been prevented from finding the signs, symbols or emblems that could otherwise represent our instincts or figure or transpose our 'instinctual object-goals'. Women's own sex instincts, Irigaray continues, are thus 'subjected to a particularly peremptory repression' that can only be translated into a 'silent and cryptic script of body language'. Our relation to the mother, our sexuality, as well as the relationships between women, she concludes, remain unconscious and unexplored.

Despite the masculine attempt to appropriate or repress women's difference, Irigaray nevertheless views women's sexuality as a potential threat to the patriarchal structure. Perceived as 'nothing', as 'a fault, a lack, an absence' beyond man's 'system of autorepresentations', the fact that women might have other desires outside the masculine 'rule of visibility' questions the very existence 'of the mirror charged with sending man's image back to him'. Woman, this 'nothing', this 'hole in men's signifying economy', thus embodies the possible destruction, splintering and 'break' in the patriarchal system, menacing the very order of mastery and 'meaning dominated by the phallus': 'that master signifier whose law of functioning erases, rejects (and) denies the surging up' of all 'heterogeneity'.[23]

The m/other's voice: Hélène Cixous

Hélène Cixous, like Luce Irigaray, questions the assumptions that underlie psychoanalytic thinking. In 'Sorties' in *The Newly Born Woman*[24] she suggests that psychoanalysis is based on a ' "natural", anatomical determination of sexual difference–opposition' that implicitly backs 'phallocentrism's position of strength'.

Whilst Cixous, like Irigaray, believes that the sexual differences between men and women have important psychic consequences, she argues that these 'cannot be reduced to the ones that Freudian analysis designates'. She too refutes the 'voyeur's theory' of traditional psychoanalysis as 'a story made to order for male privilege', insisting that sexual difference cannot be delineated 'simply by the fantasised relation to anatomy, which depends to a great extent on catching *sight* of something'. Unlike Irigaray however, who believes women's difference cannot be 'figured' at all within the current (masculine) system of representation, Cixous finds in psychoanalysis a useful description for the way sexual difference is organised within patriarchy, and hence an opportunity to challenge and defy its law. Thus, whilst she criticises psychoanalysis for its 'mirror economy' and complicitous privileging of man's narcissistic need 'to love himself', she believes its theories should not be rejected out of hand. She sees Freud as the heir to a long tradition of phallocentrism, but suggests that his model offers a helpful account of how the innate bisexuality of every human being is structured under a patriarchal system according to a single, masculine libido. She condemns the (masculine) insistence on and allegiance to 'castration', with its reverence for 'glorious phallic monosexuality', but argues that 'we have no *woman's* reason' to comply with its scheme of repressions. She suggests women's relation to the origin engenders a freer and more expansive 'economy' than is currently possible for men.

Cixous also values Freudian psychoanalysis for its 'discovery' of the unconscious. She writes in the series of 'Conversations' at the end of *Writing Differences*[25] that in the same way that women cannot refuse men's discovery of aviation, so we cannot ignore Freud's theory of the unconscious. She sees Freud's work on the unconscious as important on a number of counts. First, since the unconscious is composed of whatever is repressed by the (father's) law, it is both alien and potentially threatening to the patriarchal structure. It is other – feminine – constantly menacing the construction(s) of the (masculine) subject, as well as his attempts to symbolise him-self in language. Like Julia Kristeva, Cixous suggests that the unconscious continually impinges on and disrupts language, through the unconscious and body-drives, in the unconscious transpositions of subject and object that occur, for instance, in dreams, and in such unconscious expression as slips of the tongue and word-play.

Like both Luce Irigaray and Julia Kristeva, Cixous sees in language the key to change, and she urges men and especially women to 'write' our unconscious knowledge and desires. She stresses the role of the unconscious in her own writing, which she believes exists as a rich treasure-house of alternative possibilities.[26] She argues that the abolition of the present order depends on a new structuring of the relationships between self and other, and she highlights the inscription of the unconscious in this transformation. Cixous suggests that the unconscious also plays a vital role in reading, both in shaping our responses to the unconscious – as well as the conscious – motivations that create a text, and as the subtext to our own reading process, profoundly influencing the identifications, resistancies and questions that propel us as readers.

Cixous believes there is a link between the creation of an other, feminine order and the language of childhood. Women in particular, she stresses, carry from the relation with the mother the memory of an other love, which functions as a nourishing and vital force capable of overcoming the father's law of castration. She suggests that this m/other love is kept alive as a voice:

> singing from a time before law, before the Symbolic took one's breath away and reappropriated it into language under its authority of separation .... Within each woman the first, nameless love is singing (p. 93).

Like Julia Kristeva, she sees the mother's role as preparing the child for language, and she suggests that the continuing echo of the mother's voice permeates women's language, containing the potential for new inscriptions of the relationship between self and other:

> Text: my body . . . it is the equivoice that, touching you, affects you, pushes you away from your breast to come to language, that summons *your* strength; it is the rhyth-me that laughs you; the one intimately addressed who makes all metaphors, all body(?) – bodies(?) – possible and desirable . . . the part of you that puts space between yourself and pushes you to inscribe your woman's style in language (p. 93).

Cixous re-reads Shakespeare's *Antony and Cleopatra*[27] as an example of an attempt to create a new equality between self and other. Both Antony and Cleopatra, she suggests, 'have abandoned . . . the miniscule old world', with 'its rivalries' and 'tournaments of the phallus', to struggle against 'all the ancient and reductive means of thinking life that . . . threaten to enclose it, slow it down'. The realm of Antony and Cleopatra, she writes, is beyond 'the fatality of absence' and the 'evasions that only sustain desire by default' located by psychoanalysis as the determining elements in human development. At the opposite extreme to the lack posited at the heart of love by the phallocentric order, Cleopatra's love, Cixous stresses, entails an other economy of relations in which the wound of 'distance, parting, separation' is 'healed' through the movement of perpetual reparation: 'where love is the only value . . . there is no loss'. 'The one equal to the other', Cleopatra, and guided by her influence Antony, embody an other love in which the gift is valued: 'the more you give, the more you are, the more you give, the more you have. Life opens up and stretches to infinity' (p. 124).

An interesting feature of Cixous' reading of *Antony and Cleopatra* is the relationship she sees between Cleopatra's gift of love and the way this 'gift' is given in/to the text, both through the richness of Shakespeare's language, and through the richness of what this language signifies: Cleopatra's 'body'.[28] For Cixous, the link is particularly potent since it highlights the role of language and the body in the construction of gender: though it is Cleopatra in Cixous' reading of the play who nourishes the love-relation, the author of Cleopatra's (woman's) body is a man.[29]

Freud's theory of psychoanalysis, and particularly its Lacanian rewrite in terms of language, has thus influenced the work of a number of French feminist theorists. Both Hélène Cixous and Julia Kristeva see the account provided by psychoanalysis as offering a useful model for the way patriarchy functions and perpetuates itself, governing our identities, the roles we play, and our relationships with others. Luce Irigaray, whose rejection of the masculine premise of psychoanalystic thinking radically challenges its theories, also continues to refer to its descriptions as an empowering starting-point for change.[30] A number of questions remain however. According to Lacan, the 'truth' of the unconscious is the fundamental experience of division which creates the unconscious and the individual subject. Since this division occurs under the jurisdiction of the phallus as the crude marker of difference, there is the question as to whether the unconscious is also marked by this (sexual) division. Is there a feminine – as opposed to a masculine – unconscious? For Luce Irigaray, woman's unconscious has been repressed by a phallocentric order to the extent that it can only exist in the 'silences' that inform the gaps and borders of a male-oriented world. Annie Leclerc, whose *Parole de femme* is discussed briefly in

Chapter 1, similarly sees the unconscious fantasies and desires which are given cultural expression as predominantly male, and she cites war, hero-worship and screen violence as examples. To Hélène Cixous, the unconscious is inherently feminine since it acts as the heterogeneous other place that constantly disrupts the masculine subject's drive for unicity. She does not however suggest that this means men's and women's unconscious are the same, since the unconscious is not fixed at the moment of its creation but continues to incorporate whatever is repressed by the individual. Since this repression is currently the product of a patriarchal system, Cixous argues that this repression will inevitably be different for women and men.

But there is another dimension to this question. One of the key differences between Freud, Lacan and the French women writers who read their work, is the issue of whether the pre-Oedipal exists independently of and/or prior to Oedipal law, or whether it is created *by* it. If, as Lacan argues, the pre-Oedipal is a *function* of the law, then the unconscious must always remain subject to it, and cannot ultimately overthrow it. This would seem to represent the position of Julia Kristeva who, while she sees the pre-Oedipal forces of the semiotic as existing prior to and continuing to create important checks on the law's functioning – thereby opening the symbolic to new possibilities – does not finally envisage its removal.[31] In this case, the only means of challenging the current order would be through the construction of a *different* symbolic – such as the one envisioned by Luce Irigaray – and which would be so far outside the structures of patriarchal law as to raise the question as to whether it could ever counter and replace it. For Irigaray, an other order cannot be expressed – or even effectively imagined – from our present position. If on the other hand the law is not seen to always and forever determine the course of human subjectivity, and the pre-Oedipal is acknowledged to exist both prior to the law's intervention and in its own right, then it becomes possible to imagine those forces associated with the pre-Oedipal as presenting a direct challenge to the patriarchal structure from within.[32] For Hélène Cixous, women's problematic relation to the law becomes a potential threat to its continued operation, whereas for Lacan woman's difference is itself created by (phallic) law, and can only be given expression within the symbolic by relinquishing its other status, and becoming – or attempting to become – 'same'.[33]

OTHER WORDS

Psychoanalysis, and the account it gives of the individual, has also influenced French women's fiction. This influence is reflected in the choice of subject-matter, in the inclusion of the other of unconscious expression, in the incorporation of dreams, and in the very different approach to writing itself. Unlike mainstream Anglo–American feminist fiction, in which women's political, social and cultural challenge to the status quo are thematically expressed, the explosions of linguistic and textual convention of French women's writing can themselves be viewed as a challenge to the system in which to speak entails submission to the Law.

The mirror of separation: Irène Schavelzon

Novelist Irène Schavelzon's *Le Réduit* ('The Retreat'),[34] explores the psychoanalytic model from a woman's perspective. *Le Réduit* is the story of the marriage between 'he' and 'she', told from the viewpoint of she, and in such a way that it both echoes and confounds Lacan's notion of (man's) symbolic. The home of the newly-married couple is full of mirrors in which 'I see myself as I want others to see me' (p. 16); as the days pass, she finds herself becoming increasingly estranged through her desire to 'mirror' his desire for her. In this world of mascarade (p. 71), in which even the guests are only 'the grotesque representation of what they believe themselves to be' (p. 88), she is powerless (p. 91): his desire binds her to him separating her from her other self (p. 95). This separation, in which she feels the woman he desires in her, which is only part of her (p. 133), 'killing' her (p. 64), is linked to *his* language: 'it seemed to her that her own voice was only the echo of his' (p. 28), 'he forced her to cut her language into pieces so that she would only say what he wanted to hear: "Yours, I am yours"' (p. 33).

It is at this point in the text that she discovers the *réduit* – the retreat – where she begins to lose the definitions that have been imposed on her (p. 131), and to fabricate her own language (p. 37). This other language begins in silence (p. 86), with the rediscovery of her body. Inside the retreat, she confronts the fear that informs the coded world in which she has lived (p. 53): 'the fear of learning that nothing belongs to us, that there is no before life and no after life'

(p. 85) which menaces us as individuals. Mirroring the 'liquid womb' (p. 105) and formlessness of the newly-born (p. 112) – as well as its attendant dangers (see p. 105) – the retreat becomes a *chora* in which the voice of her body can be heard: 'poundings, mixture, sorting, warmth' (p. 131) through whose 'thick blood flow' (p. 112) and 'continual unfurling of signs, of forms' (p. 136) she is gradually able to recompose 'a forgotten alphabet' (p. 112).

The final image of *Le Réduit*, of she close to death, destroying and vomiting all the written and spoken words that have lived in her (p. 140), is both apocalyptic and an example of the potential dangers of such a position. Whilst she is ultimately delivered from the constraints of his desire and language, we are given no real alternative in the text beyond a retreat into silence and a possible 'language of the body'. Thus, while the image of woman's capacity to (re)create herself in an other symbolic may indeed be potentially revolutionary – she is described on the last page of the text as 'no longer in the retreat, but everywhere out of time' (p. 140) – the question remains as to whether woman's removal from the political, social, cultural and linguistic arenas in the way writers like Schavelzon envisage, will only compound the male-dominance of the system in which women must nevertheless continue to live. If our retreat also entails our withdrawal from direct political and social intervention, then our refusal to speak his language on the grounds that this does not speak us/her *may* reinforce woman's subordination within the patriarchal schema.[35]

A way out of the triangle: Hélène Cixous

Much of Hélène Cixous' fictional writing can also be read in the light of psychoanalytic theory. The opening pages of her novel *Angst*,[36] for example, give a vivid account of the process of separation from the m/other:

> Cut. You say I. And I bleed. I am outside . . . I no longer have what I once had ..... You're not there any more . . . I still want to have . . . To hold on to what is going to disappear .... The body, here. Separate ....
>
> My mother puts me down on the ground . . . 'Wait there for me. I'll be back straight away.' My mother goes out ....
>
> As soon as I am put down I begin to shudder; I am still trusting, sense buzzes in my ears (pp. 7–9).

As in *Le Réduit*, Cixous explores in *Angst* how men's language and desire appropriate and thus obliterate women's sense of self: 'He saw in me everything he claimed he didn't have; I didn't recognize myself' (p. 132). Unlike *Le Réduit*, however, Cixous suggests in *Angst* that there is a way round the (father's) law of castration. The 'scar' is recognised as 'a Forgery, but from his own hand' (p. 209) and Cixous urges: 'on all fours then, crawl between the table of the law' (p. 184), 'reduce the six hundred and thirteen commandments to naught' (p. 169).

Crucial to this defiance are the resources of the unconscious. Cixous draws on her own unconscious experience to envision a new order of relations between self and other:

> With all my dreams to help me I tried to create another scene for love, ignoring the laws . . . I tried with the help of all my visions to draw the flickering image which would make it possible to overcome separation (p. 99).

Dreams, which are 'free from any laws' (p. 148), are vital in overcoming our 'fear', giving us access to an other world in which we may approach the 'inner, secret, grasped life with words' (p. 149).

Women's privileged relation to the mother as source of plenitude and creation similarly offers a way through the law's restrictions. 'Bring yourself into being' (p. 19), Cixous writes, 'You've got the belly and the love' (p. 21): 'Close your eyes and open your mouth and out pops the little child' (p. 21).

Literature, because it incorporates dreams and the other of the unconscious, also provides a space in which an other order may be inscribed. Cixous describes in *Angst* how reading *Tristan and Yseult* inspires her to imagine a couple – 'a man, a woman' – who are intent, not on the acquisition of power or the obliteration of differences, but on living differently (p. 100). In a long passage which typifies the lively, humorous and playful style of much of Cixous' fictional writing, she details the dangers that beset her attempt to follow Tristan and Yseult beyond the fate laid down for them by the law:

> They were being watched. The tunnel was swarming with people who hated them. Not only the police but the whole of society .... I projected them outside in one go. Two thunder-claps. Saved. As soon as they were

> in darkness there was a commotion while I invented their flight. A prisoner of these dark times, in the midst of preparations for repression, I played the fool as if I had nothing to do with them. I played the idiot while troops were massing at the openings, ridiculous armies with cross-bows which could nevertheless kill if you came within reach. I turned base and mediocre like them, in order to invent in secret beings who are not tolerated in reality, in order to get near the frontier without being stopped; to back up to the gate, nonchalantly .... Imagine their journey. Work with feverish brain to give them the means to go where no one has ever been before (pp. 100–101).

The problem for Cixous does not, however, end there. As soon as she attempts to translate her vision into language, the vision changes:

> Every time I have wanted to tell the truth I have lied. It couldn't come out. I chose to use analogies which I vaguely felt would save the truth .... If I did succeed it would mean I had failed. I would have brought it down to my level (pp. 115–16).

But though failure may currently be inevitable, Cixous does not believe this means we should relinquish the attempt and adhere to the law's constraints. On the contrary, she suggests that it will only be by throwing off all the constructions of self – 'prudence, caution, foresight, career, position' (p. 139) – that ensure the law's continued operation, that we will make the imaginary 'leap into the dark' that will create a new symbolic:

> All ties had been cut, with knife, soul, teeth . . . I listened to the other language .... I answered with my blood ....
>
> If I hadn't devoted all my energies to renouncing everything every moment . . . if I hadn't got rid of myself, of every last wish, even the tiniest thought, the plane in which I was flying . . . in silence could never have taken off. If I had made as if to turn round, to look overboard, it could not have passed into the infinite. It would have crashed (p. 191).

From mother to daughter: Chantal Chawaf, Emma Santos and Jeanne Hyvrard

One area of development that recurs repeatedly in contemporary French women's writing is the relationship between mothers and daughters. For the sake of continuity, and in order to be able to discuss in more detail texts which may be unfamiliar to readers, I have chosen to explore this theme in five novels already introduced: Chantal Chawaf's *L'Intérieur des heures*, *Elwina, le roman fée* and *Le Soleil et la terre*, Emma Santos' *La Malcastrée* and Jeanne Hyvrard's *Mere la mort.*[37]

According to Freud, the Oedipal crisis involves the girl in a series of complicated manoeuvres vis-à-vis her mother. As a result of the father's intervention in the mother–child relation, Freud suggests that the girl switches her attention from her mother to her father, blaming and even hating her mother for not embodying the organ she now perceives to symbolise power. Since however the daughter cannot hope to compete with her mother for her father's love, Freud argues that the girl finally aligns herself with her mother in an uneasy identification with the mother's (female) sex.

This account of the daughter is echoed in Chantal Chawaf's recent novel *L'Intérieur des heures*,[38] a story about a mother and her adolescent daughter. The father is almost wholly absent and, confronted by what she perceives to be her mother's lack, the daughter retreats into a private world of fantasy:

> Her steely blue eyes rolled in an inner sky, seeming to fear madness less than the terrifying exterior and, journeying inside her anguish, the little one fled the reality she did not want to see (p. 70).

The mother's desperate attempts to bring her daughter back to earth are shown only to exacerbate the problem, visibly displaying her 'lack': 'this wound that the girl could not bear to guess at' (p. 70). The result is a web of jealousy and regressive fantasy which inhibits both women's independence:

> 'She [the daughter] hated the mark of another's imprint, this man, her father, her rival whom she took to be the conqueror of her mother forever conquered with whom the child could no longer identify herself but who she continued to love' (p. 70).

> I could work, said the mother. But I would have to leave you.
> – I need you! the little one gloomily persisted. This is not the moment to abandon me (p. 80).

> daughter and mother . . . imperfectly separated, they cleaved one to the other (p. 70).

In Emma Santos' *La Malcastrée*,[39] it is the mother who initiates the daughter's separation: 'My mother's criminal hands castrated me' (p. 53). Unlike *L'Intérieur des heures*, where the daughter's 'dream of regressing' back to the 'impossible origin' (p. 329) of unity with the mother is neither abandoned nor finally realised, *La Malcastrée* stresses the need for self-definition and its expression in language (p. 66). Although the central character's retreat into the (maternal) body initially confounds her doctors' attempts to 'cure' her and make her 'normal', this regression ultimately leaves her with no perspective from which to view herself or others:

> I need to be defined, completed. I am a mass, mostly liquid. I am the colour of whoever takes me. I have no breasts, no roundness to my hips. I am a broken heap, anything but a woman (p. 66).
>
> It's hard to be alone before a world in bits . . . myself in pieces (p. 67).

Like Hélène Cixous, the problem for Santos is that this definition can only take place in the language that has come to figure absolute separation from the m/other: total division between body and words[40].

Jeanne Hyvrard's *Mère la mort*[41] focuses on the language spoken with the mother prior to separation. As the title 'Mother Death' suggests, the mother's role is here seen to be a highly ambiguous one. On the one hand, the mother provides nourishment and shelter for her child (p. 49), symbolising plenitude and new beginnings; on the other, she must initiate her daughter's entry into an order where 'she' cannot exist (p. 49), or else paralyse or devour her child.[42] For Hyvrard, the answer lies in the language of the mother's body before separation: 'the language of your arms wide open in my night' (p. 57). Deriving from the union between mother and daughter, and rooted in the knowledge that 'Everything is my body. Even the word. Especially the word' (p. 140), this m/other language, will, Hyvrard suggests, refuse the arbitrary divisions of man's symbolic. Countering the absolute severance from the m/other decreed by the masculine – whose game it is to 'kill the other' (p. 96) – and acknowledging the relationship between body and words, it will, Hyvrard writes, be a 'language which liberates . . . which brings me back to living beings' (p. 44).

In Chantal Chawaf's *Elwina, le roman fée*,[43] the separation between mother and daughter is the text's starting-point. The process is explored through the character of Françoise, friend to Elwine, and herself a mother with a baby daughter.

> Mother and daughter never again physically linked one by the other, flesh of my flesh which bleeds, never again will your skin have the odour of creamy milk and my mouth your taste of veined butter and bitter moist salt, never again will you hold me like before against your breast, you will not brush against me with your young woman's hair, you will not warm me again with your voice in my blood (p. 27).

Elwine's efforts to write are depicted as her attempt to write the book of Elwina, the mother. Her imaginary transformation of a city into air, for example, is portrayed as her endeavour to transpose the stifling codes of the city in which she must live into m/other love:

> Her mother lives there perhaps . . . myth of life queen of our hearts and we are born to call, to ceaselessly call for love for here below we are choking, love is lacking (p. 27).

The action of writing is shown to link Elwine to the mother: 'The milk of writing flows from her chest, nourishes the emptiness, smoothes it, softens it. Elwine no longer feels alone' (p. 12).

The union is also the theme of Elwine's writing. She tells her publisher Pierre Duval: 'I want to speak of the other reality, the one we lost before we even knew it, to remind myself of what we have forgotten' (p. 15). Unlike *La Malcastrée* and *Mère la mort*, which, whilst they both envision an other language of the mother, do not themselves express this, the book of *Elwina* offers a writing in which mother and daughter, language and body, are no longer separate (see p. 99). The writing of *Elwina* the mother gives birth to meaning for Elwine:

> The more Elwina, the mother, (be)comes apart, the more something of a style, something of a language comes together for Elwine, for the daughter, in her flesh, in this progressive separation of desire and its object . . . And, in the same way and in proportion as the origin effaces itself, something of this effacement traces itself, inscribes the hollow, inscribes the emptiness and opens, opens language to the unsayable, in the same way, too, as Elwine establishes herself, she discovers her reason for living, her only reason for living in this fleshly movement thrusting towards the abstract which little by little is born from her, saves her,

> substitutes for the lost birth a birth endlessly renewed. The sense of Elwine's life is born from a mother language (p. 82).

Unlike *L'Intérieur des heures*, this mother language is neither the result of prohibitive dependency or regressive merging with the mother (p. 118); nor does it remain confined to the body since this would perpetuate our silence and compound our 'fear' (see p. 129). In contrast Elwine's writing is portrayed as her attempt to translate the knowledge and communication of union with the mother into an other symbolic:

> And from a place of separation, of death, of murder, of suffering, we pass with Elwine to this transformed peaceful place, where violence and frustration no longer impede need, desire, and where, without blocking, without boundaries, sensibility can evolve towards the other, towards love, allowing life, by crying out, by creating, by glorifying, to prevail over death, over the inevitable separation (p. 151).

Chawaf's *Le Soleil et la terre*,[44] unlike the texts presented thus far, is written from the viewpoint of the mother. In a passage which vividly demonstrates the rich material quality of much of Chawaf's writing, the mother's role is depicted as that of giving birth to independence and language in the child:

> When my milk is no longer enough for you, my daughter, my thing so soft, so small against me, then, with the veins of a fern, I will make you a dress of lace and with a shell of a hazelnut, I will make you a boat to cross the lake and leave the forest and you will go to the village and eat the most tender lamb from the stables and cheeses and grow, grow big. I sing the lullaby, I find the words, their tenderness, to give you my voice to suckle (p. 7).

The mother's words, which here 'name' the daughter, are shown to be the result of a transmission from mother to daughter (re)learnt by the mother in her daughter's birth:

> Blood flows from one body to the other, from one epoch to another (p. 8).

> And the language that I learn from your touch takes root in the senses, in the sensory organs, follows the chains of neurons which link the senses to the brain, then, from my head, I name you (p. 76).

Unlike the separation and loss, with their attendant effects of hierarchy, tyranny and death, which engender men's discourse (p. 85), the language of the mother is offered as a solution to the violence and war that threaten the world of the text. For Chawaf, women's sex-specific connection to the origin of life, embodied in the union between mother and daughter (p. 8), is here shown to contain the potential for an other order. This issue of women's difference, in its relation to language and a new symbolic, is one of the major issues of French feminism, and it is to this question of sexual difference that I now turn.

3

Theories of sexual difference

A long history has put all women in the same sexual, social and cultural condition. Whatever inequalities exist among women, they all undergo, even without clearly realizing it, the same oppression, the same exploitation of their body, the same denial of their desire.

Luce Irigaray

If you are woman, you will resemble ideal woman; and you will obey the imperatives that mark your line. You will channel your desires, you will address them where, how, and to whom it is proper. You will honour the laws.

Hélène Cixous

Women merely 'equal' to men would be 'like them', therefore not women. Once more, the difference between the sexes would be in that way cancelled out, ignored, papered over.

Luce Irigaray

A DESIRE FOR DIFFERENCE

In Freud's later work, as in the work of Jacques Lacan, the Oedipal crisis serves as an explanation for the way an individual's desire, created and maintained through the (lost) object/(m)other, and acting as a strong motivating force on the individual, is organised according to a pre-established social and symbolic system. The phallus, as object of the castration law, is emblem (first signifier) of this division. In his 'Three Essays on Sexuality',[1] Freud argued that there is no natural difference between the sexes, and he stressed that boys and girls must learn to perceive themselves as different and to desire others. Drawing on Freud's theory, Lacan makes two further points which are important here. Developing Freud's insistence that normality is at best an idealised fiction, Lacan suggested that a child's adoption of a sex and gender role is neither intrinsically linked to biological sex, nor, once a role has been accepted, is it necessarily secure. Secondly, since the boy, unlike the girl, possesses a physical equivalent of the phallus, the girl's relationship to the symbolic order is complicated in a way that the boy's is not. The fact that the girl has no means of representing within herself even her lack – she has no penis to embody the phallus that stands both for the lost object/(m)other and for the act of signifying this – places her in a problematic relation to the symbolic code since, Lacan suggested, she cannot herself figure within its order and thus only exists according to *man's* definition of her there.

These accounts of difference have prompted a number of responses from French feminists. Lacan's notion of the fluctuating nature of gender has influenced the work of Hélène Cixous, and her account of a masculine and feminine libidinal economy; while his insistence that woman cannot herself figure within the patriarchal symbolic is rejoindered by Luce Irigaray's belief that women must create an alternative symbolic universe of our own. This issue of difference is also one of the major areas of contention between French and Anglo–American feminists,[2] and raises a number of questions for writing, both in relation to whether it is necessary to be a woman in order to write in an other way, and in conjunction with the attempt to create new forms.

Women's position: Julia Kristeva

Julia Kristeva suggests that women are currently offered two diametrically opposed positions within the patriarchal schema. In *About Chinese Women*[3] she argues that women can at present choose either to remain tied to the mother and refuse to enter the symbolic system, or we can attempt intervention in the political, social and cultural arenas by entering the symbolic order and assuming those values our society aligns with the masculine. She believes neither of these options presents a satisfactory position for women. Fixation on the mother, she writes, confirms women in the role of (silent) other excluded from or relegated to the margins of social and political intervention, whilst identification with the father is achieved at the expense of the maternal relation and the suppression of body-drives.

Kristeva sees a link between these two positions open to women and the two generations which have marked the development of the women's movement. She suggests that the first generation of feminism has been an egalitarian one in which women have tried to minimise or deny sexual differences, and that this has been followed by a second phase in which women have drawn attention to, explored and celebrated what they have perceived to be our differences from men. As in her description of the paths open to women under patriarchy, Kristeva warns of the dangers inherent in both types of feminism. Like a number of French feminist writers, she believes there is an implicit trap in all forms of direct political and social action, since any such intervention is necessarily framed by the very logic of power the activist is seeking to challenge. In an article entitled 'A New Type of Intellectual: The Dissident',[4] Kristeva suggests that even the potentially subversive doctrine of Marxism is caught in this trap since it ignores the actual motivations of the human subject. It remains blind to the 'critical points' of 'human experience', which 'cannot be reduced to political causality'.[5] Like the feminism rooted in equality and which seeks direct political and social intervention, it becomes, Kristeva stresses, another master discourse and must, if it is to have any real impact, broaden its conception of humankind from beings determined in relation to (economic) production, to include our relationship to reproduction and the symbolic order.[6] Any theory seeking fundamental changes in the functioning of the political and social structure, she writes, must include an account of sexual difference as this marks the human subject's relation to the symbolic contract: which *is* the social contract. She concludes that Marxism and the feminism derived from egalitarian principles and a policy of political and social action must incorporate the role of sexual difference in the creation of human subjectivity as this has been outlined by psychoanalysis.

Kristeva's critique of the feminism which seeks to maximise women's differences hinges, not on the dangers of recuperation by a masculine order, but on the difficulties she sees in attempting to isolate intrinsic differences from those produced by the symbolic structure. If the feminine exists in the way radical feminists seeking to stress women's differences suggest, she argues, it exists only in relation to the symbolic for it is only thinkable within its terms. It is, like everything else, necessarily subject to symbolic law as we currently conceive this. Relegated by the symbolic to the position of 'excessive or transgressive other', it is, Kristeva stresses, only as this is designated by the symbolic function that 'the feminine can exist, speak, think or write itself for both sexes'.[7]

Kristeva suggests that the way forward for women depends on recognising the law of castration and sexual difference as the organising principles of Western patriarchy. She does not believe this means women should abandon the fight for equality, but argues that we must combine our struggle for equal political, social, economic and cultural rights with an understanding of our sexuality. In particular, she suggests that we should explore our sex-specific relation to procreation, since she sees motherhood as offering women the potential experience of an other that is not based on appropriation and the need for self-definition, and which allows individual differences to exist, that may provide a model for a relation to otherness beyond the one imposed by patriarchal law, and hence for a new form of subjectivity.

In addition to a potentially different relation to the other arising from women's sex-specific experience of pregnancy, birth and motherhood, Kristeva sees two further possibilities for change deriving from women's sexuality. Citing Freud's insistence that the 'ultimate law' is the 'law of death', she suggests that women's privileged relation to the origin of life means women are less afraid of death than men, and hence are less circumscribed by its law.[8] She also argues that women's biological, menstrual and hormonal cycles

– in addition to our actual or potential experience of maternity – mean women have a different relationship to time. In an essay entitled 'Women's Time',[9] she compares what she describes as the 'linear' time of man's symbolic as this is represented by the chronology of history and linguistic structure, with the more cyclical knowledge of time which she believes many women, and particularly mothers, share. Developing this distinction, Kristeva points in the essay beyond a feminism which assumes a masculine position in the search for equality, and a feminism which ignores the reality of the symbolic in the attempt to situate women beyond its law, to a new generation of feminism that will work to (re)formulate women's experiences with the (linear) constructions of the patriarchal system. 'The time has come', she writes, 'to emphasize the multiplicity of female expressions and preoccupations so that from the intersection of these differences there might arise, more precisely, less commercially, and more truthfully, the real fundamental difference between the sexes.'

Finally, Kristeva argues that however women's differences are currently conceived of, or whatever their actual or potential contribution to transforming the symbolic may be, women, because of the way we have been positioned by the patriarchal schema, are in a different relation to its law from men. For Kristeva, this relation is a potentially dissident one, since she suggests women's association with the feminine has forced us into the position of other, with little to gain from the continuation of patriarchal rule.

An other symbolic: Luce Irigaray

Like Julia Kristeva, Luce Irigaray believes women's sexuality has been appropriated and defined by men in ways which ignore or reduce its specificity. 'Women', she writes in the title essay of the collection *This Sex Which Is Not One*,[10] 'are marked phallicly by their father, husbands, procurers. And this branding determines their value in sexual commerce. Woman is never anything but the locus of a more or less competitive exchange between two men'. Irigaray cites the insistence of Freudian psychoanalysis on 'visibility' as an example of how men's definitions have determined both the sexual and social order, which, she suggests, have transformed woman's sex into the 'horror of nothing to see'. She sees this emphasis as deriving directly from the (sole) adoption of an economy alien to women's pleasure; women, she stresses, gain more pleasure from touching than they do from looking.

Irigaray explores what she describes as the 'highly anxious attention' paid to the erection of the male organ in the West as a further illustration of the extent to which the prevailing sexual imaginary is foreign to women. She argues that Western society's repression of women has been so successful 'that one would have to dig very deep indeed to discover beneath the traces of this civilization, of this history, the vestiges of a more archaic civilization that might give some clue to woman's sexuality'. She concludes by suggesting that what we would find would 'undoubtedly have a different alphabet, a different language'.

As a figurative illustration of the different ways men and women experience pleasure, Irigaray suggests that whereas men need a 'mediating instrument' to 'touch themselves', woman '"touches herself" all the time, and moreover no one can forbid her to do so, for her genitals are formed of two lips in continuous contact' (p. 24). 'Within herself', Irigaray writes, '"she" is already two': a 'two' that is only reducible by force to the 'one' of male law.

Irigaray links the disconcertingly double nature of women's sex to women's relegation to the negative or 'reverse' side of the visible and morphologically designatable male form. 'The value granted to the male form', she writes, 'excludes the one that is in play in female autoeroticism': 'whence the mystery that woman represents in a culture claiming to count everything, to number everything by units, to inventory everything as individualities'. Irigaray argues that unlike men women derive our pleasure 'precisely from this incompleteness of form'; our sexuality, she writes, *is* plural, 'always something more and something else' to however this is accredited to us. She suggests, for this reason, that women's pleasure presents a threat to the linearity of masculine law, diffusing its momentum towards a (single) 'goal-object', and undermining its 'fidelity to a single discourse'.

Like Kristeva, Irigaray finds in women's sexuality the potential for a different relation to otherness. Woman, she suggests, 'is indefinitely other in herself': the other is already 'within her' and 'autoerotically familiar' to her. She believes this capacity for alterity gives women access to an economy other than the one currently in force, founded not on the masculine preoccupation with ownership and property, but on feminine comprehension of proximity. Since women, she argues, 'derive pleasure from what is so near' that it 'makes all discrimination of identity, and thus all forms of property, impossible', woman, she suggests, enters into the 'ceaseless exchange of herself with the other' – 'without any possibility of identifying either'. This potential for otherness, she concludes, 'puts into question all prevailing economies'.

Irigaray suggests that women's inferior position within the patriarchal symbolic enslaves men almost as much as it enslaves women. In an article entitled 'Sexual Difference' translated in *French Feminist Thought*,[11] she argues that men are inevitably constrained by the power invested in whatever they designate as separate/other. Citing Descartes' account of the 'passion' of wonder, she stresses that a result of the masculine hegemony is that 'the passions have either been repressed, stifled and subdued, or else reserved for God'. She sees a re-interpretation of the whole nexus of relations between subject and other as the prelude to a true relation between the sexes. The existing space between the sexes, she writes, has been filled with 'attraction, greed, possession, consummation, disgust etc., and not with that wonder which sees something as though always for the first time, and never seizes the other as its object'. She argues that this remodelling of the relationship between self and other is the necessary prerequisite to a meeting between the sexes that would be a 'celebration and not a disguised or polemic form of the master-slave relationship'.

In 'This Sex Which Is Not One', Irigaray perceives a link between the multiplicity and diffuseness of women's pleasure and the way this has been reduced by the dominant sexual imaginary, and the way women's speech has traditionally been interpreted by masculine culture. The classic image of a woman speaking, she writes, is of a woman setting off in all directions, leaving 'him' unable to discern any coherent thread to her meaning:

> Hers are contradictory words, somewhat mad from the stand-point of reason, inaudible for whoever listens to them with ready-made grids, with a fully elaborated code in hand (p. 29).

She suggests that men's attempt to trap women by asking for a precise account of what we mean is worse than useless, since this only forces our meaning into a format that irrevocably changes its essence. She stresses that the only way to hear women's meaning is:

> to listen with another ear, as if hearing an 'other meaning' always in the process of weaving itself, of embracing itself with words (p. 29).

In the 'Questions' section of *This Sex Which Is Not One*,[12] Irigaray writes that:

> in order for women to be able to make themselves heard, a 'radical' evolution in our way of conceptualizing and managing the political realm is required (p. 127).

She suggests in 'This Sex Which Is Not One' that women's exclusion from the symbolic contract has:

> put woman in the position of experiencing herself only fragmentarily, in the little-structured margins of a dominant ideology .... what is left of a mirror invested by the (masculine) 'subject' to reflect himself (p. 30).

Like Julia Kristeva, she warns of the dangers in allowing women's difference to be 'reabsorbed and reduced by masculine practice and discourse'; if women's liberation takes place within 'men's language, men's politics, men's economy', she writes, if women's 'aim were simply to reverse the order of things, even supposing this to be possible', then history would simply repeat itself, 'would revert to sameness: to phallocratism'. Any attempt to substitute feminine for masculine power will, she insists, be doomed to failure:

> because this reversal would still be caught up in the economy of the same, in the same economy – in which, of course, what I am trying to designate as 'feminine' would not emerge ('Questions', p. 130).

She concludes that women must get rid of the language which structures the symbolic contract if we are to avoid becoming fixed or congealed by its definitions.

Irigaray sees the way forward in women's exploration of our 'pleasures'. She suggests that one means of achieving this would be for women to separate from men in order to 'discover the love of other women': without the 'imperious' dictates of a culture which places us 'in the position of rival commodities'. Women, she argues in 'Questions', need to 'constitute a place where they could be "among themselves" ', in order to learn to (re)formulate our desires, and forge for ourselves 'a social status that compels recognition'. Only then, she writes, could women come into being as something other than the 'scraps' and 'scattered remnants of a violated sexuality': only then might women begin to perceive what women might be like, and what a 'woman's society' and 'language' might mean.

In 'Volume-Fluidity' in *Speculum of the Other Woman*,[13] Irigaray reiterates her insistence that difference has only ever existed according to masculine parameters, with the result that the feminine has been construed 'as the inverse, indeed the underside, of the masculine'. She links this appropriation of the feminine to language. In language, she argues, signs acquire meaning through asserting their 'spatial distinctness' from other signs, and by 'decisively cutting up the whole matter of language', including the blanks. She suggests that in the same way that the feminine has been silenced and used to bolster the masculine sexual and social imaginary, so, in language, the existing space has been employed to create the (masculine) subject's (self-)assertions. 'Those things that are not said or said between the lines', she writes, 'have already been given meaning', with the effect that 'the "subject" will thus be able to exploit the other, fragment her, speculate her – and find in her nothing but the same sameness' (p. 235). She argues that women must renounce masculine language, since any attempt to speak its logic will inevitably determine what we say, and formulate an alternative symbolic of our own.

In 'The Power of Discourse and the Subordination of the Feminine',[14] Irigaray suggests women should 'assume the feminine role deliberately', and convert women's subordinate position through making 'visible' – by jamming the machinery of 'onto-theo-logic' – 'what was supposed to remain invisible'. Like Julia Kristeva, she warns against the dangers of reabsorption, insisting that if women's campaigns 'aim simply for a change in the distribution of power, leaving intact the power structure itself', then women risk 'resubjecting themselves, deliberately or not, to a phallocratic order'. Irigaray rejects the political and economic theories of Marxism for this reason, suggesting that its doctrines are unable to address the real issues of women's oppression since they derive from 'a definition of power of the masculine type'. Like Kristeva, she does not however believe that this means women should renounce the fight for 'equality in the sphere of civil rights', but stresses that we should attempt to articulate 'the double demand' 'for equality *and* difference'.[15] She suggests that at present there are two paths women might take. One is for women to endeavour to become men's 'equal', in which case we would enjoy the same economic, social and political rights as men, but would, she believes, still be required to adopt the 'masquerade' of femininity as this has been prescribed by the masculine. The other is for women to reject the masculine system of (self-)representation, and to 'become speaking subjects as well' and in our own way. She believes this production of an other symbolic would have radical implications for both sexes, undermining the foundations of the patriarchal schema and opening this to the possibility of change:

> that would not fail to challenge the discourse that lays down the law today, that legislates on everything, including sexual difference, to such an extent that the existence of another sex, of an other, that would be woman, still seems, in its terms, unimaginable (p. 85).

Masculine and feminine: Hélène Cixous

Hélène Cixous, like Luce Irigaray, takes issue with the account of sexual difference given by Freudian psychoanalysis. In 'Sorties'[16] she argues that the psychoanalytic reliance on its own description of sexual 'essence' is reductive, since it derives this description from the very model of biological destiny which has hamstrung men as well as women through the centuries. Both sexes, she writes, are caught 'in a web of age-old cultural determinations' so complex as to be almost unanalysable, and she suggests that the most useful way of approaching psychoanalysis today is as a theory of how sexual difference is organized in relation to patriarchal law.

Cixous sees the two possible responses of acceptance or refusal of the law in terms of the gender economies of masculine and feminine. In her essay 'Extreme Fidelity' in *Writing Differences*,[17] she illustrates her argument with reference to the story of Perceval in the Arthurian legend *Quest for the Holy Grail*. As a young man, she writes, Perceval is taught to obey a law which is unproven and which he does not understand.[18] Arriving at the court of the Fisher King, Perceval, in obedience to the law, does not question the passing of the lance or the dripping blood until the crime he should have prevented has already been committed. Cixous contrasts Perceval's classically masculine position of adherence to the law with the feminine response exemplified by Eve in the Garden of Eden. Unlike Perceval, who refuses his desire to ask questions since this would contravene what he has been taught, Eve, in the biblical version of Genesis, follows her desire and defies God's incomprehensible prohibition not to eat from the tree of knowledge, thereby creating for herself and the world the possibility of knowledge, innovation and uncensored choice.

For Cixous, these two responses of masculine allegiance to the law and feminine willingness to risk its prohibitions, exemplify the two poles of behaviour open to every one of us. For convenience, and as an approximation of the way these positions are adopted by men and women within an order where men ostensibly have more to gain from allegiance to the law than women, Cixous chooses the labels 'masculine' and 'feminine' to suggest the way these positions tend under patriarchy to divide. However, as she stresses in 'Extreme Fidelity', the terms are merely markers and can, and perhaps ought, to be exchanged for others. Although Cixous believes at present that women, because of the position to which we are relegated and the way this position is confirmed socially and culturally as well as politically, are more likely to adopt a feminine response than men, the point for Cixous is that we all perpetually fluctuate between different gender roles, sometimes assuming defensive, masculine postures that seek to close-down, appropriate and control, at other times accepting a more open, feminine response willing to take risks, and at other times combining elements of each.

Cixous suggests that biological sex differences play an important role in determining our choice of gender economy, and provide a potential impetus for transforming the (patriarchal) status quo. She argues that patriarchal law has defined and thus appropriated sexual difference, privileging and imposing male constructions and an attendant masculine response. Like Luce Irigaray, she believes women's sexuality has been repressed, excluded or neutered in this process, and she sees women's (re)discovery of our bodies and unconscious desires as an important step on the road to challenging the patriarchal monopoly. For Cixous, the differences between the sexes entail the possibility of different insights, understanding, and ways of relating. Like both Irigaray and Kristeva, she finds in women's sex-specific experience of pregnancy and childbirth the potential for a radically different approach to the other, to subjectivity, and love. Drawing on her own experience of pregnancy and childbirth, she writes:

> It is not only a question of the feminine body's extra resource, this specific power to produce some thing living of which her flesh is the locus, not only a question of the transformation of rhythms, exchanges, of relation to space, of the whole perceptive system.... It is also the experience of a 'bond' with the other, all that comes through in the metaphor of bringing into the world.... There is a bond between woman's libidinal economy – her *jouissance*, the feminine Imaginary – and her way of self-constituting a subjectivity that splits apart without regret (from an unpublished lecture given in 1982).

As an example of the diametrically opposite responses of masculine and feminine, Cixous relates these two positions to attitudes to giving. The classic masculine response to giving, she writes, is to give in relation to what will be received, an attitude she compares to the 'open extravagance' of femininity. Unlike the 'stingy narcissism' of masculinity, she stresses, femininity gives beyond the needs of selfhood, without measuring what is given in terms of what will be returned.

The search for a feminine relation to the other is the central preoccupation of Cixous' work. Like Luce Irigaray and her insistence on (feminine) proximity, Cixous believes a feminine approach to the other involves, not the (masculine) appropriation or destruction of the other's difference in order to create the self in a masterful position, but locating and maintaining the 'right distance' in which self and other can co-exist as equals. In *Le Livre de Promethea* ('The Book of Promethea'),[19] Cixous details the efforts of a writer to construct a relationship with Promethea that will not annihilate her difference through the 'murderous' practices of literary and social convention. Her admiration for the Brazilian writer Clarice Lispector, which she documents in the French–English *Vivre l'orange/To Live the Orange*,[20] is based on her respect for Lispector's attempts not to employ or deform the other of the text for her own ends. Cixous' recent cycle of history plays, written for the Paris-based Théâtre du Soleil, *L'Histoire terrible mais inachevée de Norodom Sihanouk roi du Cambodge* ('The Terrible But Unfinished Story of Norodom Sihanouk King of

Cambodia')[21] and *L'Indiade ou l'Inde de leurs rêves* ('Indiada or the India of their Dreams'),[22] are similarly concerned with the devastating effects of appropriating, controlling or destroying difference through colonialisation, segregation, apartheid and war.

Like both Julia Kristeva and Luce Irigaray, Cixous warns women of the dangers of employing masculine procedures in our struggle for equality. She believes women must continue the fight for equality in the political, social and cultural spheres,[23] but argues that this fight must be accompanied by the search for an other (feminine) schema.

Cixous' insistence on a 'feminine' writing – an *écriture féminine* – is fundamental in this respect. For Cixous, a feminine writing has two distinct possibilities. First, since she believes women are currently closer to a feminine gender than men, she urges women to write the pent-up forces of our sexuality and desire, thus 'filling in the hole' of masculine thinking and initiating changes in its government through the inclusion of women's experiences. Secondly, she believes a feminine writing will transform the structures of language and culture, and hence of our social and political systems, by refusing masculine positions of censorship and appropriation and implementing a new pattern of relations between subject and other. As with the adoption of a feminine gender, and despite her insistence that women are presently closer to the feminine than men, Cixous suggests that such a writing is potentially the province of both sexes.[24]

The sexual origin: Eugénie Lemoine-Luccioni

Unlike Julia Kristeva, Luce Irigaray and Hélène Cixous, whose writings, albeit with very different emphases, span the bridge between biological and psychological notions of difference and the need for political intervention, the work of psychoanalyst Eugénie Lemoine-Luccioni offers an interpretation of sexual difference rooted in a theory of the body. In *Partage des femmes* ('Women's Division/Share'),[25] Lemoine-Luccioni explores the effects of primary loss on men and women. Drawing on the work of Jacques Lacan, she suggests that there is a difference in the way men and women experience the loss which founds the symbolic order because of each sex's different bodily relation to the way this loss is figured. Men's possession of a penis, she writes, gives men a direct bodily relation to the phallus, and she believes this makes it easier for men to comprehend and deal with loss and hence to secure their identity as 'one' (p. 9). For men, real and potential loss are embodied by the penis, whereas, for women, Luccioni argues, this remains in 'the register of the imaginary' (p. 9). Luccioni suggests that this different bodily relation to the code of the symbolic mean men and women seek to make good our loss in different ways. Men's more confident creation of their identity – as 'one' – with its attendant implications for the other – woman – is, she argues, a consequence of their possessing a bodily equivalent which visibly represents the way loss is signified during the Oedipal crisis, and which is also the organ through which man's own (sexual) desires are transmitted. This congruence of physical and psychic–symbolic elements, Luccioni concludes, confirm men in their superior position, an ordering that woman's libidinal and psychic–symbolic energies do little to undermine. Woman's lack of the means to physically represent our loss, Luccioni suggests, blurs both its functioning and the unified identity it ultimately entails. She believes the boundaries between self and other are less clearly demarcated for women, and stresses that this makes it hard for women to challenge men on their own terms. Unlike Hélène Cixous, who finds in women's more fluid relation to loss the opportunity for transformation, Luccioni sees this fluidity as propelling women to seek an identity *through* our relationships with men.

For Luccioni, this difference precedes any possibility of the symbolic having been created by men to dominate women. Luccioni suggests that women's physical ability to give birth has placed women in a (fantasised) position of 'truth', since she argues that men perceive women as knowing the secret of the origin. She sees this register of 'fantasy' – in which each sex stands for the fantasy of the other – as the centre of the relationship between the sexes (p. 7). Women appear to men to *have* knowledge and 'possession' (p. 8), whilst women's experience of division *(partage)*, confirmed in childbirth, creates men in a (fantasised) position of 'unity'.

Luccioni argues that this division, derived from biological sex-differences, is so fundamental that 'no sexual revolution' will ever change the terms of its divide. 'Man will always love what is put in place of loss', she writes, and 'woman will love whatever makes one'. She believes this different relationship to loss and the other (sex) mean men and women have a different attitude to the world. She suggests that whilst men's desire to secure their loss gives them a more active, questing desire for knowledge and possession, women's experience renders this of lesser importance. No matter how curious or passionate women may be, Luccioni stresses, we will never have the same desire for knowledge and possession as men, since 'in some measure, on the [subject of the] origin, [woman] already knows'.

Although Luccioni acknowledges that the paradigms and systems of our society are masculine ones, she does not suggest that this means these must change (p. 11). Unlike those French feminists who see positive opportunities for change arising from women's sex-specific experience of motherhood, Luccioni believes women's experience of division – especially in its most extreme form during childbirth – compels women to seek a unified identity through our relationships with men; a desire which, she writes, tends to perpetuate rather than challenge the prevailing schema.[26]

THE BODY POLITIC

The issue of sexual difference is also explored in contemporary French women's writing. Responses to this question range from an insistence on the role of education in the creation and transformation of sexual differences, to a celebration of *women's* difference in its revolutionary potential to bring into being an other world.

Re education: Annie Ernaux, Marie Cardinal, Benoîte Groult and Chantal Chawaf

Annie Ernaux's *La Femme gelée* ('The Frozen Woman')[27] is the story of a thirty year old married mother looking back over her life and reflecting on how she was taught to be a woman. Ernaux's insistence on the role of education in the creation of women's difference links *La Femme gelée* to a mainstream of Anglo–American feminist fiction.[28] The novel opens with the woman remembering the refrain of her childhood:

> every morning, daddy-goes-to-work, mummy-stays-at-home, she-prepares-a-succulent-meal, I mumble, I repeat along with the others without asking questions (p. 16).

As a daughter, she must be like her mother – 'she's the one I must be like because I am a little girl' (p. 16) – and she recalls how this image was reinforced by the 'identikit' of motherhood given by her teacher at school: 'this silent devotion, this perpetual smile, and this effacement before the head of the family' (p. 60). Even though the woman's mother did not actually conform to this stereotype:

> ten years later, I'm the one gleaming and mute in a kitchen, amongst the strawberries and the flour, I've got inside the image and it's killing me (p. 61).

The woman remembers the:

> imaginary body, the one that began to dance in front of me during adolescence, the slim body with the harmonious proportions, the desirable bust, the appealing-mysterious-saucy-madonna face (p. 63).

This image, which 'nothing at school countered' (p. 80) and all her subsequent relationships with men confirmed (p. 89), is still the one mirrored back at her, in books and magazines. As a woman, she reflects that the choice offered her was, as now, 'this or solitude' (p. 90).

The woman recalls how even her adolescent sexuality was circumscribed by her gender. At seventeen, she was 'close . . . to sexual freedom and a glorious sensuality', but this freedom was denied her, and sex became a defensive game in which, like an animal prepared for slaughter, she was forced 'to cut my body into territories', each zone demarcated as 'permissible' or 'forbidden'. 'Each pleasure', she recalls, became 'defeat for me, victory for him' (p. 96). For her discovery of the other was a sin.

The woman remembers how all her efforts to talk, listen, share the interests of the men she became involved with, understand them, were subsumed by her gender coding: 'I shaped my body in the way they wanted, I love you in black, do your hair in a chignon, you'd look good in a purple dress' (p. 104). The only way for her to succeed was by becoming adept in feminine ways: 'killing whatever resists this . . . the desire to be really me' (p. 90).

The woman's attempts to break free of her feeling that she is 'without substance, unreal' (p. 118) by completing her academic education and realising her ambition to become a teacher, are finally prevented by the pressures of her role. At the end of the novel, Ernaux's woman can see no way of escaping the 'frozen woman' whose face she perceives reflected back to her at every turn (p. 182).

Like Annie Ernaux's 'frozen woman', Marie Cardinal, in her autobiographical text *Autrement dit*,[29] traces the way men's laws have constrained and influenced her as a woman.[30] She links her own personal experience to the effect men's laws have had on women throughout history, suggesting that, as a result, women no longer 'know that their "nature" is what politics and economics want it to be' (p. 120). As an example, Cardinal recalls how, at the beginning of the twentieth century, the industrial revolution in France needed women to work in the factories:

> they proved by A + B that artificial milk was best and that if they were good mothers and good wives they would stop breast-feeding and go and give their men a hand in the factories (p. 120).

This she compares with the current climate of high unemployment – *Autrement dit* was published in 1977 – in which, she argues, 'as if by chance' there is a wealth of evidence forcing women to believe the contrary:

> if you are good mothers and good wives, you must in all haste return home and stay there, it's nature that wants this (p. 120).

For Cardinal, man's 'education' has become such an integral part of our identities that she questions whether it will ever be possible to separate what is culturally induced from what is natural (p. 168). Like a number of French feminists, she suggests that writing – *with* the body – may offer a means of exploring this divide (see pp. 201, 213).[31]

Benoîte Groult, in *Ainsi soit-elle*,[32] is similarly interested in the education that has shaped us as women. 'We must finally cure ourselves of being women', she writes, 'not of being born women, but of having been brought up as women in a universe of men'

(p. 34). Groult recalls her own experience of growing up as a girl and young woman in France. Like Annie Ernaux's 'frozen woman', she remembers the effects constantly needing to please and conform to men's expectations had (p. 18); like Marie Cardinal, she relates her experience to the laws that have restrained women through history (p. 42). Unlike Annie Ernaux and Marie Cardinal however, and unlike mainstream Anglo–American feminist writers, Groult's purpose in *Ainsi soit-elle* is not the institution of an equality that minimises or ignores sexual difference, but the creation of an equality that respects and values differences (p. 149). She looks forward – not to the disappearance of sexual differences – but to a time when men will no longer play the appropriating male role; and both sexes – 'dazzled' by the encounter with their similar but different equal – will discover 'in this marvellous difference all the magic of life' (p. 213).

Chantal Chawaf's *Le Soleil et la terre*[33] also explores the role of education in re-creating sexual differences. In *Le Soleil et la terre*, this education, even though it is shown to derive from a male-determined schema, is also presented as the enemy of men. The tales of the war 'heroes', for example, whose 'glorious' deeds punctuate the narrative, are revealed as a key factor in perpetuating the war and 'preventing the new man, the man of life, from being born' (p. 45).

For Chawaf, man's education cuts both women and men off from the source of life (p. 71), although she believes women may redress this imbalance by drawing on the experiences that have been excluded by men. This knowledge, she suggests, may reteach men a language grounded in respect for and celebration of the other's difference (p. 59). Unlike Eugénie Lemoine-Luccioni, who locates the fulcrum of women's desire in the search for a unified identity *through* our relationships with men, Chawaf sees the specificity of women's desire in this dissolution of the self which she values as a positive force for change (p. 107). In *Le Soleil et la terre*, she stresses that this desire may reverse the destructive patterns of a world 'based on contempt for the human body' (p. 54), offering in its place the model for a new order founded – not on a repressive hierarchy of death – but in a love relation of affirming life (p. 58).

Celebrating differences: Michèle Perrein, Marguerite Duras, Xavière Gauthier and Michèle Montrelay

Michèle Perrein's novel *La Chineuse*[34] explores the theme of sexual difference against the very different cultural backdrop of South-East Asia. In Perrein's novel, a young French woman, Camille, journeys through the war territories of Vietnam in the aftermath of the break-up of the relationship with her lover Clément. Through Camille, *La Chineuse* examines sex and gender roles within the context of Camille's personal loss and the wider framework of differences that structure South-East Asian society. Being a woman is something Camille has had to learn: 'it isn't simple being a woman. You discover it bit by bit' (p. 17), an education she compares to the colonialising of the Asian people who 'do not know, at first, what differentiates them' from the whites, and who must learn, as she had to, that 'man – preferably white – is the gold-standard' (p. 184). Despite this education, Camille admits her confusion over the issue of sexual difference: 'I know neither what a male is nor what a female is' (p. 23). Watching the Vietnamese women, she feels an instinctive empathy that cuts through her ties to the men of her own 'party' (p. 87), and realises that this empathy is linked to a primary bond with the women against the war: 'no war is ever woman's war' (p. 139). Camille travels to Saigon, hoping that here she will 'at last understand something definitive about men and why, living, they kill each other' (p. 144). Reflecting on this issue, she decides that the truth of man's difference lies in his physical strength and his willingness to perceive others as objects: 'Man knows a woman will never rape him. A woman is never sure that she will not be constrained' (p. 228). Presented with a young female prostitute by a male companion, although Camille is attracted by the girl's delicate beauty, she finds she is unable to treat the girl as an object in the way her male companion has done (p. 170). As Camille travels, memories of Clément come flooding back, and she begins to understand that the reason for the break-up of their affair was that she was never considered by Clément to be his equal: 'you had shown me . . . that for you a woman *was only a woman*' (p. 193). Her role was that of an accessory, her individuality negated and denied (p. 194).

Despite Camille's hope for an equality that will end the hierarchy of differences (p. 185), *La Chineuse* ends in ambiguity, as the war in

South-East Asia escalates. The last place Camille visits is Cambodia, where she discovers in the different rhythms and attitude to life, in the different relationship to time and emotion, the model for a new life (p. 234): a hope that is shattered by the outbreak of war in Cambodia and her forced return to a Paris where difference as hierarchy still dominates (p. 286).

Marguerite Duras and Xavière Gauthier's *Les Parleuses*[35] also emphasises a new correlation of sexual differences. Whilst both writers stress the negative effects man's domination has had on women (see p. 20), they see women's different bodies entailing a fundamentally different experience of feeling (pp. 19, 71, 154). Both writers argue that a women's movement based on the struggle for equality and aiming for such changes as an increase in the number of women in management and government positions will merely result in women becoming copies of men (p. 162). For Duras and Gauthier, as for a number of French feminist writers, the way forward lies instead in exploring, celebrating and inscribing differences, in writing as well as in art (pp. 50, 210)[36].

Difference is also the theme of a collection of essays by psychoanalyst Michèle Montrelay. In *L'Ombre et le nom* ('The Shadow and the Name'),[37] Montrelay locates in women's sex-specific experience of pregnancy a unique state in which the (masculine) boundaries between self and other are broken down.[38] 'Pregnancy', Montrelay writes, 'ignores the usual mode of (ac)counting' that structures masculine relations: 'when we are expecting a child, we cannot say we are two. Still less one' (p. 137). Like Julia Kristeva, and Camille's response to the women of South-East Asia in *La Chineuse*, Montrelay suggests that, except in those cases where the foetus is experienced by the mother as a 'foreign body', mother and child are 'suspended together' for the duration of pregnancy 'in the same force of life', a state which entails a different relationship to time and the real world. During pregnancy, Montrelay argues, time takes on a different 'floating' dimension which is at odds with the masculine scaling of time into past, present and future. Pregnancy encapsulates the start of life and does not incorporate the past. This blurring of the divisions between self and other, Montrelay stresses, which modifies the mother's relation to the real world (p. 137), also includes the possibility of an other mode of symbolising this connection which does not depend on total separation, and hence involves the potential for a new relationship to language, ourselves, others and the world.[39]

In relation to the other: Madeleine Chapsal

Madeleine Chapsal's autobiographical *Une femme en exil* ('A Woman in Exile')[40] examines the role of education in creating sexual differences and sees in the exploration of intrinsic difference a positive force for change. In *Une femme en exil*, Chapsal argues for an exchange between the sexes that will value the other's difference and thus bring into being the potential of both sexes:

> In order to exchange what we really have to exchange: in order for you to make a woman of me and for me to make a man of you, in order for you to give me my virility, which is in you, for you to reconcile me with this. And in order for me to allow you, finally, to accept your femininity. In order for the two of us to come together (p. 193).

For Chapsal, this exchange between masculinity and femininity necessarily involves a re-examination and shift in our sexual education (p. 239) as well as a new attentiveness to the body as a source of experience and knowledge (p. 174). This knowledge and experience, Chapsal stresses, has become distorted by the code of language, which is the enemy of change (see p. 15) and the medium through which to inscribe new structures. As an example of how language reduces and denies our body experience, Chapsal remembers the dances she attended as an adolescent. As she and her partner dance:

> no word is pronounced, but each gesture becomes a sign. If anyone had consulted me to ask me if I was enjoying myself, I would not have known what to reply; eyes gazing into space, I felt completely attentive to what my body understood' (p. 124).

She links this experience of language to the lectures she heard as a student, where words were employed by the lecturers to endorse a predetermined position (p. 91), a use of language she contrasts to the sensation of encounter that came through her own reading (p. 92) and writing (p. 15).

Chapsal constantly calls into question her attitude and treatment of others, reminding herself again and again that she must 'leave others to themselves' (p. 32), cease 'murdering' others' potential (p. 179), 'not weigh on anyone' (p. 157), learn 'to enter into contact . . . to speak [the others'] language' (p. 95). She believes language, despite the way it currently restricts and gets in the way of our relationships with others, will play a vital role in initiating the changes necessary for the foundation of a new order and system of exchange (see p. 96). In particular she sees writing as the vanguard of this revolution, since she insists writing offers an opportunity for experimentation presently denied us in our relationships with others:

> In order to draw near others, to reconnect with them, to regroup, to come amongst them, to gain admittance, I began writing, continue writing, go on writing (p. 221).

French feminist responses to the question of sex and gender differences thus take a variety of forms and include accounts of the role of difference in the creation of identity and our relationships with others. According to Freud and Lacan, sex and gender are the product of division from the lost object/(m)other as well as from the other sex. The ego, through its various cultural supports, functions to conceal this division figured by the phallus, thereby covering the early complexity of the child's sexual life and the heterogeneous impulses of the adult sexual drive. Only the unconscious, by impinging on the subject's conscious behaviour and symbolic expression, threatens the arbitrary and tenuous nature of this division. For Lacan, more explicitly than for Freud, the categories of man and woman are the effect of language. Language, as the medium of the (father's) law, defines woman as the negative or other of man, with the result that, for Lacan, the notion that women's difference can be conceived or expressed in an other way is, literally, non-sense. For a number of French feminist writers, this impasse is altogether too convenient since it confirms women in the role of acquiescence and inaction. For Luce Irigaray, the patriarchal order is the product of an exclusively male libido and mode of perception, and she refuses to agree that this means the present structure must always predominate or that women's difference cannot be construed as such. For French feminists like Irigaray, the multiplicity, diffuseness and potentially different relation to the other of women's sex-specific experiences challenges the mono-logic of patriarchal rule, offering a space from which to articulate a *differently* structured schema. Julia Kristeva, in an interview about her text *Polylogue*,[41] endorses Lacan's insistence on the role of language in the creation of sexual identity, arguing that language and the symbolic present an 'invincible weapon' against the child's 'premature separation from the world of the mother and the world of things'. Language, Kristeva stresses, provides a 'network of drives, signifiers and meanings' in which individual identity – including sexual identity – can be 'constantly remade'. Unlike those French feminists who see the way forward for women in the formation of a separate language, Kristeva advocates the inscription of a different ethics from within 'the language of so-called phallic communication' itself. This issue – as to whether women can or should create a separate language or whether we should work for change from within the existing structure – is the subject of the next chapter.

4

A woman's language?

What can be said about a feminine sexuality 'other' than the one prescribed in, and by, phallocratism? How can its language be recovered, or invented? How, for women, can the question of their sexual exploitation be articulated with the question of their social exploitation? .... How can they free themselves from their expropriation within patriarchal culture?

Luce Irigaray

From the moment that she begins to speak, to exist, she has to face problems which are all masculine and this is what puts her in mortal danger – if she doesn't use them, she doesn't exist, if she does use them, she kills herself with them.

Antoinette Fouque

So, urgently and anxiously, I look for a scene in which a type of exchange would be produced that would be different, a kind of desire that wouldn't be in collusion with the old story of death.

Hélène Cixous

For the theorists and writers whose work is included in this book, the dominant ideology in the West is both male-determined and repressive, subordinating whatever is defined as different – other – in ways which appropriate and suppress its other status. Woman is defined in relation to man according to this schema, our difference functioning to confirm men's position as master. In this second chapter on women and language, I turn more specifically to women's role in language to examine, in the light of post-structural and psychoanalytic accounts of the creation of difference in language, what a 'woman's language' might mean.

Unlike the efforts of Anglo–American feminists to initiate changes in women's inferior position through such strategies as countering the male dominance and exclusion of words like 'chairman' and substituting the more neutral formulation 'chairperson',[1] many French feminists see such tactics as irrelevant, since they argue that such cosmetic changes do little to alter the underlying power structures which continue to promote men at the expense of women. Luce Irigaray, for instance, suggests that part of the aim of masculine language is to make itself *appear* universal, and she argues that this endeavour to remove obvious male bias and neutralise language not only serves patriarchy's purpose but is also dangerous, since it gives women the *impression* of change. For French feminists like Irigaray, women will only begin to speak *as women* by refusing the current order altogether, since to adopt this order, which exists to express *men's* perceptions, modes of organisation, needs and desires is necessarily to speak *as a man.*

The questions such assertions raise can be summarised as follows. First, what does it mean, given that language shapes our knowledge of the world, to speak *as a woman*? If, as Irigaray suggests, the current order utilises, defines and obliterates women, how can we begin to conceive ourselves in ways which escape its schema? Is our task to *deconstruct* the hierarchies that inform language? Or is it to refuse the existing power structures altogether and to formulate a new language derived from a *different* perception, experience and desire? If it is the former, what path should our challenge take? Will women's inscription of our differences in the gaps and margins left uninhabited by the masculine undermine its hegemony, as some of the writers included here suggest? Can women's naming of our different body experiences, as Annie Leclerc believes, transform the patriarchal structure? And if we are to take the second of these options as our task, where is this other – feminine – language to come from? From women's biological experience and knowledge? From a different relation to the m/other and a language in which the bond between words and objects, such as Jeanne Hyvrard suggests, remains intact? How can we equate this other language with Lacan's insistence that woman's privileged access to the body and a mode of communication beyond symbolic law is itself a misconception and a *product* of language? What are we to make of his assertion that men and women are the *result* of language, and that either sex can change places and locate itself on the other side of this sexual (linguistic) divide? Is it necessary to *be* a woman in order to speak as one? And what of the argument that the formulation of a woman's language will strengthen the existing status quo, which continues to denigrate women? What should the aim of a woman's language be?

CHANGING LANGUAGE

Before turning to the work of Julia Kristeva, Luce Irigaray, Hélène Cixous, Michèle Le Doeuff, Catherine Clément, Michèle Montrelay and other French feminist writers on this subject, it is worth returning briefly to the writings of Jacques Lacan, whose theories of difference in language provide a context for French feminism. According to Lacan, language functions to cover the fundamental loss and division that initiates our entry into the symbolic order and our recognition of ourselves as subjects, by appearing to offer a unity which it nevertheless indefinitely postpones. Within this order, Lacan stresses, woman is cast in the position of other, *produced by* language as that which guarantees man's status:

> As negative to the man, woman becomes a total object of fantasy (or an object of total fantasy), elevated into the place of the Other and made to stand for its truth.[2]

As a result, Lacan suggests, woman is both excluded from and elevated *beyond* language; since woman only exists in language *as* she is so defined, her position as other – as 'what (man) is not' – means she necessarily escapes his (this) definition. Lacan does not however believe that this means women have an other essence or language which could destabilise or reverse this process, since, he writes, our other status is itself an effect of language and there is no pre-symbolic reality to which we could (re)gain access outside language.

The revolution in language: Julia Kristeva

For Julia Kristeva, language is the key to change. In both *Revolution in Poetic Language*[3] and the English collection of her work *Desire in Language*[4] she shows how reading and writing can transform the symbolic order. Kristeva outlines the scope of her project in an early essay first published in 1971 and reprinted in *Polylogue* and *Desire in Language* entitled 'How Does One Speak to Literature?'[5] with a series of questions. How, she writes, can literature engender a 'shattering' of the (masculine) subject, and bring about fundamental changes in the structure of Western capitalist society? How can the (literary) text break down existing ideologies to formulate new meanings, and attempt to create new relationships between subject and object, self and others, the symbolic and the real?[6]

Kristeva distinguishes[7] between a pre-Oedipal phase of human development in which drive-charges predominate, and the subsequent repression and control of drive-energies brought about through entering the symbolic. For Kristeva, the pre-Oedipal or semiotic phase is marked by drive-energies that are expressed in the child's babblings, their attempts to copy sounds, and gesture and body movements. The constraints imposed on drive-energies during the Oedipal phase are the necessary precondition for the creation of independent subjecthood and the acquisition of language. Without these constraints, the human being cannot function in the real world of social and linguistic relations.

Even before the mirror phase, Kristeva notes that the rhythms and articulations of semiotic drive-energies prepare the child for speech.[8] Language is acquired at the expense of repressing instinctual drive-energies and a continuous relation to the mother, through holding in check primary (drive-governed) processes which become subordinate to it. Following Freud and Lacan, Kristeva argues that the force of drive-energy continues to exert pressure on the individual even after Oedipalisation is complete. This continuing pressure of the instinctual drives affects the signifying process, bringing with it the possibility of change. The expression of semiotic energy alters the structure of the symbolic, threatening the status quo. Poetry, Kristeva writes, because of its comparative freedom from the rules that govern language, enables the fullest expression of the semiotic within the signifying order, and thus reactivates the link to the 'repressed, instinctual, maternal element'.[9]

To illustrate the ways in which drive-energies manifest themselves in literature, Kristeva cites the various deviations[10] from the grammatical rules of language that characterise some forms of modern poetry. She sees these deviations as 'articulatory effects',[11] the result of primary processes that return language to its source. In some modern poetry, she writes, rhythmic patterns take precedence over grammatical rules, and these rhythms perform an organising function that is different to the one of conventional syntax, in which the status of the subject and ego are guaranteed. Kristeva suggests that any attempt to deviate from conventional syntax disrupts the signifying order, but argues that it is in modern poetry that this disruption is most extreme. Here semiotic activity is expressed not only in linguistic or semantic deviations, but in the rhythm, tone, and even the graphic layout of the page. Modern poetry, she writes, is neither an 'imaginary discourse of the self', nor a 'discourse of a transcendental knowledge', but a 'pulsation' of 'sign and rhythm', 'consciousness and instinctual drive'.[12] It destroys accepted beliefs and traditional modes of signification, preparing the way for revolutionary change.

As an example of the effect semiotic activity can have on the signifying process, Kristeva looks at the 'rejection' drive in the context of poetic creation. In *Revolution in Poetic Language*, she suggests that the violence generated by the rejection drive can prevent stasis, or, as she expresses this in her essay 'The Ethics of Linguistics',[13] safeguard the writer from the 'rust' of automatic formulation.

Kristeva gives a more detailed instance of the results of semiotic activity in literature in her discussion of the nineteenth century French poet Stéphane Mallarmé. In *Revolution in Poetic Language*, she shows how the musical rhythms of Mallarmé's verse echo the oral and glottal sounds made by small children. These 'pleasurable' emittances, she argues, are connected to movements of the mother's body – the movements of throat, voice and breast as these are registered and given expression by the child. Kristeva suggests that the inclusion of these rhythms – linked as they are to our own memory of the maternal body – has a subversive impact, since they involve a re-working of conventional linguistic structure which in turn effects a change in the status of the (writing/reading) subject.[14] She believes that – as a result of the negative and pleasure drives gaining expression in this way – the subject is brought 'to call himself in question', to emerge 'from the protective shell of a transcendental ego within a logical system', and restore his or her connection with the repressed source of human motivation in a way that both 'rends and renews the social code'.[15] Kristeva writes:

> The text's principal characteristic and the one that distinguishes it from other signifying practices, is precisely that it introduces through binding and through vital and symbolic differentiation, heterogeneous rupture and rejection: jouissance and death. This would seem to be 'art's' function as a signifying practice: under the pleasing exterior of a very socially acceptable differentiation, art re-introduces into society fundamental rejection (*Revolution in Poetic Language*, p. 180).

On the one hand, semiotic energy motivates us to transgress the established order and take risks even at the expense of our 'death' (as subjects); on the other, the pleasure we derive from this release recasts our relation to the social–symbolic code. The modulations brought about by oral, aural, visual, linguistic and semantic play 'pulverise' the expected structure of the text, lifting the constraints that normally weigh upon us as subjects, and enabling us to explore these. What is at stake, in this type of textual creation, is the very framework on which our relationships with the world of others and our own identities as subjects are built. The incorporation of new signifying procedures both shatters and recreates the framework within which subjectivity is formed, disrupting the equilibrium of the social–symbolic code by transgressing its boundaries and recasting them in the ongoing pleasure of new creation. The poetic text, Kristeva writes, rejects the 'uniformed, opaque, and empty activity the capitalist system demands of the subject', including its inbuilt other-side – madness/delirium – and involves the subject in a new type of *production* which threatens the premises of patriarchal and capitalist law.

Running beneath Kristeva's thesis of revolution in poetic language is the distinction Barthes draws between realist writing –

in which the writer is obedient to the rules of language – and more poetic forms of expression.[16] In his work, Barthes focused attention on the writer's desire. For Kristeva, this desire is effectively repressed in most forms of writing, a state she compares to the creation of a work of art in which there is, on the contrary, a 'complex weaving' of the relationship between 'desire and the law' and 'the body, language and metalanguage'.[17] Unlike the realist writer, for whom transgression is unthinkable, the poet, Kristeva argues, writes on the borderline between nature and culture: the motivating force of the instinctual drives and their (necessary) social–symbolic repression. As a result of semiotic activity, she suggests, the poet is brought to confront these tensions, transgressing and reformulating these boundaries in their work. In this way, Kristeva continues, poetic writing takes the individual back to the point of separation between self and m/other – the semiotic and the symbolic – providing an opportunity to re-experience these divisions and hence our status as subjects in relation to the world.

For Kristeva, the poet's task can never be that of (re)creating a unified subject. On the contrary, she sees the poet's importance precisely in their ability to transmute the violence of drive-energies into an (acceptable) social–symbolic form, creating rhythmic and signifying patterns that return us to the moment of separation – the scene of castration, the bar dividing the symbolic from the real on which language and the social order is founded – and involving us in the rejection, dissolution, multiplication and transformation of these divisions.

In her essay 'Word, Dialogue, and Novel',[18] Kristeva contrasts poetic language with the monological discourse characteristic of patriarchal society. Because of the way patriarchy functions, she writes, its discourse is subject to prohibition, unable to turn back upon itself and examine its own procedure. Unlike monological discourse, Kristeva continues, poetic discourse 'analyzes itself endlessly', rejecting and transforming the signifying order through an intimate knowledge of its own process. Although it is always subject to (symbolic) censorship, Kristeva suggests that modern poetry has the capacity to change the symbolic structure, through its inclusion of the (writing) body, its use of dream-narrative, and its ability to reflect upon its own signifying operation.

Kristeva suggests the poet represents a threat to the social–symbolic order as a result of their willingness to free language from the strictures of its own conventions. In 'The Ethics of Linguistics',[19] she argues that the poet's incorporation of the semiotic in their writing liberates language 'from denotation', and makes it 'perceive what it doesn't want to say'.[20] She stresses that poetic language has often been excluded by society – castigated as dangerous: a discourse of evil – for this very reason, and in 'From One Identity to Another'[21] she writes:

> If it is true that the prohibition of incest constitutes . . . language as communicative code and women as exchange objects in order for a society to be established, *poetic language would be* for its questionable subject-in-process the *equivalent of incest*: it is within the economy of signification itself that the questionable subject-in-process appropriates to itself this archaic, instinctual, and maternal territory' (p. 136).

This, she concludes, 'simultaneously prevents the word from becoming mere sign and the mother from becoming an object like any other – forbidden' (p. 136).

Kristeva reads the poetic and prose writings of a range of writers to illustrate the ways in which semiotic energy can express itself in texts. She suggests that the impact of drive-energies can be seen in any irregularity, modulation or rhythm which breaks the anticipated structure of the text, changing the linguistic, semantic or graphic form. She reads the frequent use of exclamation marks and rows of dots in the verse of the French writer Céline, for example, as the mark of a surge of drive-energy which, she suggests, shatters the linguistic codes that normally weigh upon and control the speaking–writing subject. The 'panting', 'breathlessness' and 'acceleration' of pace of Céline's verse, she stresses, testifies to his desperate search for an other with whom to establish and exchange meaning.[22] At the opposite extreme to the 'global summing up of the world's meaning' of conventional discourse, what we experience in Céline's poetry, Kristeva writes, are the rhythms of a drive 'forever unsatisfied'.

Kristeva sees semiotic activity disrupting the usual forms of language in the active inclusion of plural meanings within a text, both in the multiplication of meanings within each word, phrase or other language unit, and in the incorporation of meanings derived from other texts. Kristeva coins the term 'intertextuality' to describe this latter process, which, she stresses, refers not only to other written texts, but to films, paintings, or any public or private text such as advertisements or the texts of individual family history. Any inclusion of fantasy or free-play with language or the status of writer or reader is, she argues, evidence of semiotic energy gaining expression in the text.

For Kristeva, the incorporation of semiotic energy in the text also has radical implications for us as readers, forcing us to disband our 'judging consciousness' and experience the jouissance of drive-rhythms.[23] In 'The Father, Love and Banishment',[24] she describes the language of those texts which actively include the semiotic as a 'language that "musicates through letters" ';[25] and she suggests that unlike those forms of language which confirm the status of the recipient, reading in this sense is 'abounding, multiple, enveloping'. She develops this argument in 'The Novel as Polylogue',[26] suggesting that poetic texts of this type not only refuse to corroborate the position of the reader as (masterful) subject, but actively call the reader into question, offering a site of 'nonidentity, nonauthenticity, impossibility and corrosiveness' whenever we seek a reflection of ourselves there.[27] She argues that the reader's participation in the rhythms and movement of a poetic text can arouse feelings of pleasure, which not only challenge the reader's neutrality, since they bring into play the drive-governed terrain of his or her sexuality, unconscious motivation and desire, but also return the reader to the rhythms, movement and echolalias of the pre-Oedipal *chora* before the splitting of the mother-child continuum, entailing 'a polymorphic, polyphonic, serene, eternal, unchangeable jouissance that has nothing to do with death and object'. It is in this context that Kristeva describes the poetic text as 'territory of the mother', since she suggests that it provides an opportunity for alternative forms of meaning, identity and pleasure to those laid down by the power relations implicit in the 'Father's Name'.

Kristeva reads Philippe Sollers' novel *H* to show how literature can challenge both writer and reader. In Sollers' novel the character, H, has no consistent identity but functions to undermine the reader, 'whisking you from your comfortable position,'.[28] Kristeva argues that the operation of Sollers' text sweeps the reader along an infinite and repeated chain of dissolution created through the exploding effects of its rhythm, linguistic and syntactic transgressions and semantic possibilities. The reader, she stresses, must work to follow this movement, refusing to succumb to the dictates of the super-ego with its desire for power and conservative identity, and 'piercing through' the symbolic barricades to re-emerge 'uneasy', 'split apart', 'overwhelmed with a desire to know, but a desire to know more and differently than what is encoded-spoken-written':[29]

> So I listen to the black, heterogeneous territory of the body/text; I coil my jouissance within it, I cast it off, I sidestep its own, in a cold fire where murder is no longer the murder of the other, but rather, of the other who thought she was I, of me who thought I was the other, of my, you, us – of personal pronouns therefore, which no longer have to do with all this (p. 163).

The purpose of this dissolution, Kristeva continues, is ultimately to force the fragmented reader to (re-)seek symbolic restoration, but to do so both with a new awareness of the processes involved and with the aim of intervention to change the real of social and political affairs.

Kristeva suggests that part of Sollers' aim in *H* is a redrawing of sexual relations. Illustrating how the text explores the possibility of a new relationship between the sexes based on sexual differences, she describes the experiment as 'a painful laboratory', entailing 'mistakes, failures and victims'.[30] Out of this laboratory, she writes, the 'I' of H and reader emerge reaffirmed, tenaciously holding on to our 'identities', but also imbued with an other knowledge – of different possibilities and constructions.

Kristeva believes there is a difference in the way men and women experience the semiotic in language. According to Oedipal theory, entry into the symbolic order is dependant on our relinquishing the mother's body. Kristeva's emphasis on the continuing impact of the semiotic on the speaking subject leads her to view the subject's relation to the mother as 'probably one of the most important factors producing interplay within the structure of meaning',[31] since, she argues, it incorporates the potential for the speaking subject to re-cast his or her relation to the world. Following Freud and Lacan, Kristeva suggests that woman's relation to language is complicated as a result of our having to identify with the mother – thereby associating ourselves with what is repressed and excluded from the symbolic order – and that this identification continues to affect the way we experience language. Whereas men's return to the semiotic *chora* is brought about through the explosion of rhythms and echolalias we have known as children which act as comforting reminders of early plenitude or, alternatively, give rise to laughter and symbolic play, Kristeva suggests that for women reactivating these rhythms threatens the tenuous nature of our symbolic construction, rendering us 'ecstatic, nostalgic or mad'.[32] She cites the work of three women writers – Virginia Woolf, Sylvia Plath and Marina Tsvetaeva – as examples of women who have attempted to disentangle this 'impossible dialectic' between language and the semiotic at great personal cost: all three writers committed suicide. Kristeva nevertheless urges that because semiotic drives influence not only our relation to language but all our relationships with the world, we must continue to work towards a (re)ordering in which the positions of both sexes might be differently construed. It is in this light that she points, seemingly paradoxically, and in a formulation reminiscent of Hélène Cixous' theory of gender roles, to the way writers like Céline have stressed that any power they have as writers derives from that part of themselves which is 'woman'. Woman's status as 'ultimate' guarantor of a 'sociality beyond the wreckage of the paternal symbolic function', Kristeva writes, means it is women who have the greatest potential to take the symbolic schema to its limits.[33]

Kristeva's exploration of the revolutionary potential of poetic language leads her to make a number of points worth emphasising here. First, she suggests that because poetic language only comes into being through transgressing the logic of conventional discourse, it can only be created in the 'margins of recognized culture'.[34] Secondly, her insistence on the capacity of the poetic text to reflect on its own constitution as a means of recasting the boundaries between subject and other – thereby presenting an opportunity to redraw the social and political schema – leads her to evaluate a text's importance not in terms of its message – as product of the text – but in terms of how this message is produced. Thirdly, Kristeva argues that the eruption of the semiotic within the signifying function with its attendant impact on symbolic creation, is the driving force behind not only the transformations brought about by art, but of all signifying procedures which entail changes in our perception of ourselves and others. The semiotic for Kristeva is thus important not only in art, but in all forms of symbolic production, including the 'metalanguages' of mathematics and science.

Following her distinction between the poetic and realist writer, Kristeva distinguishes between two types of text.[35] She calls those texts which reveal a deviation from the rules of language under the influence of the semiotic drives 'genotexts', and suggests that these deviations can be expressed in a variety of ways, affecting the genotext's rhythm, language and meaning. Kristeva labels the second type of text 'phenotext', which she describes as those texts which repress all traces of the multiple, heterogeneous and often contradictory pressures of the semiotic in strict adherence to the law.

Kristeva calls for a new mode of critical practice that will explore the dynamic of the semiotic drives and processes of creation of the genotext.[36] She labels this new mode of critical practice 'semanalysis', thereby emphasising its link to the role of the semiotic in the genotext. Paralleling her insistence that, as readers, we must abandon our customary procedures of using a text in order to construct ourselves as unified and masterful subjects, and attend instead to the processes of *how* a text means, Kristeva believes the critic must similarly relinquish the secure positions we normally adopt in relation to a text, and actively involve ourselves in its 'production'. As critics, Kristeva stresses, we must abandon the comfortable codes of conventional critical 'metalanguage': we must, she writes, 'remove our masks'. Equally, she suggests that as critics we must switch our attention away from those types of traditional and realist narrative which confirm the positions we have already taken up in relation to the symbolic order – including the construction of our own (sexual) identities and (gender) roles. We must, she argues, turn to those texts which, through the pluralising, disruptive and exploding effects of the semiotic, force us to confront, question and recast these constructions. It is in this sense that Kristeva defines the critic's task - not as commentator or elucidator of the text's meaning – but as someone prepared to initiate a new experience of reading that will cast 'a different kind of subject', one 'capable of bringing about new social relations' and 'joining in the process of capitalism's subversion'.

In *Histoires d'amour* ('Love Stories'),[38] published in 1983, Kristeva develops her exploration of the ways in which women's experience of motherhood can (re)create a relation to the other different to the one encoded by the patriarchal symbolic, by drawing a parallel between the love of a mother for her child and the 'transference love' of psychoanalysis. Both types of love, she writes, are unconditional, and directed towards the ultimate creation of those involved in the love relation as independent subjects. She suggests that further investigation into this transference love could provide the blue-print for a new type of love-relation, no longer intent on possessing or destroying the other, but concerned to nurture the other towards the realisation of their full potential.

In 'Motherhood According to Giovanni Bellini',[39] Kristeva continues this theme of the potential of women's experience of motherhood to initiate change. She describes the physical transformations of pregnancy, as well as the sensations carrying a foetus can give:

> Cells fuse, split and proliferate; volumes grow, tissues stretch, and body fluids change rhythm, speeding up or slowing down. Within the body, growing as a graft, indomitable, there is an other (p. 237).

During pregnancy, she suggests, there is an increased awareness of feeling and biological rhythm, which presents women with a strange dilemma. Whilst pregnancy makes women intensely aware of biology, this experience is not included within the symbolic sphere of social exchange.

Kristeva draws a link between this aspect of motherhood and the impasse of the poetic writer unable to transfer his or her semiotic experience into words.[40] She believes the act of giving birth presents a vivid connection with the poetic writer's struggle, since in the West childbirth remains at the threshold between biology and language, the semiotic and the symbolic. Childbirth, she suggests, like poetic writing explodes the dividing line between self and other. As an example of this process, Kristeva looks in this essay at the image of motherhood in the paintings of the Italian Renaissance artist Giovanni Bellini. In Bellini's paintings, she writes, motherhood is depicted as 'the ultimate language of a jouissance at the far limits of repression, whence bodies, identities, and signs are begotten'. She stresses here that despite the problems inherent in women's symbolic construction, women have a potentially revolutionary relation to the symbolic function *as a result of* our sex-specific capacity to reproduce – guarantee – the species beyond any breakdown in the symbolic structure; and she urges women to actively assume this role and challenge the power axis on which Western patriarchy depends.

Kristeva develops her theory of the creative potential of motherhood to (re)work changes in the symbolic structure and the model of self–other relations this engenders in two parallel texts, which outline both the 'argument' on which her thesis is founded, and her own personal experience of maternity.[41] The title of the essay 'Stabat Mater' refers to a thirteenth century poem describing the feelings of Christ's mother as she stands at the foot of the cross and watches her son die, and the essay sets Kristeva's poetic account of her own ambiguous feelings as a mother within the more conventionally written argument. This juxtaposition highlights Kristeva's difficulty in describing her experience: words, she writes, are both 'too distant' and 'too abstract' to articulate the 'underground swarming' of a mother's feelings. She suggests that language is unable to express the sensations of carrying and giving birth to a child, or the complex relationship between a mother and her child, which thus run the risk of remaining beyond the 'legitimation' language gives to our experience: 'only the law', she stresses, 'sets anything down'.

As in the later *Histoires d'Amour*, Kristeva sees in a mother's love for her child a model for a different relation to the other to that encoded by the patriarchal order, based, not on appropriation or annihilation of the other's alien status, but on loving concern for their development and growth. Attempting to record her own feelings at her son's birth Kristeva writes:

> Then there is this other abyss that opens up between the body and what had been its inside: there is the abyss between the mother and the child. What connection is there between myself, or even more unassumingly between my body and this internal graft and fold, which, once the umbilical cord has been severed, is an inaccessible other? .... No connection, except for that overflowing laughter where one senses the collapse of some ringing, subtle, fluid identity or other, softly buoyed by the waves (p. 179).

Kristeva links her experience of motherhood to the relationships that exist between women, suggesting that together women may 'reproduce among themselves the strange gamut of forgotten body relationships with their mothers'. She suggests that this affects how women use language, and she gives as an example the way women are often able to comprehend what is not spoken by other women, attending to and understanding all the extra-linguistic signs of gesture, facial expression, body language, the tone of the voice, even smells. Within this realm of the unspoken, Kristeva writes, women are finally 'set free of our identification papers and names'. She believes this experience may offer the blue-print for a new form of exchange that would no longer be dependant on individual subjectivities – with the destruction of the other this implies – but deriving instead from direct communication between bodies: 'connections between atoms, molecules, wisps of words, droplets of sentences'.

Another possible feature of this women's language, Kristeva writes, would be the avoidance of all reference to individual subject positions. She cites as examples the languages of ancient matriarchal cultures which, she stresses, did not use personal pronouns but left it to the recipient to distinguish protagonists according to the context. Kristeva suggests that such features might become elements of 'an underwater, trans-verbal communication between bodies', and she asks: 'a woman's discourse, would that be it?' One result of this new women's discourse, Kristeva concludes, might be the creation of a new heretical ethics or 'herethics' – a new and subversive relation to the other no longer bound by the power structures of death, but reflecting instead a new life.

As an example of how poetic writing may influence and disrupt the symbolic order, Kristeva points to the revolution affected at the end of the nineteenth and beginning of the twentieth century by modernism. Placing the work of such writers as Lautréamont, Mallarmé, Joyce and Bataille in their political, social and economic context, she illustrates the way their writing challenged the prevailing ideology of the day. Their achievement, she suggests, was that of finding a form in which to convey the operations of 'the machine, colonial expansion, banks, science, Parliament – those positions of mastery that conceal their violence and pretend to be mere neutral legality'.[42]

In 'The True-Real',[43] Kristeva develops this idea further by suggesting that the modernist revolution in art and thought has been its willingness to explore the processes by which we become (symbolic) subjects. She argues that these processes – which include language – define what is true or real and what is not. Since part of the symbolic function is to conceal the means by which subjectivity occurs, Kristeva again stresses the daring of writers who have risked their own creation as subjects to explore both the origin and continuing impact of these operations.

Kristeva suggests that we normally employ language to confirm our position as independent and capable subjects, and she cites as an example the way we repress, distance ourselves from or defend ourselves against anything which disturbs us by analysing and 'making a judgement upon it'. This reaction, she argues, is helped by the mechanism of language, which operates to sever a word from its referent, unless we actively choose the poetic response and work to maintain the link between word and flesh.[44]

Kristeva also argues in this essay that the acquisition of symbolic status, derived as it is from a break in the m/other–child continuum, is tantamount to 'murder', and as such is often represented as the killing of a man, prisoner, slave or animal. Christianity, she writes, is one such example, since its doctrine depends on the murder of Jesus Christ. She suggests that this representation in turn functions to prohibit the eruption of desire and the semiotic within the political, social, cultural and religious arenas, thereby curtailing any potential disruption to the status quo.[45]

In 'A New Type of Intellectual: the Dissident',[46] Kristeva stresses the need to take on board 'the closed nature of society and its safety mechanisms'. Like a number of French feminist writers, she suggests that one way of challenging this hegemony would be to 'give voice to each individual form of the unconscious, to every desire and need'. She believes that this attack on the social–symbolic order may take three forms. First, she designates the 'rebel', who, since he or she attacks the balance of power directly and on its own terms, 'still remains within the limits of the old master-slave couple'. The second type of dissident Kristeva describes as the 'psychoanalyst', who, in the search for a language founded on metaphorical identification with the other – rather than the 'metonymical displacement' of desire of patriarchal relations – works towards a transformation of the patriarchal state. The third type of dissident, Kristeva suggests, is the writer, who, instead of focusing on the extra-linguistic laws that operate through language, chooses to concentrate on the process of language itself, 'overturning, violating, [and] pluralizing' the linguistic function 'to set the law ablaze', and pave the way for revolution.

In the interview with Françoise van Rossum-Guyon,[47] Kristeva suggests that 'writing ignores sex or gender' by displacing its constitutional differences in the process of signification. As a result of the mechanisms of displacement and condensation which structure language, she writes, 'a strange body comes into being, one that is neither man nor woman' but a product of the heterogeneous 'drives, signifiers and meanings' that constitute language and the speaking subject, which is constantly being 'remade and reborn'. Unlike Jacques Lacan, Kristeva believes the subject covers the loss and division that create our entry into language 'not by positing the existence of an *other* (another person or sex . . .) or an *Other* (the absolute signifier, God)', but by participating in the processes of congruence and separation which comprise linguistic symbolisation. For Kristeva, these processes are always – necessarily – influenced by social factors and the prevailing ideology, and she concludes that where it might therefore be possible to locate a language 'peculiar to women' is in examining the effect ideology and social forces have on women, which influence women's language. Kristeva stresses here the difficulty of determining, at the present time, whether these differences are the result of women's biological experiences, our sociological positioning, or the way women's psychological make-up is dictated by the current order. She writes:

> in speaking of these characteristics, for the moment I find it difficult to say if they are produced by something specific to women, by socio-cultural marginality, or more simply by one particular structure (for example hysteria) promoted by present market conditions from among the whole range of potential female qualities (p. 112).

Despite her hesitation as to the causes of the possible differences in women's language, Kristeva details a number of 'stylistic and thematic elements' which she suggests recur in contemporary women's writing with a greater insistence than in texts by men. She argues, for instance, that contemporary women's writing often 'displays' the body in ways which challenge its 'careful disguise' by patriarchal culture: 'they invite us to see, touch and smell a body made of organs'. She also suggests that women's writing shows a marked 'lack of belief in any project, goal or meaning', a fact which she attributes to the lack of any 'single Other' to sustain women's dissatisfaction; women's writing, she stresses, calls – paradoxically – on 'a host of others to fill this vacuum'. She suggests that women's writing is often concerned with 'reformulating love', a preoccupation she links to women's search for 'other-love(s)' and to the exploration of the mother-daughter relationship which, she stresses, occupies a central place in women's fiction in contrast to the 'public veil and dismissal' this relationship has received at the hands of the Christian religion.

Considering the style of women's writing, Kristeva argues that whilst this is often emotionally charged, the charge remains latent, a fact she explains by suggesting that 'the notion of the signifier as a network of distinctive' – and discriminating – marks is insufficient for women, and she stresses that the force of emotion thus fails to find adequate expression. She argues:

> It is as if this emotional charge so overwhelmed the signifier as to impregnate it with emotion and so abolish its neutral status, but, being unaware of its own existence, it did not cross the threshold of signification or find a sign with which to designate itself (p. 113).

As a result, Kristeva suggests, 'the expression (more often than in texts by men) falls short of the emotional charge which gives rise to it'. Kristeva argues that women writers are on the whole less concerned with the formal considerations of composition than men. She stresses, for example, that where women do orchestrate their work to comply with the requirements of artistic and linguistic arrangement, the result is 'an artificially imposed structure that smacks of word-play or crossword puzzles' or else reveals a sparing use of words and an 'elliptical syntax' which, she insists, is 'congenital to our monological culture'. Although Kristeva does not cite specific examples, the word-games and puns of Hélène Cixous or Monique Wittig, and the blanks and silent spaces in the work of Marguerite Duras or Michèle Ramond are evoked by her description.

Françoise van Rossum-Guyon quotes Kristeva's insistence on women's marginal and potentially dissident position to the social and political status quo as a consequence of our exile from power. She places this insistence – which she takes here from an interview with Paul Enthoven printed in the French magazine *Le Nouvel Observateur* – alongside Kristeva's suggestion, also contained in the Enthoven interview, that women are ultimately more concerned with preserving life than anarchy because of our role in reproduction. In reply Kristeva reiterates her belief that the purpose of a revolution in language is not the total release of ungoverned drives, but knowledge of the processes by which we are created – and create ourselves – in language. Her emphasis connects with her insistence, expressed in 'The Ethics of Linguistics',[48] that the free-play of unleashed semiotic forces could lead to the regimes of fascism. The impetus of the semiotic, for Kristeva, is thus a means of confronting the reality of our situation as subjects and the mechanisms by which the socializing structures of language and the symbolic operate.[49] It is in this light that she defines the task for women:

> the time has perhaps come for each and every woman, in whatever way we can, to confront the controversial values once held to be universal truths by our culture, and to subject them to an interminable analysis' (p. 116).

Such an analysis, she suggests, might finally bring about the pluralisation of *languages* necessary to tackle the crisis endemic in the Western world.

A feminine poetics: Luce Irigaray

For Luce Irigaray, the language revolution is the creation of an other symbolic in which women's differences can at last come into play. In an article entitled 'Sexual Difference',[50] she reiterates her belief that the masculine has dominated 'every subject and discourse' in the West, and she stresses that women's aim must be the institution of an order in which sexual differences can exist. If women fail to build this foundation, she warns, 'will not all the concessions gained by the women's struggle be lost again?', and she urges 'we must re-interpret the whole relationship between the subject and discourse, the subject and the world, the subject and the cosmic, the microcosmic and the macrocosmic' if we are to devise a framework in which 'a sexual encounter would be a celebration, and not a disguised or polemic form of the master-slave relation.' She believes this framework will entail a radical reassessment of our relationship to space, time, procreation, children, the mother and others. Like Julia Kristeva, she suggests that the new order will involve a relation to the other no longer intent on 'seizing, possessing, or subduing' the other 'as *object*'; and she argues that the key to this inauguration will be a 'new poetics', the 'production of a new age of thought, art, poetry and language' no longer circumscribed by 'the shadow or orbit of a God of the Father who alone lays down the law, or the immutable mouthpiece of a single sex'.

In her replies in *This Sex Which Is Not One* to the questions raised for readers by *Speculum of the Other Woman*,[51] Irigaray makes the following statement concerning the impetus for her work on women and language:

> I am a woman. I am a being sexualized as feminine. I am sexualized female. The motivation of my work lies in the impossibility of articulating such a statement: in the fact that its utterance is in some way senseless, inappropriate, indecent. Either because *woman* is never the attribute of the verb to be nor *sexualized female* a quality of being, or because *am a woman* is not predicated of I, or because *I am sexualized* excludes the feminine gender (p. 148).

'The articulation of the reality of my sex', Irigaray continues, 'is impossible in discourse' such as this is currently construed. Woman, she stresses, must speak either as sexualised (male) subject *or* as asexualized (female) other, formulating meaning to conform to the requirements of the master's discourse or else accepting that her words remain unintelligible.

As an example of the effect this embargo has on women, Irigaray cites the fact that in Western patriarchal culture mothers and daughters have no adequate means within the dominant language to identify themselves in relation to each other. As a result of patriarchal logic, she argues, a mother and daughter are perceived as 'neither one nor two, neither has a name, meaning, sex of her own'; and she concludes 'here "for example" is one place where the need for another "syntax", another "grammar" of culture is crucial' (p. 143).

Irigaray stresses that the feminine must acquire its own distinct mode of expression. She suggests that one way for this to happen would be for women to bypass the specular economy of masculinity, and to explore our own 'economy of flow'. Women's different relation to others, she writes, contains the potential for a new form of exchange based on 'modalities' fundamentally un-like those currently in force.[52] She urges women to examine 'the processes of specula(riza)tion that subtend our social and cultural organization', and to create in their place a different pattern of relationships between 'subjects' to those reproduced by (a) man's reflection in a (flat) mirror. We must, she writes, challenge the status of this 'mirror', and explore what 'it may have kept suspended . . . what it may have frozen of the "other" 's flowing'. Only by inaugurating a new order of specularisation, she concludes, will women be able to formulate the relation 'of woman to "herself" and to her like'.

'Language', Irigaray writes, 'has always led women astray', and she insists that its present form continues this general trend 'of deviation, and of reduction, in the artifice of sameness, and of otherness'. She repeats her insistence here that women's exploration of our pleasure, accruing, not from the (imaginary) reflection of (speculated) images, but from a direct 'relation to fluids', can proffer glimpses of 'those as yet unterritorialized spaces' where a feminine desire might at last come into play. This (feminine) mode of relations, she writes, might then form the basis for a discourse that would reject 'all closure or circularity' and privilege 'the "near" rather than the "proper" '. This, Irigaray argues, would necessarily entail 'a different relation to unity, to identity with self, to truth, to the same and thus to alterity'. Woman's sex, *because* it is outside the current (masculine) 'economy of representation', might then prove 'capable of interpreting this economy', and thus articulating the real difference between the sexes without this resulting in the subjection of one sex by the other.

In 'The "Mechanics" of Fluids',[53] Irigaray develops her insistence that the 'fluidity' of women's sexuality may undermine the masculine schema. Woman, she writes, has been made the 'projective map' of man, functioning as the interval necessary to maintain his definitions and order of individual relations. This fluidity has become 'fixed and congealed' as a result, although Irigaray stresses that since this has never been wholly solidified by the ruling symbolics, it still contains the potential to jam the mechanism of man's theoretical machine. For 'that woman-thing', Irigaray writes, 'speaks. But not "like", not "the same", not "identical with itself" nor to any x, etc. . . . What she emits is flowing, fluctuating. *Blurring*'. She sees in this 'speech' the pattern for a new form of communication, based not on preserving the 'empirical representative' of the male organ as the 'model of ideal functioning' by means of which all desire is reduced to 'being or having this ideal', but on a 'transgression and confusion of boundaries' in which individual 'unities' become 'hardly definable as such'. Like Julia Kristeva's insistence on learning to read in a new way and Hélène Cixous' belief in the importance of attentive listening, Irigaray stresses here that 'one must know how to listen otherwise than in good form(s)' in order to hear what women have to say.

In what has become the most famous of the essays from *This Sex Which Is Not One* 'When Our Lips Speak Together',[54] Irigaray warns that if women do not attempt to speak our own language, and continue to 'speak to each other as men have been doing for centuries', then 'we will miss each other' and 'fail ourselves'. 'If we keep on speaking sameness', she writes, we will merely perpetuate the current schema and our position within it as 'spoken', 'speaking machines'.

As an example of the way language imprisons, gags and exiles women from the possibility of speaking as ourselves, Irigaray shows how even the apparently innocuous and generous statement 'I love you' is predicated onto a model of power relations in which the 'I' seeks to master the 'you'. Whenever a man addresses a woman – or another man – with this phrase, Irigaray suggests, the words are positioned between the two polarities of 'gift' and 'debt'.[55] Contained within the meaning of the phrase are the preoccupations of the masculine, dedicated to the reproduction of sameness and the attendant positioning of others. The phrase is not given freely, but implies bargain, debt, opposition, control. Irigaray compares this to the 'I love you' of women, which, she suggests, cannot operate in the same way. Not only do women not divide into the neat couple of 'I' and 'you' necessitated by the phrase, but, she writes, the hierarchy of relations figured by the phallus and (supposed) unicity of male desire are confounded by the plurality of woman's sex: women, she argues, 'are always several at once'.

Given the dominance of the masculine, Irigaray questions whether it will ever be possible for women to escape its 'compartments, distinctions and oppositions', to 'put "I love you" differently'. How, she asks, can women begin to designate ourselves, when the only spaces open to us are those of 'deficiencies' and 'lacks'? How can we 'touch' ourselves and each other when our bodies have been 'cut up' and our pleasures denied, or else appropriated by a system that regards even our virginity as something to be penetrated and possessed? Irigaray's reply is once again to urge women to refuse the order in which we have been 'passed from master to master', and to express the multiplicity of our sex which, she believes, will of itself challenge the oneness of masculine truth and hence the circularity of its logic. She looks to the love between women to provide a model for this new exchange in which, she argues, 'nothing is privileged': 'why only one song, one speech, one text at a time', when the passage from the inside out, from the outside in, in the passage between us, is limitless' and 'without end'? Stressing the openness, multiplicity and fluidity of women's sex, Irigaray looks forward to a form of communication in which nothing will be programmed and one will no longer be the master of others.

In 'Questions',[56] Irigaray stresses the difficulties in attempting to define a feminine economy and language from within the current order. Even trying to imagine the form a feminine language might take is, she warns, neither 'simple nor easy', since it will necessarily be composed of different elements to those allowed into play by the existing structures. She nevertheless believes a number of outlines may be tentatively imagined. She suggests for example that the new language will refuse the rigid divisions between subject and object created by phallocentrism, to create in their stead a '*nonhierarchical* articulation' of differences in which ' "oneness" would no longer be privileged'. She also believes the new language will entail a less possessive relationship to others, and she suggests that nearness and proximity may instead become its keynotes:

> in such an extreme form that it would preclude any distinction of identities, any establishment of ownership, thus any form of appropriation (p. 134).

The new syntax, she writes, might thus dispense with 'proper meanings' and 'proper names'. She reiterates her insistence that the 'gestural code' of women's bodies might provide a blue-print for the new order: what women ' "dare" – do or say' when we are among ourselves.

Irigaray suggests that the function of the new language will be 'to cast phallocentrism, phallocratism, loose', so that it will 'no longer, all by itself, define, circumvene, circumscribe, the properties of anything and everything'.[57] She insists that precisely for this reason, it is crucial for women to create a language in which to express our sex, but she also argues that this is important for men. Whilst dominance has given men power, she stresses that this has been at the cost of their sex:

> So long as men claim to say everything and define everything, how can anyone know what the language of the male sex might be? So long as the logic of discourse is modelled on sexual indifference, on the submission of one sex to the other, how can anything be known about the "masculine"? (p. 128).

In this way, Irigaray writes, the creation of a woman's language is to the advantage of us all.

Writing the other: Hélène Cixous

For Hélène Cixous, there is a difference in the way men and women use language. In 'Sorties',[58] she suggests that women do not repress the unconscious to the extent men feel obliged to do, and she believes this attention to the unconscious affects women's language. She argues that women involve the body in the process of communication to a greater degree than men. In a passage that has strong links with Kristeva's theory of the semiotic, Cixous stresses woman 'has never ceased to hear what-comes-before-language reverberating', and she argues that the pre-symbolic rhythms of the relation to the mother, as well as the rhythms and music of the mother's voice, permeate women's language. Like Luce Irigaray, Cixous inverts and then re-values the criticisms often levelled – by men – at women's language, and she suggests that the circularity, questioning and apparent waste of women's speech is not only something 'we like', but that it derives from women's (positive) refusal to summarize in accordance with the 'objectivising' principle of the phallus, allowing instead 'the time a phrase or thought needs'.

In an exchange with Catherine Clément at the end of *The Newly Born Woman*,[59] Cixous, like Clément, insists that, under the current system, women must adopt the dominant mode of communication in order to make ourselves heard. Cixous and Clément disagree however as to the effects this communication has on women and whether its model will always be in force. Cixous stresses the dangers of the present structure, and looks forward to a time when its claim to 'universal truth' will be dislodged by 'thousands of different kinds of feminine words'. Clément, on the other hand, finds this plurality and disruption hard to envisage: 'I see no way to conceive of a cultural system in which there would be no transmission of knowledge in the form of a coherent statement'. Unlike Cixous, Clément believes language can only ever operate by 'moving one square to the place of another', and she stresses that 'real change cannot happen at this level'.

For Cixous the revolutionary potential of language lies in writing. Writing, Cixous suggests, presents a 'boundless space', in which the hierarchy of masculine relations might at last be transcended and overturned. In 'Sorties', she links this revolutionary potential to women's writing, urging women to inscribe our knowledge of the body and m/other-love which, she stresses, cannot fail to challenge the existing schema. She also suggests that as a result of women's different biological and social experiences, it is easier for women to admit the other than for men; like Luce Irigaray, she looks to a feminine writing in which the movements of depropriation, de-personalisation and other-love will offer an alternative to the masculine state.

Like Julia Kristeva and Luce Irigaray, Cixous suggests that an important component of the new language will be the way words are listened to. Like Julia Kristeva, Cixous sees a new type of reading practice as essential if we are to move away from those postures which ignore the meanings of a text in order to select those elements which confirm the status of the reader. For Cixous this new type of reading comprises three interrelated strands. First, she suggests that in the same way that differences shape who we are, so these differences influence and affect the way we read. Our sexual, social and cultural experiences and expectations are brought into play as we read, and, Cixous stresses, we need to work towards a practice of reading that will actively acknowledge this participation of the self.

As an example of the importance of self-identification in reading, Cixous describes how, as an adolescent, the fact that the only characters with whom she felt able to identify were male had a detrimental effect on her developing sense of herself as a woman:

> where am I to stand? what is my place if I am a woman? I look for myself throughout the centuries and don't see myself anywhere (p. 75).

She suggests that this lack of female characters with whom she could identify alerted her both to women's subordination and to the possibility that the marginalised and repressed elements in texts might nevertheless be attended to and heard.

As an example of this second point, Cixous outlines how, reading Freud's case-study of Dora, she became aware of other voices in the text: 'I heard voices sighing in the text – voices of people who, in the chain, were finally those on whom weighed heaviest the great weight of silence, those who were crushed'. She suggests that by listening to these other voices, she was slowly able 'to bring center stage obliterated characters, characters repressed in notes, at the bottom of the page, and who were for me in the absolute foreground'.[60] The result of this other reading, Cixous concludes, was a very different understanding of the text to the one Freud intended.

Linked to this deconstructive[61] practice of reading is Cixous' insistence that we must develop an approach to the text that will no longer seek to master and appropriate its meanings in order to corroborate the pre-established position of the reader, but will begin instead from a knowledge of the experiences, expectations and needs we bring to the text and attend to its many different voices. She suggests that the process of 'inhabiting someone' that can come through reading in this way – refusing masculine positions of closure, and allowing the self to be traversed by another's initiatives and actions – might thus create an alternative 'scene of exchange' in which the existing structures would at last be overturned.

Plural meanings: Michèle Le Doeuff

The work of French philosopher Michèle Le Doeuff reflects the preoccupations of feminists like Hélène Cixous and adds to the debate on women and language. In a text translated in *French Feminist Thought* as 'Women and Philosophy',[62] Le Doeuff explores the way in which our system of thinking 'creates itself in what it represses', engendering an opposite or other from which it must then 'endlessly . . . separate, enclose and insularize itself'. Within the patriarchal schema, Le Doeuff suggests, this other is demarcated 'feminine', a definition which philosophy recreates: 'whether we like it or not, we are within philosophy, surrounded by masculine–feminine divisions that philosophy has helped to articulate and refine'. Le Doeuff stresses, however, that we do not as women have to identify ourselves with this position: 'we are constantly being *confronted* with that image, but we do not have to recognize ourselves in it'. She acknowledges the dilemma this presents to women: 'from which position do we speak, then?'. She argues that this can be neither the feminine position of negated other produced by patriarchy for its own ends, nor from within the philosophical system 'since this founds the duality of masculine rationality and feminine disorder'. Instead, Le Doeuff calls for a new language that will cut across these alternatives by recognising 'the necessarily incomplete nature of all theorization' as well as the validity of another's viewpoint, and hence the limits of our own. Reading the work of the seventeenth century French scholar Blaise Pascal, she argues that his work presents 'a form of writing which does not claim to reconstruct and explain everything', but which on the contrary maintains 'a relationship to the unknown and the unthought' by consenting to be 'a tributary to a collective discourse and knowledge'. She suggests that Pascal's writing offers a model for a new collective discourse. She believes women will play a key role in pioneering this other language, and stresses that it will be through this 'plural work' that women may at last create a place for ourselves within philosophy.

SPEAKING AS A WOMAN

Despite the differences that exist between French feminists on the subject of women and language, their writings nevertheless present a number of preoccupations in common when compared with the work of Anglo–American feminists. The insistence on language as the locus for change for instance, differs radically from the emphasis of a mainstream of Anglo–American and other feminists on political and social reform of the existing system. The notion that this system, created and maintained by language, cannot express woman, and the suggestion that change may come from those areas beyond language, as well as the proposition that this change will necessarily entail a re-ordering and re-valuing of differences, are also unlike the more material approaches of Anglo–American and other feminisms. These preoccupations, represented here by Julia Kristeva, Luce Irigaray, Hélène Cixous and Michèle Le Doeuff, are also shared by other French feminist theorists, critics and writers.

Re creating the subject: Catherine Clément

In her book *Miroirs du sujet* ('Mirrors of the Subject'),[63] Catherine Clément explores the subject's relation to language and the world. She suggests that the mirror of self-recognition of the social–symbolic structure acts as a protective 'screen' against the 'in pieces-pleasure' of the pre-symbolic state, enabling the subject to live (pp. 19, 23). She argues that all subsequent cultural acquisition continues this 'fundamental protective function' (p. 19). Clément reads Marguerite Duras' novel *Lol V. Stein* as an example of this function. Drawing on Lacan's account of the object lost by the subject as the price of entry into culture, Clément stresses that this object can never be articulated since it remains beyond the order of cultural expression, and she suggests that Duras' writing, and particularly the absences in Duras' texts, serve to figure this loss (p. 130). The writing of *Lol V. Stein*, Clément stresses, reveals itself to be an act of 'unflagging metaphoric defence' against 'pulsional menace' (p. 130).

Clément argues that in addition to its necessary protective function, culture is also the medium through which ideology is created and transmitted. She believes that any form of cultural transformation must take into account this contradictory role, recognising the importance of the 'orthopaedic-identity' society constructs for the individual *as* it effects changes in this structure. Clément looks forward in the light of her analysis to a cultural revolution, the 'ambiguous' function of which will be to initiate new structures whilst protecting the individual from the traumas of the real (p. 23).

Like both Julia Kristeva and Luce Irigaray, Clément sees a possible model for a new type of cultural production in psychoanalysis. She explores the mode of communication Freud refers to as 'construction', in which nothing is silenced, everything is expressed, and through apparent side-tracking a story gradually unfolds, seeing in this 'dispersion' and 'disorder' the possible genesis for a new discourse. This language Clément writes, would circulate as between analyst and analysand like 'an oral writing' 'without an author', challenging the 'logocentric mythology' of contemporary forms to create 'a speech that no longer belongs to two, but which passes into another register' (p. 15).

Inscribing the feminine: Michèle Montrelay

Michèle Montrelay, in the collection of her essays *L'Ombre et le nom: sur la féminité* ('The Shadow and the Name: On Femininity'),[64] also reads Marguerite Duras' *Lol V. Stein* in conjunction with her work on women and language. Montrelay suggests that it is impossible to read *Lol V. Stein* as one would another book: 'this novel dispossesses you of thinking', she writes, 'one is no longer master of one's reading'. She describes the fluid movement of Duras' writing, and argues that this fluidity holds the reader in the 'indefinite', liberating us from our concern to 'fix the classic references of an identity'. In Duras' novel, Montrelay suggests, 'the games of looking, of show . . . no longer hold'. Here, on the contrary, 'one is . . . in the space of ecstasy, of dispersion'. She compares Duras' writing to that of the nineteenth century realists Guy de Maupassant and Gustave Flaubert whose texts, she stresses, operate to cover over the lack at the heart of language, by attempting to transform this lack into an object which writing can then metaphorically express. In *Lol V. Stein*, Montrelay argues, the focus is not that of recreating the lost object, but shifts instead to engage with the way language *means*. Unlike Catherine Clément, who sees the absences in Duras' writing as recalling the lost object, for Montrelay the innovation of *Lol V. Stein* is the way words circulate and endlessly suggest each other, in active involvement with the linguistic play.

In a second essay in *L'Ombre et le nom* 'Parole de femme: sur le transfert de l'hystérique' ('Woman's Speech/Word: On the Hysteric's Transference'),[65] Montrelay suggests that this attention to the way language means must also include recognition of the spaces in language if it is to have a revolutionary effect. She writes: 'a signifier defines itself by its position in relation to other signifiers, and by the spaces it leaves open'. For Montrelay, this 'and' is crucial, and she argues that a feminine language must incorporate these spaces of non-sense, since these escape classification and hence the structures of the symbolic system.

In a later essay in the collection 'Textes à l'infini' ('Texts to Infinity'),[66] Montrelay links this notion of a feminine discourse specifically to women. She suggests that man's possession of a physical equivalent of the phallus – 'the privileged organ' – means men have a different relationship to the symbolic. Men, she argues, use language to recreate and maintain their 'separation from the Other'. Women, on the other hand, experience language differently. In the essay 'Recherches sur la féminité' ('Researches Into Femininity'),[67] she suggests that women's primary identification with the same body as our own makes it difficult for women to distinguish 'between her own body and the one that was the "first object"', and she argues that language, which in the first stages of life is an extension of the mother's body, retains this quality for women: 'words . . . are the extension of herself . . . . A woman is not separate from words'. As a result, Montrelay believes women have a less detached relationship to language. Words, she writes:

> are not these objects which one approaches, touches and manipulates, with this passionate curiosity, made of pleasure and respect, which is the characteristic of man-the-writer (p. 152).

For Montrelay, this different relationship to language poses women with a number of problems and options. It is for instance perfectly possible for women to write as men: 'one feigns the distance. One pretends to be "separated" and to have pleasure in their way'. Or, Montrelay argues, we can simply allow language to function, 'advancing' words and letting them speak our meaning without attempting to intervene. She suggests that neither of these options presents a satisfactory solution, since neither course takes into account women's sex-specific relationship to words.

In 'Textes à l'infini', Montrelay points to the work of a number of women whose writings, she suggests, offer a way out of this 'double impasse'. She cites the work of Chantal Chawaf and Jeanne Hyvrard as examples, and reads Chawaf's novel *Rétable, la rêverie* to demonstrate how in Chawaf's writing everything is brought into play: 'words, the body, anguish, the passion of the woman writing'. Chawaf's texts, she writes, 'speak, sing, cry out', refusing to offer 'any contour on which the eye could come to rest'. Desire is thus endlessly diffused, since there is no object or image but only the ceaseless unfolding of thoughts and impressions. Montrelay believes this movement is highly disconcerting to the reader, since, in Chawaf's work, the reader finds themselves in an 'element' in which 'the individual, the event no longer hold sway'.

In the final essay of the collection, 'La Dernière Femme?' ('The Last Woman?'),[68] Montrelay calls for a women's language that would draw on such models, refusing to recreate an image or object or to capture or transfix its interlocutor. She suggests that this feminine 'discourse' might then transform the present system, since it would no longer operate as a defence or trap but – 'with words, colours, sounds, "ideas", with images of the body that . . . dance this side of the specular image' – would 'fill out' and inhabit the 'forgotten spaces' of memory, language and m/other-love.

Writer Danièle Sallenave chooses the form of a dialogue between 'He' and 'She' in her text *Conversations conjugales* ('Conjugal Conversations')[69] which illustrates differences in the way men and women use language. In *Conversations conjugales*, 'He' is constantly pressing 'Her' to speak in concrete terms, suggesting that 'it would help you to confront things head on if you were to call them by their name' (p. 46). The incomplete, tentative nature of 'Her' speech is in contrast to 'His' brutal directness; it is as though Her words seek to circulate round and explore the object of her thoughts rather than to name and contain this:

> *She*: Finally, it's very agonizing all the same.
> *He*: Dying? Probably.
> *She:* Not dying. To... to...
> *He*: Say it. Say it for once.
> *She*: (Laughing. Confused.) I don't know any word well' (p. 63).

The effect, in Sallenave's text, is one of two parallel discourses that do not finally engage or communicate with the other, and which barely conceal the disastrous consequences the couple's non-communication has on their conjugal relationship.

An other culture: Marguerite Duras

In *Les Parleuses* ('The [Women] Speakers'),[70] a book based on a series of tape-recorded conversations between Marguerite Duras and writer Xavière Gauthier, Gauthier suggests that there is a development in Duras' writing from the more masculine approach of the early work to an increasingly feminine style of writing. She argues that Duras' early writing is more closely and consciously interwoven: 'there is not yet the place of a lack', she stresses, 'the space is not yet . . . either large or silent enough' (p. 13). Gauthier compares this to Duras' later work where, she suggests, the writing changes to incorporate silence (p. 49) and the circulation of a specifically feminine pleasure and desire (pp. 47–8). In response Duras stresses that she believes writers must relinquish the various means that present themselves to us as subjects to secure our identity, and 'enter inside, let the self be carried by this (his)story . . . which is, after all, others' (his)story' (p. 65). A writer, Duras insists, must become 'a chamber of echoes' (p. 218), constantly seeking to span the difference between ourselves and others in a 'movement towards the other' which necessarily involves 'rubbing out' the self (pp. 209–10).[71] Both Gauthier and Duras agree that this writing is at the opposite extreme to that of the writer whose identity precedes what is written: 'anyone who believes himself to be master of himself, of his desires, who is whole and secure, with a will and all that, is lost' (p. 55) Gauthier insists, and she argues for an abdication of this 'illusion of speech and decision' (p. 64) towards a 'shedding of everything that is, finally, accessory' (p. 60). Like a number of the writers referred to here, she believes this entails 'listening to what goes on inside us', including our unconscious voice (p. 64). Discussing Duras' novel *L'Amour* ('Love'), Gauthier suggests that Duras expresses here not (only) the love-*story* – the 'repetition' of 'outside events' (p. 64) – but also the 'not-said' of this relationship – 'everything that circulates through this love' – which it would be 'brutal to name' (p. 67). Gauthier believes this circulation of desire – 'from one to the other and which does not belong to one rather than the other' (p. 54) – in which there is no possession (p. 41), and in which individual masks are finally stripped away (p. 68), is the hallmark of a feminine writing (p. 39). Duras suggests that this willingness to let the self 'be invaded' (p. 65) is something that women find easier than men, partly *because* of the way women are positioned in relation to 'transgression' (p. 49), and partly because men's (sexual) relationship to language and the world makes it harder for them to conceive and admit the blanks: they would, Duras stresses, attempt to intervene rather than 'simply . . . allow an experience to happen' (p. 19).[72] It is in this sense that Duras sees what has come to be regarded negatively in the West as women's passivity as a positive attribute (p. 71), arguing that it is precisely this passivity which enables things to unfold and which would, if a man were to become involved, immediately be covered over (p. 72). Questioned about her work in the cinema, Duras outlines how she deliberately avoids the fast pace (p. 136) and profusion of scenes characteristic of current trends, in order to allow the spaces to exist (p. 87). She compares this approach to the greater receptivity of Eastern culture (p. 143) which, she suggests, unlike the continual striving for mastery implicit in Western ideology (p. 140), does not seek to logically organise (p. 178) or police (p. 138) all its proceedings. She explains how she tries to recreate this 'attentive receptivity' (p. 146) in her films by such means as deliberately disconnecting the voices of the soundtrack from the images on screen, thus disrupting the audience's attempts to cover over and decide on what is happening (p. 89). Instead, Duras suggests, voices 'traverse' her films in ways which leave the spaces open (p. 89), giving both images and voices – as well as their audience – a life and locus – of their own (p. 96).[73]

Discomposing I and you: Monique Wittig

Monique Wittig's theoretical and fictional writing presents a number of parallels with the writers we have looked at so far on the issue of women and language. In her essay 'The Mark of Gender',[74] written in English and published in the collection *The Poetics of Gender* from the 1985 US colloquium of that name, Wittig stresses the necessity of changing language. She argues:

> One must understand that men are not born with a faculty for the universal and that women are not reduced at birth to the particular. The universal has been, and is continually, at every moment, appropriated by men. It does not happen by magic, it must be done. It is an act, a criminal act (p. 66).

Gender, she writes, as 'an element of language', undermines the apparent neutrality of the linguistic function to deny women 'any claim to the abstract, philosophical, political discourses that give shape to the social body'. She stresses that gender, as a component of language, 'must be destroyed'.

Wittig describes her own project as a writer as one of rendering the 'categories of sex obsolete in language', and endeavour she contrasts to the attempts by other French women writers to feminise language. She suggests that one means of achieving her goal would be to eradicate the 'I', which, she stresses, would 'not only modify language at the lexical level', but would also effect both 'the structure itself and its functioning', entailing a transformation at the conceptual-philosophical and political levels.

Wittig's fictional text *Le Corps Lesbien* ('The Lesbian Body')[75] offers an illustration of her project. *Le Corps Lesbien* experiments with language and literary form in a variety of ways, including blank spaces between the fragmented sections of text, interweaving a second narrative of the body in block capitals across double pages at irregular intervals, changing punctuation, and splitting the text's subject: 'I/I pass by your side, I/I shatter the tiny unities of m/y//self, threatening m/e' (p. 109).[76] This experimentation is echoed in the text's theme, as the two (feminine) bodies – the 'I' and 'you' – explore their desire for the other: the desire to merge with the other (pp. 17, 53, 118, 122); the agony of a desire that is not returned (pp. 26, 40); the pain of rejection (p. 99); the threat to the self of another's desire (p. 108). *Le Corps Lesbien* ends with a vision in which 'one' is no longer subject to or of the other, but each retains their difference to create a new superposition:

> The second moon becomes visible in her turn. Her colour is orange. Very quickly she is two thirds along the course of the violet moon. Their two spheres are of identical size. Only one travels more quickly than the other. The colours that they cast do not mix. When they are one by the side of the other two luminous cones prolong them the one violet the other orange, there is superposition in the brief moment at which they intersect (p. 179).

In *Le Corps Lesbien*, this vision is linked to a new language, in which vowels have disappeared and consonants are pronounced directly 'one against the other' (p. 116). This alternative language, which entails the 'I' relinquishing its 'hierarchical position' (p. 165), links Wittig's work to that of other French feminist writers, in their search for a language in which women will also be expressed.

For many French feminists, it is writing that offers the opportunity for change; and it is this notion of writing, as a means of disrupting and reformulating the organising principles of subjectivity and language, and as a generative force capable of expressing differences and disseminating (plural) meanings, that is the subject of the final chapter.

5

Towards an *écriture féminine*

If there's no earth, invent it, if the earth doesn't go fast enough leave it behind, take off, if there's no road, make one, invent it with feet, hands, arms, passion, necessity.

Hélène Cixous

You take pleasure with me as with you I take pleasure in the rejoicing of this reciprocal living – and identifying – together.

Luce Irigaray

Everyone knows that a place exists which is not economically or politically indebted to all the vileness and compromise. That is not obliged to reproduce the system. That is writing. If there is a somewhere else that can escape the infernal repetition, it lies in that direction, where it writes itself, where it dreams, where it invents new worlds.

Hélène Cixous

The concept of an *écriture féminine* – or feminine writing – derives from the work of Hélène Cixous, though it also has links with that of other French feminists. Before turning to their work, I return briefly to the writings of Jacques Derrida, whose theories offer a helpful context for the insistence on a writing that will *include* the repressed – feminine – other of conventional forms.

AN OTHER WRITING

Writing other meanings: Jacques Derrida and French feminism

According to the post-structuralists, language is the medium through which our experience is organised. For Jacques Derrida, the foundation of our present system in the West traces back to the Greek philosophers, who, he argues, have imposed their understanding of the world in ways which have become so deeply embedded in our culture that it is now almost impossible to conceive of the world in any other way.[1] He analyses their various attempts to posit a transcendental origin from which all meaning would ensue, suggesting that their desire for power has succeeded as a result of their creating a conceptual system encoded in language in which whatever is designated as other serves to support the dominant principle.[2]

Derrida stresses that this conceptual system operates in language only through ignoring and suppressing the way language actually works. He suggested that writing, more than speech, retains the knowledge of its creation,[3] and he employs this knowledge to unravel the complex threads of a writer's strategy. He argued that writing's own differential structure incorporates meanings beyond those the writer intended, since the process of meaning entails gaps in which other possibilities can erupt beyond the writer's control, to contradict and challenge his purpose. This 'supplement', Derrida suggests, is what gives writing its other status, since writing always contains the (unconscious) knowledge of its formation, other meanings, and the potential for the reader to interpret the text in an other way. It is this other function that underlies Derrida's insistence on the femininity of writing,[4] which, he argues, has the capacity to deconstruct the parameters of our conceptual system.

Derrida calls for a writing in the light of this analysis that will not conceal or suppress the process of its creation, but will actively incorporate other meanings in defiance of the system that seeks to impose its own authority by closing down other options. He urges writers to keep the opportunities for meanings open and plural, by attending to the metaphoric and metonymic functions of language, as well as to the heterogeneous suggestions thrown up by the signifying operation itself. He suggests that writing might in this way be freed from the restrictions of the current order, 'disseminating' meanings in ways that will inevitably dislodge the concept of a hierarchical structure, and a closed, self-referential system of meaning.

Derrida's account is reflected in the work of a number of French feminist writers. Marguerite Duras and Xavière Gauthier, in *Les Parleuses*,[5] emphasise the need for the writer to work through desire and transgression to silence logical reason (p. 178), relinquishing traditional (Cartesian) subject positions (p. 17) in a movement away from the self 'towards the other' (p. 182), and opening the text as a 'field of experimentation' (p. 18) with the potential to topple the established structure (p. 8).[6] Annie Leclerc, in *Parole de femme*,[7] similarly seeks 'to invent a word that will not be oppressive' (p. 8) and a writing 'in which each one is whole and does not hold dominion over others' (p. 69).

For writers like Annie Leclerc, this other writing is feminine not only because it inscribes what would otherwise be appropriated or repressed by (masculine) culture, but also because it involves the positive (re)valuing of *women's* differences.[8] This issue of the relationship between a feminine or other language and writing and women's sexual specificity, is viewed differently by different writers.[9] For writers like Luce Irigaray, the quest for an origin or 'first term' from which all meaning and order would ensue is *intrinsically* male, and, she believes, has led to the present system of exclusively masculine (self-)definition. For writers like Julia Kristeva, whilst she agrees that the (illusory) search for an origin is initiated by men and entails the continuing usurption of power, this quest, together with the frameworks it has spawned, are now, she writes, so embedded in our thinking that to move beyond them is to risk madness or the 'genocide' of non-communication. Like Derrida, she suggests that the purpose of writing is 'to bore from within', unsettling and challenging – though never completely destroying – the structures of the symbolic. Her approach can thus be contrasted to that of Irigaray, and to some extent Hélène Cixous, who urge women – and in the case of Hélène Cixous men – to make the imaginary 'leap' beyond the present schema to found a new 'order'. Luce Irigaray in particular sees the different composition and aims of female jouissance as containing the blue-print for an other system. For Michèle Montrelay, desire is the prerequisite for symbolisation, and, she suggests, can *only* be satisfied in language.[10] A feminine writing, Montrelay stresses, is thus one in which the writer, and hence the reader – instead of attempting to (re)create the (lost) object in words – plays with and enjoys the pleasures of the signifying procedure itself (p. 65).[11] Hélène Cixous, whilst she acknowledges that loss underpins human existence, suggests that the way this has been encoded as lack is inherently masculine, and she seeks to explore our experience through writing in ways that will enable us to view ourselves and the world differently. Cixous stresses the potential of a feminine writing to work through loss, which, she argues, will inevitably challenge the current structure of self-other relations. She urges the feminine writer to (re)claim the lived experience which the (masculine) symbolic seeks to bar.

Derrida's theories also have implications for the way a text is read. For Derrida, the prevailing system in the West is dependant on the notion that its reason is unaffected by language, creating and maintaining its order of 'truth' by ignoring the differential structure – the endless displacements and deferrals – of the signifying operation. Like the critic Roland Barthes, Derrida calls for a mode of reading that will focus on the text's formation to reveal, like the psychoanalyst, its obsessions and evasions. Derrida demonstrated how, despite attempts to conceal this process, traces of the text's creation can always be read in its 'blind-spots' – its system of imagery, its silences, its paradoxes and contradictions – in such a way as to explode its claim to mastery. He revealed how, by locating the points at which the text transgresses its own logic, and by reading its words and metaphors to discover what *else* they mean, the gap between the author's project and what the text also says may be exposed.[12]

Although for Derrida the author's intention does not in itself guarantee meaning, he nevertheless stresses that the writer's historical and social context influences the way a text is structured, since each historical and social situation produces its own discourses out of which the text is made.

Like a number of French feminist writers, Derrida believes every act of reading implies the creation of new meanings. Like Hélène Cixous, he suggests that no reading can ever be definitive, and that what a text means is only ever the product of a particular instance of reading. Like Barthes, he stresses that there can be no meta-language – no objective form of criticism free from the processes of the linguistic function – and he calls, instead, for a criticism in which the reader does not impose (his desire for) meaning, and a writing that will include the other possibilities of the signifying operation.

A woman's writing: Luce Irigaray

For Luce Irigaray the current order is so all-pervasive that she believes it is impossible, from our present vantage point, to even imagine the form an other writing might take. She does however give a number of tentative suggestions as to the possible direction of this new language. In her essay on Plato in *Speculum of the Other Woman*,[13] she suggests that there is, in Plato's work, the trace of an alternative 'mimesis' involving production rather than mere imitation, but stresses that this other form is stifled in line with a rhetoric deriving from *man's* need for 'specularisation' and *re*production. In 'The Power of Discourse and the Subordination of the Feminine',[14] Irigaray develops this notion to suggest that the new language will come through *women's* desire, inscribing the proximity, fluidity and multiplicity characteristic of the exchange between women rather than the masculine insistence on 'identity-to-self'. Irigaray believes that through this means women's writing will resist and explode the 'proper' terms and 'well-constructed forms' of conventional structures, and in such a way that it will never be 'upheld as a thesis' or made the 'object' of a pre-determined and self-glorifying position.

To illustrate the difficulties in attempting to give expression to the feminine from within the confines of the current order, and to figure some of the possible features of a woman's writing, Irigaray prefaces her essays in the collection *This Sex Which Is Not One* with a text based on a reading of Lewis Carroll's *Through the Looking Glass* and a film about the arrival of surveyors in a village prior to the building of a new road.[15] This opening text is a collage of scenes, 'characters', voices and dialogue, interspersed with other (Irigaray's?) descriptions, hypotheses and questions as to what is taking place. This multifariousness is reflected in the text's layout and typography, interweaving the different voices and fragments of italicised and non-italicised text so that it is impossible to distinguish who – if any *one* – is speaking. (Irigaray's?) text is itself prefaced with a text – the passage from Lewis Carroll's *Through the Looking Glass* in which Alice asks the question 'who am I?'. The Alice of *this* text, the text suggests, has gone 'behind the screen of representation': she has crossed to the other side.

The setting for (Irigaray's?) text is autumn, a time 'when things are still not completely congealed'. In addition all the measuring instruments, including – 'especially' – the looking glasses, which up until this point have 'controlled the limits of properties' and 'differentiated what was looked on with approval from what wasn't', have been left behind. The result of this 'oversight', the text tells us, is that it is now impossible to be certain about the extent or ownership of property, order, objectives, or to distinguish in any appropriating sense one woman from another.

At this point the text introduces the surveyor. Unlike Alice, who has been in wonderland, and whose eyes, we are told, *expect* 'appearances to alter' and 'one to turn into the other', the surveyor deals in 'specific, unquestionable, verifiable fact'. Confronted with his intervention, Alice and her friend Lucien seek a retreat – somewhere beyond the surveyor's scheming eyes. But Lucien's delight in 'tearing down the fences' between mine, yours, his and hers is disturbed by a 'detail' thrown into relief by the surveyor's meticulous sums – Alice's gift has been left lying on the bed. Lucien returns to Gladys (his wife?), now confused – in a 'legitimate' sense – about his (self) identity and that of the women he loves.

At this point in the text (the author? Irigaray?) suggests that there should be music to 'accompany the rhythm' of 'incessant transferral': the 'duplicating, doubling, dividing: of sequences, images, utterances, "subjects"'. Despite this movement, from past to present and one to the other, it is the surveyor's rule that nevertheless holds sway. Even though Alice displaces the surveyor's desire, her other status is made to function as matrix and support for *his* order: repeating and reproducing 'the projects of the one'. This is a fate shared by the text's (feminine) subject:

> *on this side of the screen of their projections, on this* plane *of their representations, I can't live. I'm stuck, paralyzed by all those images, words, fantasies.* Frozen. *Transfixed . . . So either I don't have any 'self',*

> *or else I have a multitude of 'selves', appropriated by them, for them, according to their needs or desires* (p. 17).

The text ends in darkness, since neither she (Alice?), nor 'I' (the author? Irigaray? the reader?), can live, either on *this* side – where she is made use of and suppressed – or on the other since this does not, as yet, exist: '*we would have needed,* at least, two *genres*', the text stresses, an alternative optics, an other style, a different way of proceeding.

Ending, however, leaves (the author?) with a problem. How is she to sign her name given that she has 'no right to a public existence except in the protective custody of Mister X'? Unless she signs her 'father's' name, how is she to represent herself? But to refuse to sign is to relegate herself to the unnamed and the unidentified and hence to being appropriated and forgotten; and so she compromises, signing herself: ' "Alice" underground'.

It is in the section of *Speculum of the Other Woman* entitled 'La Mystérique' ('The mystic–mysterious–hysterical–feminine one')[16] that Irigaray perhaps comes closest to outlining the form a feminine writing might take. Looking back at the languages traditionally associated with women, she sees in the visions and writings of the mystics the model for a language already attempting to express what is repressed by the 'dry desolation of reason'. She suggests that mysticism offers a means of escape from the 'disciplines' of knowledge, philosophy and science, since its tenets involve a 'flowing out' in which subject and other 'mingle', and in which 'consciousness is no longer master'.

In a passage that presents interesting parallels with Julia Kristeva's work on the function of poetic language, Irigaray suggests that at the heart of the mystical experience is a surrendering of the self as (masculine) subject. She believes this experience of self-loss – the relinquishing of 'self-identity-as-same' – together with the visions and outpourings it entails, offers women a context in which to break free from the prison within which the (masculine) subject must define himself. She stresses that these texts represent the only examples in Western culture of a writing in which women – and those men who follow ' "her" lead' – 'speak (as) woman'.

Irigaray documents the almost insurmountable obstacles that have confronted those who have attempted to follow the mystics' path. First, she argues, language is itself 'unfit to translate' the mystics' vision, which, given the predominance of philosophic discourse, can only 'at best be stammered out'. Second, the very forces that conspire to create this discourse cancel and invalidate the mystical state. Already 'caught' within an alien system of (self-) representation, the mystics' words, Irigaray stresses, are (re-) subjected to the 'configurations and chains' of that system and made to conform to its prescriptive unity.

Irigaray argues that these same difficulties continue to block women today. Just as the constricting forces of knowledge and reason imprisoned the mystics, so, she suggests, the forces that create the current order conspire to prevent all our attempts to move beyond it. Since we are (inevitably) bound by this order, she believes we cannot even begin at present to imagine what might lie outside. Only one thing, she stresses, seems clear. If we are to overthrow the masculine state, then 'all properties (and proprieties) will have to be shed': 'love, wish, affection, delight, interest, profit must all go as they are still related to a self-as-same'. Whilst Irigaray is aware that even putting this much into words 'is being too calculating, too logical', she nonetheless attempts a brief outline of a new (feminine) order in a passage which stresses many of the features of Hélène Cixous' concept of a feminine writing. The new (feminine) economy will, Irigaray writes, be founded in an economy of 'spending', in an 'expansion and dissipation of self' in which 'the richest person will certainly be the one who has most depleted the stores'. It will be an economy based on pleasure, on reciprocal living, on the sharing and overflowing of the boundaries between yours and mine. Above all, it will, she believes, be an economy in which power is abolished, a constant (r)evolution in which nothing is ever repeated or the same: a 'rejoicing' 'that can never be counted or determined by measure', in which the other is no longer at the mercy of the one.

Writing other worlds: Hélène Cixous

Hélène Cixous' notion of a feminine writing or *écriture féminine* is perhaps the area of French feminist theory most widely discussed outside France and possibly also that which is the least understood.

Like Luce Irigaray, Hélène Cixous believes the current (masculine) order is so all-pervasive that it is virtually impossible, from our present position, to 'say' what a new (feminine) 'order' might be like. In *The Newly-Born Woman*,[17] Cixous warns that any attempt to theorize *écriture féminine* in line with contemporary masculine (self-)definitions will only reduce, distort or annihilate its essential features. For Cixous, the heart of *écriture féminine* is a relinquishing of the (masculine) self, and an acceptance and inclusion of the other in ways which will necessarily call into question the prevailing ideology and its mode of perception and expression, and hence create a new 'order' to replace the patriarchal and capitalist hegemony. Like Julia Kristeva, Cixous sees writing as the locus and means of this revolution; like Irigaray, she gives women the key (though not exclusive) role in bringing this new 'order' into being.

The phrase 'write your body' has become closely associated with – even taken as the battle-cry of – *écriture féminine*. Kristeva's insistence on the potential of the semiotic drives to re-cast formal linguistic relations, and Irigaray's stress on the need for women to explore and 'write' our body experiences, relations and desires have contributed to this. For Cixous, 'writing the body' has three specific components.

First, like Irigaray Cixous stresses the ways in which women's bodies – including our perceptions of ourselves as women and our sexual experiences – have been appropriated and determined by men. She urges women to break with these restrictive definitions, and to express our discoveries in writing: 'women have almost everything to write about femininity: about their sexuality, that is to say, about the infinite and mobile complexity of their becoming erotic', she suggests in *The Newly Born Woman*. She believes women's inscription of our 'awakenings' will 'burst' the partitions and codes of the masculine symbolic, opening this up to other possibilities.

Secondly, Cixous argues that language is itself a body function. Speaking and writing involve the translation of thoughts through a complex network of chemical messages, nerve impulses and muscle movements, and Cixous suggests that this physiological activity, together with the ongoing body functions of breathing, pulse, the momentum of the body drives, stress and hormonal changes, influence our use of language. She believes a writer's attempt to repress these activities is both a falsification of the nature of the writing process, and an attempt to control meaning in compliance with the dictates of masculine law.

Thirdly, paralleling Kristeva's work on the power of the pre-symbolic *chora* to affect the subject in language, Cixous emphasises the role of the mother's body in feminine writing. For Cixous the pre-Oedipal rhythms and articulations of the mother's body continue to influence our adult experience, and like Kristeva she believes the inscription of these rhythms is a primary factor in preventing the codes of the patriarchal symbolic from becoming rigidifed and all-powerful. In her essay 'La Venue à l'écriture' ('Her Arrival in Writing'),[18] Cixous gives a clear if tangential illustration of this from her own childhood. Cixous' own mother-tongue is German, and she describes in the essay how the rhythms and expressions of the German language which she did not, in the context of a colonial French culture, learn the rules of, still inform and unsettle the languages she now speaks, and particularly the 'official' language of French.

Cixous suggests that the continuing impact of the rhythms and articulations of the mother's body affects the otherwise omnipotent stratification of the (masculine) symbolic, challenging its constitution and definitions, and hence the subject's relationship to language, the other, himself and the world. More emphatically than Kristeva, Cixous believes the non-repression and inclusion of the maternal body in writing presents a link with the pre-symbolic plentitude between self and m/other, and hence a way round the loss, exile and perpetual alienation of the masculine schema.[19] She sees in the very different motivations of mother-love the model for a radically different relation to the other, and thus the possibility for an other – feminine – economy and language 'contrary to the self-absorbed, masculine narcissism, making sure of its image of being seen, of seeing itself, of assembling its glories, of pocketing itself again'.[20] She believes the inscription of this m/other relation in writing will provide a blue-print for revolutionary change.

Cixous suggests that women find it easier than men to acknowledge the continuing impact of the m/other-bond, partly as a result of our sex-specific capacity to become mothers ourselves, a knowledge, she stresses in *Writing Differences*,[21] that women carry even if we choose not to or are unable to become biological mothers, and partly because of our marginalised position in relation to (masculine) law. She believes women's sex-specific potential to physically nurture and give birth to an other makes it easier for women to accept the disruptions (to the self) that an encounter with the other can bring. 'It is much harder for man to let the other come through him', she writes in *The Newly Born Woman* and, in a formulation reminiscent of Kristeva's insistence on the power of poetic language to challenge the subject's relation to the symbolic structure, suggests in 'La Venue à l'écriture' that 'this peopling gives neither rest nor security, always disturbs the relationship to "reality", produces an uncertainty that gets in the way of the subject's socialization'. Unlike the masculine approach, with its determined tendency 'to master. To demonstrate, explain, grasp. And then to lock away in a strongbox',[22] the feminine writer, Cixous insists, like a mother, 'looks with the look that recognizes, studies, respects, doesn't take, doesn't claw, but attentively, with gentle relentlessness, contemplates and reads, caresses, bathes, makes the other shine. Brings back to light the life that's been buried, fugitive, made too prudent. Illuminates it and sings it its name'.[23] For Cixous, this willingness to encounter and 'sing' the other, without seeking to appropriate or annihilate the other's difference in order to construct and glorify the self, is the keynote of *écriture féminine*. 'Writing is the passageway, the entrance, the exit, the dwelling-place of the other', she writes in *The Newly Born Woman*, and the feminine writer is 'the enchanted womb, the woman pregnant with all the love' whose flesh allows 'strangeness to come streaming through'.[24] She suggests that women's relegation to the margins of the patriarchal order also makes it easier for women than for men to risk the decrees of castration and experiment with and challenge its law, and means women have less to gain than men from the law's continued operation.

In both *The Newly Born Woman* and 'La Venue à l'écriture' Cixous urges women to write. She argues that women must overcome all the obstacles that stand in the way of our writing – 'history, my origin, my sex', 'no legitimate place, no land, no fatherland, no history of my own' – and, relinquishing the old structures, and risking the unknown, 'seek out the shattered, the multiple I' to 'emerge from the one self, shed the old body, shake off the Law'.[25]

For Cixous, unlike Luce Irigaray, the concept of femininity and hence of an *écriture féminine* is not however uniquely linked to sexuality. In 'La Venue à l'écriture', Cixous suggests: 'woman, for me, is she who kills no one in herself, she who gives (herself) her own lives: woman is always in a certain way "mother" for herself and for the other';[26] and whilst she reiterates her insistence that the questioning and apparent waste of women's speech and our willingness to incorporate the 'unmanageable' forces of the unconscious are crucial elements of an *écriture féminine*, she does not preclude the possibility of femininity existing in men. In *The Newly Born Woman* for example, she cites as an illustration of *écriture féminine* the work of the French playwright Jean Genet. In Genet's writing, Cixous argues, there is an abundance of other as well as continual variety and movement. She stresses that Genet's writing constantly changes shape as a result of this movement, so that his work is never arbitrarily fixed to represent (only) one truth or viewpoint. She quotes the work of the German dramatist Heinrich von Kleist as a second example. 'Not only is he capable of these transformations', she suggests, 'but he insists on passing through the bodies and souls' of those others who are 'stretched to the limit' in his writing: 'those closest to the lifesprings and therefore closest to life's origins, which is to say, to body, flesh, desire'.[27]

Écriture féminine is then, for Hélène Cixous, the endeavour to 'write the other' in ways which refuse to appropriate or annihilate the other's difference in order to create and glorify the self in a (masculine) position of mastery. It entails relinquishing the (symbolically constructed) self – 'a writing . . . without you, without I, without law'[28] – and an attention to the body, including the forces of the unconscious and sexuality. For Cixous, 'writing the other' also means the inscription of what is repressed by the masculine in its economy of death and obliteration. In 'La Venue à l'écriture', she describes writing as 'a way of warding off death, of thwarting forgetfulness' – 'if I write you are not dead' – and she argues that this inscription is vital both in the sense of our needing to create something in place of the abyss opened up by the prospect of death, and as a result of our duty to keep alive those others killed by *his*tory, tyranny and political violence.[29] She suggests that in this way (a feminine) writing may finally implement an 'order' in which death will no longer predominate.

In her critical work, Cixous gives a number of indications as to how this writing may be achieved. In 'La Venue à l'écriture', she contrasts those procedures of naming which function to perpetuate the masculine schema with a 'naming' that is akin to loving, and which serves 'to transmit: to make things loved by making them known'. In the Danish writer Karen Blixen's novel *Out of Africa*, one of the characters, Count Schimmelmann, argues that things only begin to exist in the world once they have been named and classified by man.[30] Hélène Cixous, in her readings of the Brazilian writer Clarice Lispector,[31] whose work she sees as the most important example to date of an *écriture féminine*, compares such colonizing attitudes to those of Lispector's 'G.H.' She quotes as an illustration the following passage from Lispector's *The Passion According to G.H.*:

> I have avidity for the world, I have strong and definite desires, tonight I'll go down and eat, I won't use the blue dress but the black one. But at the same time I don't need anything. I don't even need a tree to exist. I don't impose my need on things, they exist without my asking them, demanding them to be there.[32]

Cixous' concept of an *écriture féminine* as a writing of the other includes Derrida's insistence that language – and especially writing – brings with it its own riches and body of meanings. 'As soon as you let yourself be led' by writing, Cixous suggests in 'La Venue à l'écriture', 'as soon as you let yourself go' beyond the codes of the (masculine) symbolic, 'words diverge' and 'meanings begin to flow'. Like Derrida, Cixous stresses that any attempt to fix the meaning of a text is both impossible and reductive; and she urges writers to actively incorporate the myriad rhythms, sound-patterns and suggestions thrown up by the writing process itself.

This is a strategy Cixous follows in her own writing. The French title of *The Newly Born Woman*, for example, '*La Jeune Née*' – literally, 'The Young (feminine) Newly-Born' – includes a number of other meanings which are picked up and played on in the text. A French ear also hears 'Là je n'est' in 'La Jeune Née' – 'There I'm not' – a meaning which is echoed in the text's insistence that woman is always elsewhere to where the (masculine) symbolic wishes to define her. *Jeune* can also be divided into *Je une* – 'I (feminine) one' – a division which is reflected in the emphasis on the feminine 'I' as (new) subject. This attentiveness to the way language adds to and disrupts the signifying procedure, suggesting other possibilities for the writer to try, also has a bearing on the way writing is read.

Cixous sees the type of textual composition woven from the multiple and heterogeneous possibilities generated by the writing process as challenging the rules of (linear) logic, objective meaning, and the single, self-referential viewpoint decreed by masculine law. She believes (feminine) writing has the potential to undermine and present an other alternative to this law, and the hierarchy of linguistic, social and political relations the law creates. Like Luce Irigaray, Marguerite Duras and others, Cixous suggests that one of the ways in which (feminine) writing can bring into existence a new order is for the writer – and the eventual reader – to pay attention to the (silent) spaces – the 'not-said' – of the signifying operation. 'Writing is working; being worked; questioning (in) the between (letting oneself be questioned) of same and of other', Cixous writes in *The Newly Born Woman*, and she stresses that (feminine) writing must include the (symbolic) (re)presentation of this questioning by allowing those elements which do not adhere to the rigid codes of the masculine to speak. She believes that time is a key factor in this process, and she urges the writer – and the reader – not to hurry over any of the stages which might otherwise lead to an other insight, knowledge, or means of expressing these, in the (fallacious) struggle for greater achievement. Cixous again cites the work of Clarice Lispector as exemplary in this respect, stressing how Lispector refuses to shy away from the difficult, the painful or the ugly in her work, allowing herself instead the time she needs to confront the feelings generated by these, and to attempt to comprehend, transform and learn from her reactions.[33] Cixous suggests of the feminine writer in *The Newly Born Woman*:

> She comes out of herself to go to the other, a traveller in unexplored places; she does not refuse, she approaches, not to do away with the space between, but to see it, to experience what she is not, what she is, what she can be (p. 86).

This willingness to traverse the spaces left uninhabited by the masculine and to seek to encounter the other in all its various forms is, Cixous stresses, an approach which fundamentally challenges the defences necessitated by the (illusory) struggle for mastery and meaning.

Alongside her insistence that a feminine writing remain open to the other as *other*, Cixous also emphasises the need for the feminine writer to acknowledge and incorporate herself. A feminine economy and writing does not, Cixous argues, mean a negation or obliteration of the self, since this would merely reverse the dialectic between self and other, but entails, on the contrary, the relinquishing of the self's appropriation of the other, and an honest – loving – appraisal of the self's own needs, desires, prejudices, predilections, questions, blind-spots and fears. Cixous writes:

> when I write, all those that we don't know we can be write themselves from me, without exclusion, without prediction, and everything that we will be calls us to the tireless, intoxicating, tender-costly-search for love (p. 100).

She stresses the role of the unconscious in writing, which, she suggests, brings an other voice that disrupts any claim to a single or objective 'truth', and provides a 'jewellery-box' of alternative meanings, possibilities and directions for the writer to consider: 'these pearls, these diamonds, these signifiers that flash with a thousand meanings, I admit it, I have often filched them from my unconscious'.[34]

Cixous argues that this opening to the other in writing will have a radical impact on traditional literary genres and forms. The incorporation of writing's own (other) processes will, she suggests, have a transforming influence on the 'beginnings, middles and endings' narrative of so-called realist fiction; the writer's attempts to deconstruct his all-powerful, all-knowing 'I' and to include the other – of the signifying function, the body, objects, other people – will explode conventional notions of character as a stable, unified construct whose actions and behaviour can be predicted, manipulated and made use of. Cixous believes time will lose its pseudo-realistic quality, to echo more closely the ways we actually experience time in life. Finally, she suggests that a feminine writing will refuse to prioritise and select from the range of meanings to work to include *all* meanings, and especially those which destabilise and threaten the meaning we hope we have achieved and wish to impose on the reader. An illustration of this last point can be found in Cixous' own French–English text *Vivre l'orange/To Live the Orange*.[35] In *Vivre l'Orange*, Cixous describes her sudden realisation of the magnificence of an orange as she is working on a piece of writing. Her realisation is informed by a description by Clarice

Lispector she had previously been reading, and is interrupted by a telephone call reminding her that women are marching in the streets of Paris in support of women in Iran. This interruption in turn leads her to remember the Nazi concentration camps in which so many people lost their lives. Cixous' dilemma is that of inscribing all these elements in her writing: 'to be able to arrive alive awoman in front of an orange full of life, we must be able to live six million cadavers'.[36] She stresses that this endeavour to incorporate *all* meanings – and particularly those which are painful or difficult – is the keynote of feminine writing, in its struggle to approach, comprehend and learn from the various forces that compose life, and in its search to prevent the forces of holocaust from happening again.

Linked to Cixous' notion of an *écriture féminine* is the question of the reader's response. In 'La Venue à l'écriture', Cixous emphasises both the crucial role played by the reader in bringing the text to life – 'reading: writing the ten thousand pages of every page, bringing them to light' – and the inevitably limited nature of each reading, which can never exhaust all the possibilities of a text. 'Writing is never read: it always remains to be read, studied, sought, invented', Cixous stresses.[37] In 'Conversations' in *Writing Differences*, she develops her account of reading further.[38] She suggests that like the feminine writer the feminine reader must remain open to the meanings of a text, without seeking to impose 'his' preconceptions or desires, or attempting to make sense of the text in order to construct 'his' position as reader. She stresses the need for the reader to be attentive to all the various ways in which a text means, including our own desire for meaning, as well as the way this desire – and hence our reading – change. She suggests that a feminine reading implies a *collectivity* of readings, in which different interpretations are placed alongside each other, as well as the choice of those texts that deal in an open and questioning way with the fundamental issues of our existence, which shape our perception of ourselves and others, and hence influence our capacity to resist or create a better and more equal way of life.[39]

Cixous' fiction offers a practical illustration of her concept of *écriture féminine*.[40] In *Le Livre de Promethea* ('The Book of Promethea'),[41] Cixous describes her project as that of 'heaving a great hymnic cry of pleasure (*jouissance*) in order to make, in the leather of the old sclerotic language, an opening' (p. 12). *Le Livre de*

Promethea, Cixous tells us, is both 'a book of love' (p. 21) *for* Promethea (p. 51), and a book of all the difficulties (p. 20) of loving – in life as well as in writing. On the one hand, there are all the difficulties involved in finding an approach to the other that will not violate the other's difference (see for example p. 11), on the other there are difficulties of writing itself, which can both help create this approach (p. 22), and undermine the rigid definitions of the old order (p. 171), but which brings with it its own traces of the law. As in *Vivre l'orange/To Live the Orange*, the difficulties that confront the writer have even greater implications however. In addition to the ('personal') difficulties involved in changing economies (p. 99) in order to create a love relation that will ensure the happiness of each, there are also the difficulties of loving whilst keeping alive the knowledge of others' suffering (pp. 98–9). In *Le Livre de Promethea*, it is Promethea herself who provides the writer with examples. Promethea, we are told, 'won the soul of H, without taking her, by not taking her, by giving herself' (p. 183); she has left 'uncut the cord that links words to the body' (p. 184). In the light of Promethea's lead, and her own love for Promethea, the writer tries a variety of approaches. She attempts for instance to keep herself in a state of permanent receptivity (p. 15), attending to the passage of words through her body (p. 102), and pursuing her vision of a place 'without walls or bars' (p. 175) by refusing to reread (p. 110) or impose an order on what she has written (p. 22). She also deliberately splits her role as writer into two: 'I . . . reserved myself two places in the text (so as to be able to slip constantly from one to the other)' (p. 19), thus relinquishing her (writer's) claim to mastery, and freeing her (writing) 'I': 'I abandons herself. I abandon myself. I surrenders, loses herself' (p. 28). This splitting of the authorial self enables the writer to approach Promethea more openly (p. 51), and allows for the inscription of the other in the text: 'the author of what I describe is not me, it is the Other' (p. 245).

THEORIES AND PRACTICE

The concept of a feminine or other writing is also reflected in the work of a range of French women writers.

Feminine echoes: Christiane Rochefort, Marie Cardinal, Annie Leclerc, Jeanne Hyvrard and Chantal Chawaf

The notion is echoed in the work of the various writers discussed so far.

Christiane Rochefort's *C'est bizarre l'écriture* ('Writing is bizarre'),[42] the author's meditation on her own writing process, presents interesting parallels with the concept of *écriture féminine*. Rochefort outlines how time and again her readers 'give me back another book', often very different from the one she thought she had written, and she asks 'where then is the truth of the book?' (p. 10). She examines the way language carries ideology (p. 134), and urges the writer to move beyond the mechanical repetition of received language (p. 133), which has been poured into our memories since babyhood (p. 132), and which comes first to the writer (p. 133), since to use it 'without examination or shattering revision . . . we express the reigning mode' (p. 134). For Rochefort, the writer's task is to dismantle this received language, 'losing' its 'manufactured, factory-produced' words and phrases (p. 132), and working to employ language in another way (p. 133). She presses the writer to resist the temptation to become the 'brilliant subject' of their work (p. 17), suggesting that as soon as the ego is allowed into a sentence it 'coats' everything in it (p. 103), and to vanquish the 'constant tendency' of 'the intellect to take power' (p. 88). Rochefort emphasises the role of the body in writing – writing is a biological process, she argues (p. 74) – as well as the 'primacy of the unconscious' (p. 82). She details how, for her, writing is 'organic, not intellectual' (p. 33), and she stresses the importance of biological rhythm and respiration in the process of composition (p. 70). She suggests that this 'physical rhythm' combines with the operation of writing, with the result that body and writing interconnect to dictate the words to her (p. 89). She describes one such experience from her notebooks, recalling how, on an occasion when 'I was not thinking', '"I" left the circuit – FINALLY! – things happened *of their own accord*, writing accepted the relay from thinking, the prefect went out into the fields' (p. 89). The change is accompanied by a change in pronoun: '"ONE IS WRITING" – and opening today the notebook for reference I notice the use of an impersonal form to signal this turning-point moment' (p. 89). Rochefort believes that this writing 'without personal possessives' is the writing to which every writer should aspire; like Hélène Cixous, she urges writers to conquer their fear (p. 17) and burrow like moles through the restrictive codes of self and language, to create through their writing 'all these kingdoms which are not of this world ... because one dare not admit the possible' (p. 101). Books with too much 'I', Rochefort writes, 'gorge' their characters; and she stresses: 'once the I has been eliminated, it's necessary to come back as the writer, by another door, or rather by a staircase' (p. 117) in order to achieve the 'relationship of alterity' (p. 103) between (writing) subject and object (p. 17) in which 'the respect owed to every creature' may finally be accorded (p. 101).

Rochefort's fictional texts provide illustrations of these preoccupations. *Les Petits Enfants du siècle* ('The Grandchildren of the Century')[43] for example, perhaps one of Rochefort's most popular and accessible texts, includes numerous references to language. There are the phrases – 'white, smooth and closed like an egg' (p. 17) – which the central character, Josyane, is taught at catechism, and which she finds impossible to swallow (p. 18). There is Josyane's realisation of the way language can generate meanings we did not intend or expect (p. 39), as well as her detailed examination of the components of which language is made:

> The handkerchief which you gave me when I had the cross is white.
> 'The handkerchief is white', principle proposition;
> 'The', definite article;
> 'Handkerchief', common noun masculine singular, subject of 'is';
> 'Is', verb to be, 3rd person singular, indicative present;
> 'White', adjective masculine singular; attribute of 'handkerchief';
> 'Which you gave me', subordinate proposition, compliment of 'handkerchief';
> 'Which', subordinate conjunction;
> 'You', personal pronoun, 2nd person singular, subject of 'gave';
> 'Me', personal pronoun, 1st person singular, indirect compliment of 'gave' (p. 24).

Les Petits Enfants du siècle ends with a vision paralleling that of other French feminist writers. Surveying the perfect order of the newly-created city spread out beneath her (p. 129), Josyane finds herself longing for 'disorder and shadows' (p. 130). Josyane's vision is accompanied by her recognition that we spend our lives in search of the 'Other' we lack (p. 151), as well as by an answer to the question that has pursued her since school:

> 'What do you want to do in life?' – Love. Love, there, that is what I should have replied, in Guidance. What did I want to do in life? Love. Deep down it's very simple (p. 155).

Marie Cardinal, in response to a question by Annie Leclerc in *Autrement dit*,[44] outlines how for her writing is a mixture of 'jouissance' and 'struggle' (p. 54). Like Christiane Rochefort, she suggests that the struggle is directed partly against the self – as she works through the various motivating impulses of her own desire (p. 54) – and partly against the rigid code of language, which excludes so much of what she wants to convey:

> How to transmit to my beloved manuscript the eloquent mimicry of the body and the face that accompanies speech, the silences, the tone and music of the voice, the look filled with unexpressed words which are nevertheless comprehensible, the hands, like trays of fruit, full of mute phrases (p. 71).

Whilst Cardinal rejects the idea of there being a masculine or feminine writing linked to each sex (p. 82),[45] she stresses the connection between words and the body: 'words live, they are made of flesh and bone, blood and tears, laughter and fear' (p. 174); 'I write with my body' (p. 201). She believes the aim of writing must be the subversion of the current schema (p. 222), and argues that the ultimate responsibility for a text's meaning lies not with the writer but the reader (p. 121).

Annie Leclerc, questioning and listening, endorses Cardinal's views on writing (see p. 211), emphasising in her 'postface' to the conversations the role of the body in writing (p. 213) and our potential to overcome the fear of birth which, she suggests, founds the present system (p. 213), and give birth (p. 214) through writing to what is currently unexpressed: 'so that the real is somewhere modified, expanded' (p. 215).

Jeanne Hyvrard's *Mère la mort*,[46] with its insistence on the mother, death, and a new (feminine) language that will overturn existing grammar (p. 19), also echoes the tenets of *écriture féminine*. In *Mère la mort*, Hyvrard explores the way men's 'fear of the tiny beating in women's bellies' (p. 21) has resulted in their seizing power through language, and repressing the origin, the mother, death, the body and love:

> words, nothing but words. Cement. To cover over their [masculine] emptiness. Cement. In order to recognize themselves as from the same clan. Cement. In order to take possession of us (p. 22).

The text searches for an other language that will break down these (masculine) self-constructions (p. 26), dependant on a mirror economy and the other's destruction (p. 96), to create, in their place, a language that will spell the subject's dissolution (p. 141) and *include* the 'unnameable' of the m/other, birth and death (pp. 57–8). This m/other language, Hyvrard suggests, will be the gift of women, linking men and women back through the mother to overcome the effects of separation (p. 22):

> In our bellies in blood, we will give them back their death so that they [masculine] may be reborn with us. We will deliver them from their anguish because love has no end . . . We will deliver them from their jealousy . . . . We will deliver them from their appropriations . . . . We will deliver them from their fear and our confinement (p. 154).

Chantal Chawaf's writing can also be read in the context of an *écriture féminine*. In *Elwina, le roman fée*[47] for example, there is constant emphasis on the link between the body and the writing Elwine is struggling to create. Despite the insistence of her publisher, who tells Elwine: 'the body does not exist, my little one. When you have understood that the body does not exist, you will have understood eternity' (p. 11), Elwine's writing is like 'milk . . . streaming from her breast, nourishing the void' (p. 13). Her pages are:

> blood, flesh, nerve endings, they are of the body, they are a part of my body, it is not yet completely detached from me, everything is vibrating in my stomach, in my belly, in my intestines, all these words, all these phrases, their living red, their pink flesh, it's like life, it's like my life, it's like more than my life, as if I were rejoining someone who has always been lacking from me, as if I were going closer than one ever goes even when one is caressing, when one is touching, when one is embracing (p. 14).

Elwine's writing is a dark, inner 'hole', which 'one enters blind, feeling one's way instinctively' like a newly-born (p. 35). Pitted against a society in which all trace of femininity is inhibited by 'dreams of power, fame and money', and in which language censures (p. 85), Elwine searches for 'an ideal of love that does not know the reality of hatred and suffering and which aspires towards a language from the other world' (p. 36). The name Elwine gives to her writing is that of Elwina the mother, and as the process of writing takes Elwine closer to the mother so her writing opens to take 'less and less the name of Elwina and more and more all the possible names, the inexhaustible names of life' (p. 64):

> And, as the origin effaces itself, something of this effacement traces itself, inscribes the hollow, inscribes the void and opens, opens language to the unsayable (p. 82).

In Chawaf's *Le Soleil et la terre*,[48] the struggle is against the phallic language of order and the law (p. 54) which, with its system of injustices, its repression of femininity (p. 114) and abuse of women (p. 52), its 'contempt for the human body' and 'general indifference to life' (p. 54) is shown to have created the tyranny and violence that have led to war. Against this language, the text posits an alternative writing of the mother (p. 76), the body (pp. 76, 118) and love (pp. 18, 77), with the potential to inscribe 'a zone beyond the forbidden' in which the (masculine) schema of differences has not yet come into force (p. 81). It is, the text suggests, by 'returning to the origin' of language (p. 89) and life (p. 121), and by risking the chaos this return inevitably entails (p. 89), that we may evoke 'your words, the other words, the words of other [feminine] languages, of other places, other politics' (p. 86) in which the system of binary oppositions no longer exists (p. 107) and the barriers between individuals are dissolved (pp. 83, 107). It is, Chawaf argues, only by re-forging the link between words and objects that we can reverse the present order of abstraction (pp. 84–5) – in which the obliteration of the m/other has become not only possible but necessary – to create in its place a new inscription capable of healing the world (p. 77) from its destructive course (p. 89):

> and I will unite with you . . . and we will circulate one in the other, without danger, without obstacle, without traps, without restraint, without incompatibility, without hurting ourselves, and it will be an

> Egg-World, a world ready to hatch . . . unified only by the flesh of its bodies linked biologically, tenderly . . . in vital solidarity, in which society, instead of preparing to make us inhale an atmosphere of death, will accept its human body, return to its human body, re-enter its human body, its veins of blood, and live, instead of exploiting, instead of prohibiting, instead of destroying life (p. 125).

Other forms: Chantal Chawaf, Marguerite Duras and Monique Wittig

In addition to its very different preoccupations and aims, *écriture féminine* also entails a new form to writing. Chantal Chawaf's *Le Soleil et la terre* and *Elwina, le roman fée*, for example, employ a fluid structure in which sentences sometimes run for an entire page[49] and within which the 'subject' is consequently submerged, as well as a movement of constant self-questioning.[50] In Chawaf's *L'Intérieur des heures*,[51] the girl's dreams are incorporated into the body of the text, collapsing the division between objects and language,[52] a blurring which is echoed in the confusion of subject pronouns.[53]

The writing of Marguerite Duras similarly involves startling formatic innovations. Her recent text *L'Amant*, translated into English as *The Lover*,[54] includes a number of elements characteristic of an *écriture féminine*. There is, for example, an emphasis on the body as a source of knowledge,[55] and on a writing which is inclusive rather than (self) publicising.[56] There is the recurring image of a mirror, in which the adolescent self sees and recognises its own reflection:

> I . . . look at myself in the shopkeeper's glass, and see that there, beneath the man's hat, the thin awkward shape, the inadequacy of childhood, has turned into something else .... Has become . . . a choice of the mind. Suddenly it's deliberate. Suddenly I see myself as another, as another would be seen, outside myself . . . available to all eyes (p. 16, see also p. 7).

This mirror symbolises the images carried by the ego (p. 14), which are imposed on the self (p. 14), as well as the images reflected back to the self by others (p. 21, see also pp. 17, 19).

The formal composition of *The Lover* echoes the concerns of feminine writing. The text is split into fragments, interweaving recollections from the past with commentary and blank spaces, so that whilst there is progression and a sense of increasing understanding, no definitive or temporal order is imposed on the text by the narrator. Instead the narration follows the thoughts of the central character – who remains unnamed – sometimes picking up the thread as 'I', sometimes as 'she', and sometimes as though from a 'neutral' (the author's?) perspective (see for example p. 11). This shifting voice is reflected in the questioning movement of the text (see for example p. 16), highlighting both the partial and necessarily incomplete nature of what can be told (see p. 11), and implicating the reader's own recollections and understanding in the process of the text's formation.

It is perhaps Monique Wittig's work, of those writers discussed so far, which offers the most vivid illustration of the formal innovation of *écriture féminine*. Her *Les Guérillères*[57] for instance, includes a number of the concerns of *écriture féminine* and displays a startling array of formal experimentation. The women of *Les Guérillères* – the (feminine) 'they' – the *elles* – of the text – are searching to end the old order that has held women 'prisoners of the mirror' (p. 40). Their aim is to 'institute disorder' (p. 40), overturning the present system (p. 189) to create 'a new world' (pp. 121, 184) of relations (p. 154) expressed in 'a new language' (p. 189). Like a number of the writers referred to here, Wittig suggests this new order will come from women. She believes this will involve a positive (re-)valuing of women's sex (see pp. 11, 24, 61), as a source of pleasure (p. 290), as 'the emblem of fecundity and the reproductive power of nature' (p. 42), and as the symbol for a new culture in which the current schema of difference and the oppressive hierarchy of the masculine will no longer hold (p. 97). This new culture will necessitate a re-telling of the myths and stories that have hereto told the 'his'tory of the world. The story of Genesis, for example, is re-interpreted by *les guérillères* to praise Eve's desire for the apple (of understanding) (pp. 116–17), in a way which reveals 'his' 'trick' of banishing Eve from paradise and making her his slave (pp. 158–9, see also pp. 31, 35, 60–1). The song of the siren is remembered as 'a continuous O' which evokes, 'like everything that recalls the O, the zero, or the circle', woman's sex (p. 16). The symbol of the round table in the King Arthur legends is also given a new significance (p. 62). *Les Guérillères* is composed of a weave of women's/feminine voices, and the heterogeneous voices, like the echoes that superimpose themselves on Lucie Maure's recital, filling the gaps and spaces between her words (p. 17), continually suggest the possibility of other meanings and perspectives. Like other French feminist writers, Wittig stresses in *Les Guérillères* that these other meanings will emerge in the intervals of the masculine system:

> 'They [feminine] say, the language that you speak is made of signs which properly speaking designate what they [masculine] have appropriated for themselves. What they [masculine] have not put their hands on, what they [masculine] have not pounced on like birds of prey with manifold eyes, that will not appear in the language you speak. That only manifests itself in the interval which the masters have not been able to fill with their words of owners and possessors, it can be looked for in the hiatus, in everything that is not the continuation of their discourse, in the zero, the O, the perfect circle that you invent (p. 164).

At the same time, *Les Guérillères* warns against the dangers of constructing a new ideology in place of the old (p. 80), emphasising the constant need to 'return to zero' and begin again (p. 88).

These concerns are tied to the text's form. The insistence on the feminine, on women and on circles as the (positive) symbol of woman's sex, is expressed both in the continual reference to these (see, for example, 'the game of circles', p. 84), in the lists of women's names that appear at various points in the text (see p. 15), and in the series of circles repeated at intervals on otherwise blank pages (for example p. 8). Part of the text is set in block capitals 'IN AN OTHER WRITING'/'AGAINST MEANING', incorporating what is 'OUTSIDE THE TEXT': the 'MYRIAD CONSTELLATIONS' of meanings that appear in the parentheses and 'LACUNAE LACUNAE LACUNAE'/'MARGINS SPACES INTERVALS' (p. 205). The text also incorporates long lists of objects, which are presented in an unpunctuated form without any attempt to organise or order (for example pp. 11, 13). Many of the sentences repeat this format, offering the reader a multiplicity of possibilities without punctuation, enabling the rhythm – and the reader – to create their own 'order':

> They [feminine] say, I refuse from now on to speak this language, I refuse to mumble after them the words of lack lack of penis lack of money lack of sign lack of name (p. 153).

Les Guérillères is composed of a series of fragments interspersed with blanks, which, like the books read by *les guérillères*, interleave words with 'symbols of the circle, of the circumference, of the ring, of the O, of the zero, of the sphere' (p. 61) with space for the women to write their own accounts (p. 17). Whilst the fragments contain movement and a sense of progression (for instance, the [re-] valuing of women's sex which is at first seen as necessary is later regarded as a temporary step on the road towards greater physical integration [p. 102]), like the 'great register' left open on the table, 'it is pointless to open' the text 'at the first page and look in it for an order of succession' (p. 74). Like the song the women sing to commemorate Medusa's story (p. 35), in which there is no 'logical' meaning, *Les Guérillères* is a book the recipient 'may take . . . at random' and 'find something by which one is concerned' (p. 74).

The new wor(l)d: Geneviève Serreau, Marie Redonnet and Michèle Ramond

I would like to conclude with reference to the work of three further writers whose texts exemplify the thematic concerns and provide innovative illustrations of the formal experiments of *écriture féminine*, and thus demonstrate its impact on a wide range of contemporary French women's writing.

Geneviéve Serreau's *Un enfer très convenable* ('A Very Agreeable Hell')[58] comprises different versions of a journey to the 'other side' (p. 18). Not only is each version different, offering a multiplicity of individual perspectives each written in a different voice, but each account also includes the stories of other journeyers (see for example p. 137), and gives contradictory information (see p. 29). The different styles emphasise the impossibility of an objective viewpoint, and implicate the reader in a different way. La Grélue's account for instance is virtually unpunctuated, and this, together with the colloquialism of the stream of consciousness style, draws the reader directly into her story, leaving it to us to punctuate and make sense of her meaning. Tibulle's experience on the other hand is recounted after his return from his descriptions by those who have stayed behind, and thus offers a different temporal perspective to La Grélue's account, and although Tibulle is often quoted directly his story is shot through with the tellers' own cynical efforts to understand.

The purpose and descriptions of the final destination of the journeyers can be read as a metaphor and parable of *écriture féminine*. Each of the journeyers has their own reason for going. Tibulle expresses his as a dissatisfaction with the restraints of his present life (p. 17) and a belief that the other side will fulfil his dream of Utopia, entailing the 'dispossession of old man' and men's rebirth (p. 18). Jéricho explains his purpose as one of finding a 'path that will take me away from me' (p. 66), whilst La Grélue describes her motivation as that of wanting to add up to more than the zero she has always equalled in the old world:

> for as I had learned with amazement from elementary school one could go on forever increasing the number given even up to a billion billion if one was multiplying it by zero that never gave anything but zero in virtue of I don't know what mathematical contagion of nothingness so much so that being certain of the multiplying zero that was me I was equally sure that whatever the multiplicand as they say to end up zero, and that's why my project or plan or dream or programme in short my goal in going to the other side was in particular to transform if possible this multiplying zero into something with more body to rise even if it was only to the height of one so as to henceforth prevent it all inevitably capsizing in absolute non-entity, it wasn't too much too ask is it too much to ask? (p. 77).

The description of the other side, although fleeting and contradictory, can also be read in the context of *écriture féminine*. All that is known of the other side – which is situated 'beyond the frontiers' at 'the outermost boundaries' of the known world (p. 17) – is derived from the conflicting accounts of a handful of travellers (p. 17). These accounts range from those who talk of another Eden, to those who find it impossible to *say* anything at all (p. 17), to those who, like the tellers of Tibulle's story, doubt its very existence.

There are also echoes of *écriture féminine* in the reasons we are given for the failures of the journeyers to reach the other side. Some spend so much time and energy focusing on all the practical difficulties that they forget their reason for going (p. 141). Clotaire and Gontran, two travellers Tibulle meets at one of the outposts on this side, have simply lost their desire to go any further (p. 110). They prefer the comparative security of the 'permitted limits', and their lassitude infects Tibulle. Although no actual prohibition prevents Tibulle from leaving the outpost, he feels guilty, as if he is violating some invisible decree each time he thinks of going on:

> Nothing but his own scruples and this vague unformulated threat which hung over each inhabitant of the House as soon as they took the least initiative, and even if they submissively conformed to the permitted customs and behaviour (p. 109).

Language is a key element in the account of the different journeys. In addition to the multiplicity of voices, each journeyer is confronted by another language. Jéricho encounters a dumb boy who communicates through body language (p. 49), and Clotaire and Gontran have an invented language of their own: 'Fluft drin yalerick, said Gontran .... Take care of Quinbus Flestrin' (p. 109). La Grélue is influenced by Cuné, whose stories seem like the 'sparse ends' of a submerged history which lacks the necessary words to be told (p. 119). In Cuné's accounts, 'the dates and the precise locations . . . the whens the wheres and the whys' are not allowed to obstruct what she has to say.

It is Tibulle's description of what happens to him on the border that perhaps most closely echoes the tenets of *écriture féminine*. Tibulle prefaces his account by reminding his interlocutors that the words he is obliged to use – because 'there are no others' – 'restrict, immobilise, kill': 'words lack, in other words lie in bringing back to the wounding limits of time what was by nature unlimited' (p. 149). His description involves both a space and a music in which 'nothing either began, or ended, nor was aimed towards any goal because everything at each moment was newly born' (p. 149). The musical notes, whilst creating harmony, are distinct and separate from each other: 'no sound went towards the next one in order to perfect or resolve it, but existed totally for itself' (p. 150). The new space Tibulle feels he inhabits gives a different role to the body and objects. Like the notes of music, objects exist in and for themselves (p. 154). Tibulle recalls feelings of joy but also pain (p. 153), a knowledge of the reality of death (p. 154) as well as 'the pure sensation of life's flux' (p. 150). These feelings are lived by the body in 'ways infinitely more subtle and vehement than words' (p. 151), and to the amazement of his listeners, Tibulle can remember no sense of physical restraint or sexual differentiation (p. 152). Instead his desire is transformed from the desire for, to a continual satisfaction and renewal within the 'incredible pulsation of life' (p. 152).

Marie Redonnet's *Rose Mélie Rose*,[59] first published in 1987, is the story of three generations of women, Rose, Mélie and Rose, presented from the viewpoint of Mélie, though without the insistence on temporal or historical progression such stories usually entail. Instead the text offers a series of pictures, which like the twelve photographs Mélie bequeaths to her newly-born daughter Rose, it is left to the recipient to interpret, invent stories about and organise. The text is composed of short fragments interspersed with blank lines, and echoes a number of the images and themes of *écriture féminine*. There is an emphasis on birth as part of the ongoing life-cycle (see p. 11), and on the power of dreams to influence our lives (see p. 17). There is also the 'book of legends' handed on from mother to daughter and re-interpreted by each generation, and an old and new alphabet with the power to change the meanings of names (p. 39).

Unlike the simply written, almost matter-of-fact and conventionally structured sentences of *Rose Mélie Rose*, Michèle Ramond's *Vous* ('You')[60] is written in a strikingly unconventional and innovative form. The central preoccupation of *Vous* is the relationship between language, objects and the body. Here the law is recognized as 'a theory of reason' that 'weighs ... the body down' through the accumulation of everything it refuses (p. 74). In the context of this law, the 'I' searches for a space in which desire will return unchanged and 'opposites' will no longer be the ruling principle (p. 61). This space will entail 'a spontaneous blazing of language', overwhelming the law's need for genders and predicates and the self's 'desire to know and fix things' (p. 72). The form of *Vous* echoes this space. The text opens with a double blank page, beginning a narrative on page three in mid-sentence. The double blank pages are repeated at irregular intervals through the text, and the narrative is resumed in each case in mid-sentence and sometimes mid-word, and always at a different point from where it was broken off (see for example pp. 21–4). Ramond's sentences also break with all the conventional rules of sentence construction, placing different propositions alongside each other, incorporating half-lines of blank space, and experimenting with the textual lay-out:

> It's in my prehensile, loving, murderous eye's line of vision, that the object grows and takes on relief.
> It's in the waiting, . . . the love, the tracking, that the tree grows
> in the trance that the object is transfigured.
> in the betrayal[61] of my mouth and my eye (p. 20).

The thematic preoccupations and particularly the formal experiments of *écriture féminine*, with their explosions of conventional narrative procedure, their dislocation of the writing subject and engendering of a new relationship between subject and object, their emphasis on a multiplicity of meanings created through word-play and transgression of the rules of language and textual layout, are in striking contrast to the 'realistically' conceived female protagonists in their struggle for political, social, economic and cultural equality with men of mainstream Anglo–American feminist writing.[62] Perhaps only in the rich tradition of feminist science fiction in Britain and America, in the crossing of sexual and gender boundaries of Angela Carter's *The Passion of New Eve*[63], for example, or the envisioning of an other world order and language in Marge Piercy's *Woman on the Edge of Time*,[64] are some of the concerns – if not the mode of presentation – of an *écriture féminine* shared.

As we approach the twenty-first century, designated by some as the dawn of the millennium of women, I believe the theories and writings of French feminism can be seen as pioneering and inspirational. Traditional Anglo–American feminist criticism of French feminism – that its insistence on language and the reconstruction of identity does not guarantee the overthrowal of oppression[65] – should not, I would suggest, prompt us to ignore this rich and challenging body of writings. French feminism, as represented in this volume, has much to offer in its relentless questioning of the processes through which we symbolise, order and understand ourselves, the world and others. As critics, its practices and approaches also have much to contribute.[66] Perhaps what is needed is an alliance between the two perspectives. As readers and writers, I believe we have much to gain from combining Anglo–American concerns with content and French feminist interest in the way this content is produced and used.[67] As feminists, the (self) questioning of French feminism and material propositions of Anglo–American feminism similarly seem a fruitful conjunction. Such a dialogue might thus overcome the pitfalls of co-option by also working on the historical and material causes of oppression, employing the deconstructive strategies of French feminism to prevent a policy of direct intervention from recreating the appropriation and destruction that have hereto marked the conceptual, political and inter-personal government of the West.[68]

As reproductive technology advances,[69] the question 'what is woman' takes on a new significance. French feminist insistence on the value of difference as a counterweight to the tyrannies of enforced homogenisation, appears in the light of developments which threaten to remove the most basic difference of all, a crucial addition to feminist programmes which may unwittingly be playing into the schema of the masters of old.[70]

Notes and references

References are given to the published English translation wherever this is available. (Readers of French can find details of French texts in the Bibliography.)

Since the discussion of male theorists is not my main focus in this study (see Preface), I have tended to keep references to their writings general, supplying details only of those texts I have found helpful in preparing my presentation. I have organized my discussion of French feminist writers around individual essays which are documented below, and in order not to overload the text with references, I have given direct page references only where quotation from an essay is substantial. References to novels or longer works are, however, indicated in the text.

Preface

1. For an introduction to the development of Anglo–American feminism in its relation to Anglo–American feminist criticism see Janet Todd, *Feminist Literary History* (Cambridge: Polity Press, 1988) p. 20.
2. See, for example, Simone de Beauvoir, 'Women and Creativity', translated by Roisin Mallaghan in *French Feminist Thought: A Reader*, Toril Moi (ed.) (Oxford: Basil Blackwell, 1987) (p. 17).
3. Claire Duchen's *Femininsm in France: From May 68 to François Mitterand* (London: Routledge and Kegan Paul, 1986) provides an excellent overview of the women's liberation movement in France, whilst her *French Connections: Voices from the Women's Movement in France* (London: Hutchinson, 1987) presents translated extracts from a number of women involved in feminist debates in France during the 1970s and 80s. For readers of French, Maïté Albistur and Daniel Armogathe's *Histoire du féminisme français: du moyen âge à nos jours* (Paris: des femmes, 1977) offers a survey of feminism in France from the middle ages to the present time. The women's group 'La Griffonne' have also published a useful year by year review of women's campaigns in France from 1970 to 1981 entitled *Douze ans de femmes au quotidien: douze ans de luttes féministes en France: 1970–1981* (Paris: La Griffonne, 1981).

4. Both Claire Duchen's *French Connections: Voices from the Women's Movement in France* (London: Hutchinson, 1987) and Toril Moi's *French Feminist Thought: A Reader* (Oxford: Basil Blackwell, 1987) include translated extracts by feminists – like Christine Delphy – who radically refute the work of some of the theorists and writers I include here.

5. This insistence on philosophy can seem strange in the context of the more material concerns of Anglo–American feminism, and it is worth noting that philosophy – including Freud's theory of psychoanalysis – is widely taught in French schools.

6. See, for example, Dale Spender's *Man-Made Language* (London: Routledge and Kegan Paul, 1980) for the classic exposition of early Anglo–American feminist work on language. For a more recent account which includes both a critique of this position in the context of French feminist theories of language and suggests a new direction for Anglo–American feminism see Deborah Cameron's useful and accessible *Feminism and Linguistic Theory* (Basingstoke: Macmillan, 1985).

7. See, for example, Mary Ellmann's *Thinking About Women* (New York: Harcourt Brace, 1968 and London: Macmillan, 1969); Ellen Moers, *Literary Women: The Great Writers* (New York: Doubleday, 1976, and London: The Women's Press, 1976); Elaine Showalter, *A Literature of Their Own: British Women Novelists from Brontë to Lessing* (Princeton University Press, 1977); Sandra Gilbert and Susan Gubar, *The Madwoman in the Attic: The Woman Writer and the Nineteenth Century Literary Imagination* (Yale University Press, 1979); Mary Jacobus (ed.) *Women Writing and Writing About Women* (London: Croom Helm, 1979, and New York: Barnes and Noble, 1979).

8. Readers of French might compare the terrain of such critical texts as Anne-Marie Dardigna, *Les Châteaux d'Eros: ou les infortunes du sexe des femmes* (Paris: Collection Maspero, 1981); Béatrice Didier, *L'Écriture femme*, (Paris: Presses Universitaires de France, 1981); Irma Garcia, *Promenade femmilière: recherches sur l'écriture féminine* (Paris: des femmes, 1981).

9. See, for example, Marilyn French, *The Women's Room* (London: Abacus, 1986).

10. Elizabeth Fallaize's forthcoming 'Contemporary French Women's Fiction' (Basingstoke: Macmillan) offers a selection of translated extracts from the work of a range of contemporary French women writers.

Introduction

1. Ferdinand de Saussure, *Course in General Linguistics* (1916), New York, 1966.

2. Claude Lévi-Strauss, *Structural Anthropology* 2 volumes (1958), London, 1968 and 1977.

3. Claude Lévi-Strauss, *Introduction to a Science of Mythology* 4 volumes (1964, 1967, 1968, 1971), London, 1970, 1973 and 1978.

4. Claude Lévi-Strauss, *The Elementary Structures of Kinship* (1949), London, 1969.

5. Michel Foucault, *The Order of Things: An Archaeology of the Human Sciences* (1966), London, 1974.

6. Georg Hegel, *The Phenomenology of Spirit* (1807), Oxford, 1979.

7. Simone de Beauvoir, *The Second Sex* (1949, (Harmondsworth: Penguin, 1972).

8. Simone de Beauvoir, *The Second Sex* p. 16. The master–slave relationship is also the subject of a novel by one of France's top-selling women writers Christiane Rochefort, *Quand tu vas chez les femmes* ('When you go to the women's house') (Paris: Grasset, 1972). In the novel, Rochefort reveals the perverse nature of this relationship through the masochistic sexual exploits of the novel's male protagonist. Although the novel at first appears to reverse the sexual politics of Beauvoir's model, the hero is in no doubt of the nature of the relation between himself and the prostitutes he employs: 'what was establishing itself between us was the only true link, that of the slave and the master' (p. 20). When he later meets the young woman to whom he will dedicate himself, he realises that the perverted tortures she inflicts on him at his bidding place him in the position of power: 'She was obeying me!' (p. 50).

9. Michel Foucault, 'The Discourse on Language' (1969), in *The Archaeology of Knowledge*, London, 1972.

10. Roland Barthes, *Mythologies* (1957), London, 1972. A useful English selection of the work of Roland Barthes is the Susan Sontag introduced Fontana Pocket Reader, *Barthes: Selected Writings*, Oxford, 1983.

11. Roland Barthes, 'Écrivains et écrivants' (1960), in *Critical Essays* (1964), Illinois, 1972.

12. See Roland Barthes, *The Pleasure of the Text* (1973), New York, 1975.

13. Luce Irigaray, *Speculum of the Other Woman* (1974), translated by Gillian C. Gill (New York: Cornell University Press, 1985). All quotations in this section on Irigaray, except where otherwise indicated, are taken from this translation.

14. Luce Irigaray, *This Sex Which Is Not One* (1977), translated by Catherine Porter (New York: Cornell University Press, 1985) p. 164.

15. 'Plato's *Hystera*', in *Speculum of the Other Woman*, pp. 243–364. All quotations in this section on Plato are taken from this essay.

16. Irigaray's use of the term *khora* can be usefully compared with Julia Kristeva's description of a *chora* (see Chapter 2 below).

17. The image is that of a medical instrument used for inspecting the cavities of the human body. Its resonance here stems from the fact that it is both a mirror and is most usually associated with the examination of women's sex.

18. 'How to Conceive (of) a Girl', in *Speculum of the Other Woman*, pp. 160–8. All quotations in this section on Aristotle are taken from this essay.

19. 'And If, Taking the Eye of a Man Recently Dead...', in *Speculum of the Other Woman*, pp. 180–90. All quotations in this section on Descartes are taken from this essay. Irigaray's reading of Descartes here revolves around his famous dictum 'I think, therefore I am'.

20. 'Paradox A Priori', in *Speculum of the Other Woman*, pp. 203–13. All quotations in this section on Kant are taken from this essay.

21. 'The Eternal Irony of the Community', in *Speculum of the Other Woman*, pp. 214–26. All quotations in this section on Hegel are taken from this essay.

22. Julia Kristeva, *Revolution in Poetic Language* (1974), translated by Margaret Waller (Columbia University Press, 1984).

23. Julia Kristeva, *About Chinese Women* (1974), translated by Anita Barrows (London: Marion Boyars, 1977). An extract from *About Chinese Women* is translated by Séan Hand in the Toril Moi (ed.) *The Kristeva Reader* (Oxford: Blackwell, 1986) pp. 138–59. Since the full English translation has for some time been out of print, all quotations in this section on Kristeva, except where otherwise indicated, are taken from this translated extract.

24. See, for example, Rosalind Miles, *The Women's History of the World* (Harmondsworth: Michael Joseph, 1988) for a comprehensive and accessible introduction to this field of feminist research.

25. Julia Kristeva, 'A New Type of Intellectual: The Dissident' (1977), translated by Séan Hand in *The Kristeva Reader* (Oxford: Blackwell, 1986) pp. 292–300.

26. Hélène Cixous, 'Sorties', in *The Newly Born Woman* (1975), (with Catherine Clément), translated by Betsy Wing (University of Minnesota Press, 1986) pp. 63–130. All quotations are taken from this translation.

27. See Aeschylus, *The Oresteian Trilogy*, translated by Philip Vellacott (Harmondsworth, 1956).

28. See Chapter Three below for an account of the relationship between masculine and feminine as modes of behaviour and intrinsic biological differences between the sexes.

29. Readers of French might be interested in consulting, for a context for this theory, Marcel Mauss' 'Essai sur le don. Forme et raison de l'échange dans les sociétés archaïques', in *Sociologie et Anthropologie* (Paris: Presses Universitaires de France, 1950).

Chapter 1 Women and language

1. This account of Derrida's work is taken mainly from the following: *Of Grammatology* (1967), translated by Gayatri Spivak (Baltimore and London, 1977); *Writing and Difference* (1967), translated by Alan Bass

(London, 1978); *Margins of Philosophy* (1972), translated by Alan Bass (Brighton, 1982). For readers of French, an excellent introduction to Derrida's work is the collection of interviews (with Henri Ronse, Julia Kristeva, Jean-Louis Houdebine, Guy Scarpetta) *Positions* (Paris, 1972). For English readers, Jonathan Culler's essay 'Jacques Derrida' in *Structuralism and Since: From Lévi-Strauss to Derrida*, John Sturrock (ed.) (Oxford, 1979) pp. 154–79, and Christopher Norris' *Deconstruction: Theory and Practice* (London: 1982) both provide useful introductions to Derrida's work. Gayatri Spivak's introduction to her translation of *Of Grammatology* (see above) is also helpful. This introductory discussion of Derrida's work will be continued in Chapter 4 below.

2. In his first published book on the work of the late nineteenth century German philosopher Edmund Husserl, *Speech and Phenomena and Other Essays on Husserl's Theory of Signs* (1967) (Illinois, 1973) Derrida contests the idea that philosophy can work back to any direct experience or meaning prior to language. He refutes the work of the early twentieth century German philosopher Martin Heidegger, for example, for his belief in an 'originary' meaning predating linguistic organisation.

3. See, for instance, French feminist insistence on the body as a source of knowledge unmediated by language (Chapter 3 below).

4. Luce Irigaray, 'Women on the Market', *This Sex Which Is Not One* (1977), translated by Catherine Porter (New York: Cornell University Press, 1985) pp. 170–91. All quotations in this section are taken from this essay.

5. Luce Irigaray, 'Cosi Fan Tutti', *This Sex Which Is Not One*, pp. 86–105. All quotations in this section are taken from this essay except where otherwise indicated.

6. Luce Irigaray, 'The Power of Discourse and the Subordination of the Feminine', *This Sex Which Is Not One*, pp. 68–87. All quotations in this section are taken from this essay.

7. Luce Irigaray, 'Commodities Among Themselves', *This Sex Which Is Not One*, pp. 192–7. All quotations in this section are taken from this essay.

8. Luce Irigaray, '"Frenchwomen", Stop Trying', *This Sex Which Is Not One*, pp. 198–204. All quotations in this section are taken from this essay except as indicated.

9. Hélène Cixous, 'Sorties', *The Newly Born Woman* (1975), translated by Betsy Wing (University of Minnesota Press and Manchester University Press, 1986) pp. 63–132. All quotations in this section are taken from this essay.

10. For an account of Cixous' thesis that women's potential to conceive, carry and give birth to another human being involves a potentially different relation to the other to that which has characterised masculine relations see Chapter 3 below.

11. Hélène Cixous, *La Venue à l'écriture*, with Catherine Clément and Madeleine Gagnon (Paris: Union Générale d'Editions, 1977). The quota-

tions in this section are taken from a manuscript translation of Cixous' title essay by Deborah Carpenter (with Ann Liddle) forthcoming from Harvard University Press.

12. Hélène Cixous, *Angst* (Paris: des femmes, 1977). All quotations in this section are taken from the English translation by Jo Levy (London: John Calder, and New York: Riverrun Press, 1985).

13. Marie Cardinal, *Autrement dit*, with Annie Leclerc (Paris: Editions Grasset, 1977).

14. Nathalie Sarraute, *L'Usage de la parole* (Paris: Editions Gallimard, 1980).

15. Annie Leclerc, *Parole de femme* (Paris: Editions Grasset, 1974).

16. This issue of the role of the body in language will be the subject of Chapters 2 and 3 below.

17. Monique Wittig, *Les Guérillères* (Paris: Editions de minuit, 1969).

18. These textual strategies will be explored in Chapters 4 and 5 below.

19. Chantal Chawaf, *Le Soleil et la terre* (Paris: Société Nouvelle des Editions J.J. Pauvert, 1977).

20. Chantal Chawaf, *L'Intérieur des heures* (Paris: des femmes, 1987).

21. See note 15 above.

22. Chantal Chawaf, *Elwina, le roman fée* (Paris: Flammarion, 1985).

23. This can be compared with similar passages in *L'Intérieur des heures* on pp. 30, 245 and 255.

24. Writing – *écriture* – is feminine in French.

25. '*La* langue maternelle'.

26. 'There are too many words, too many words of the other language but never enough words of this language spoken by life' (p. 153).

27. Andrée Chedid, *Le Sommeil délivré* (Paris: Flammarion, 1976). All quotations in this section on Chedid are taken from the English translation *From Sleep Unbound* by Sharon Spencer (Ohio: Swallow Press, 1983 and London: Serpent's Tail, 1987).

28. Jeanne Hyvrard, *Mére la mort* (Paris: Editions de minuit, 1976).

29. See note 17 above.

30. See also p. 44.

31. Emma Santos, *La Malcastrée* (Paris: Editions des femmes, 1976); first published by Editions Maspéro, Paris, 1973.

32. Madeleine Chapsal, *Une femme en exil* (Paris: Grasset, 1978).

33. 'I remembered my promises: not to weigh on anyone, not to hold on to anything, ever, to remain light, to ceaselessly restore people to themselves' (p. 157).

34. These questions will be explored in detail in Chapters 4 and 5 below.

Chapter 2 The (feminine) unconscious

1. See, for example, Kate Millett, *Sexual Politics* (1969) (London: Virago Press, 1977) (pp. 176–203).

2. Christine Delphy, one of the founders of the French feminist journal *Nouvelle Questions Féministes*, is for instance critical of what she sees as the preoccupation with psychoanalysis at the expense of redressment of women's historical and social oppression. See *Close to Home*, translated by Diana Leonard (London: Hutchinson, 1984).

3. Hélène Cixous, 'Conversations', in *Writing Differences*, Susan Sellers (ed.) (Milton Keynes: Open University Press, and New York: St. Martin's Press, 1988) p. 144. Another French feminist, journalist and writer Benoîte Groult, in her book *Ainsi Soit-elle* ('Let Her Be Thus') (Paris: Editions Grasset, 1975) similarly condemns Freud for having conceived 'the whole of psychoanalysis in the masculine' (p. 131), and suggests that if Freud had been equally biased and a woman s/he would have created a 'psycho-analysis' in which *boys* were disadvantaged because of their inability to have babies. Unlike the early mainstream of Anglo–American feminist critics however, she, like Cixous, sees the key to change in women's expression of the very 'pleasure' Freud has been at pains to repress (p. 116; see also p. 34).

4. Sigmund Freud, *The Standard Edition of the Complete Psychological Works of Sigmund Freud* (1900-), edited by James Strachey in 24 volumes (London: Hogarth Press, 1953–1974). My account of Freud's work is taken primarily from *Introductory Lectures on Psychoanalysis* (1916), *The Interpretation of Dreams* (1900), and *Three Essays on the Theory of Sexuality* (1905).

5. The quotation marks refer to the fact that this relation will be true even if the person who fulfils this role is not the child's biological mother.

6. The reference is to the Greek legend in which Oedipus, a King of Thebes, unwittingly fulfils the prophecy of the oracle at Delphi by killing his father and marrying his mother.

7. Juliet Mitchell, *Psychoanalysis and Feminism* (1974) (Harmondsworth: Penguin, 1975).

8. The reference is to the work of the Russian linguist Roman Jakobson, whose writing on literary language greatly influenced the Bulgarian born critic Julia Kristeva. Jakobson suggested that whenever we speak or write, we select signifiers either because they are similar to (metaphor) or associated with (metonymy) other signifiers. He described 'poetic' writing as the result of selection from both a range of equivalent linguistic choices and those possibilities generated by semantic, phonic, rhythmic and graphic 'play'. See Roman Jakobson, *Fundamentals of Language*, with Moris Halle (The Hague: Mouton, 1971).

9. My reading of Lacan is taken primarily from *Ecrits* vols 1 and 2 (Paris: Seuil, 1966 and 1971). (In particular, the essay 'Le Stade du miroir comme formateur de la fonction du jeu', *Ecrits 1*, pp. 89–97, forms the basis for my interpretation of the 'mirror'-image.) A selection of the essays in *Ecrits* is translated into English as *Ecrits: A Selection* (London, 1977). Juliet Mitchell and Jacqueline Rose's *Feminine Sexuality: Jacques Lacan and the Ecole Freudienne*, translated by Jacqueline Rose (Basing-

stoke: Macmillan, 1982), offers helpful introduction to Lacan's work for English readers.

10. Freudian and Lacanian theory can be usefully compared with other interpretations of human development, such as that given by Nancy Chodorow in her *The Reproduction of Mothering: Psychoanalysis and the Sociology of Gender* (Berkeley: University of California Press, 1978). Chodorow argues that since it is the mother who is the primary provider and caretaker of the child, it is from the mother that the child acquires their gender identity. She suggests that whereas the girl learns her identity through a positive identification with sameness, the boy learns his gender negatively as not-female, a difference which requires constant reinforcement. The overlap with Freud and Lacan comes at a later stage of child development, in which external social values give a different interpretation to gender roles.

11. The term refers to the subject's fantasised fulfilment of desire (through language).

12. Julia Kristeva, *Revolution in Poetic Language* (1974), translated by Margaret Waller (New York: Columbia University Press, 1984). This account and all quotations are taken from the 'Prolegomenon' (pp. 13–17) and the section entitled 'The Semiotic and the Symbolic' (pp. 21–106) unless otherwise indicated.

13. The bar here refers to the notion that the 'mother' is first 'other' to the child.

14. See the essay on 'Freud's Notion of Expulsion: Rejection', pp. 147–64.

15. See note 8 above.

16. Freud's theory of castration as a theory of origins can be usefully compared with that of his near contemporary Ernest Jones, who saw the determining factor in human development as 'aphanasis' – or fear of losing the possibility of jouissance. See Ernest Jones, 'The Early Development of Female Sexuality' (1927), *International Journal of Psychoanalysis 8*, pp. 459–72.

17. See Chapters 4 and 5 below.

18. Julia Kristeva, 'Giotto's Joy' (1972), in *Desire in Language: A Semiotic Approach to Literature and Art*, translated by Thomas Gora, Alice Jardine and Leon S. Roudiez (Columbia University Press, 1980; and Oxford: Basil Blackwell, 1981), pp. 221–36.

19. This insistence on the role of the body in the process of acquiring and using language links with that of French feminist writers like Emma Santos, who stresses the physical materiality of 'words' (see Chapter 1 above). Kristeva's belief in the revolutionary potential of language to challenge the patriarchal order and subject will be discussed in Chapters 4 and 5 below.

20. This account of Irigaray's work on psychoanalysis is taken from 'Psychoanalytic Theory: Another Look', in *This Sex Which Is Not One* (1977), translated by Catherine Porter (Cornell University Press, 1985)

pp. 34–67, with reference to 'The Power of Discourse and the Subordination of the Feminine', pp. 68–85, and 'The Blind Spot of an Old Dream of Symmetry', in *Speculum of the Other Woman* (1974), translated by Gillian C. Gill (Cornell University Press, 1985) pp. 13–129. All quotations are taken from these essays.

21. Irigaray's attack on the masculine bias of Freud's theory can be compared with that of Michèle Montrelay who, in an influential text *L'Ombre et le nom: sur la féminité* ('The Shadow and the Name: On Femininity') (Paris: Editions de Minuit, 1977), criticises Freud's account for its expression of a single, 'male' desire. Like Irigaray she refers to the work of psychoanalysts such as Ernest Jones, Melanie Klein and Karen Horney to stress the role of *female* anatomy in the formation of the girl's unconscious. In an essay entitled 'Recherches sur la féminité', translated as 'Inquiry Into Femininity' by Parveen Adams in *French Feminist Thought: A Reader*, Toril Moi (ed.), (Oxford: Basil Blackwell, 1987) pp. 227–4, Montrelay suggests that the (oral, anal and vaginal) feminine drives are never completely subjected by the symbolic structure, but continue to circumscribe a place or dark continent beyond the jurisdiction of phallic law (p. 235). She argues that females are less affected by this law as a result of our anatomical difference. She suggests that not only is it impossible for girls to be threatened by castration in the same way as boys, but that the very visibility of the male organ means the boy's sexual impulses are always directly exposed to the castration threat. (See also the section 'The m/other's voice: Hélène Cixous', below, and note 3 above.)

22. Even here, the mother's role is defined according to what is regarded as socially necessary. See also Julia Kristeva's account of the way patriarchal Christianity depends on the repression of the mother's pleasure – symbolised in the icon of the *virgin* mother (Introduction, above).

23. Irigaray's insistence on women's potential to overturn the premise and mechanisms of man's language will be the subject of Chapters 4 and 5 below.

24. 'Sorties', in *The Newly Born Woman* (1975), with Catherine Clément, translated by Betsy Wing, pp. 63–132. Quotations are taken from this translation except where otherwise indicated.

25. See 'Conversations', in *Writing Differences: Readings from the Seminar of Hélène Cixous*, Susan Sellers (ed.), pp. 144–5.

26. The unconscious also forms the subject matter of much of Cixous' writing, from the exploration of her own unconscious (see the account of *Angst*, below) to an increasing engagement in her more recent fiction and writing for the theatre with the unconscious forces that influence a people in history.

27. See 'Sorties' pp. 122–30.

28. See 'Sorties' p. 123.

29. Cixous' theory of the relationship between gender and biological sex will be the subject of Chapter 3 below.

30. I have not included here the influential French feminist group 'Psych et Po', whose name comes from an abreviation of 'psychanalyse' (psychoanalysis) and 'politique' (politics). Although 'Psych et Po' have played a considerable role in French feminism since the late 1960s, and particularly in French feminist intellectual debate, very few of their ideas, group meetings, discussions and writings have been published or, where they have been published, are available outside the back-issues of reviews and magazines. I have for this reason omitted their work on psychoanalysis from my discussion. Readers interested in their role in the overall development of French feminism might consult Claire Duchen's *Feminism in France: From May '68 to Mitterand* (London: Routledge and Kegan Paul, 1986).

31. See Chapter 4, below.

32. For an interesting discussion of this point, see Juliet Mitchell, *Women the Longest Revolution: Essays in Feminism, Literature and Psychoanalysis*, (London: Virago, 1984) pp. 290–2. The relevant extract is also printed in Mary Eagleton's reader, *Feminist Literary Theory*, (Oxford: Basil Blackwell, 1986) pp. 100–102.

33. These questions will be discussed in detail in Chapters 4 and 5 below.

34. Irène Schavelzon, *Le Réduit* (Paris: des femmes, 1984).

35. Toril Moi's *Sexual/Textual Politics: Feminist Literary Theory*, (London and New York: Methuen, 1985) offers a good example of this materialist-socialist critique of French feminist reliance on psychoanalystic models as a means to women's liberation.

36. *Angst*, translated by Jo Levy (London: John Calder and New York: Riverrun Press, 1985). All quotations are taken from this translation. (See also Chapter 1, above.)

37. See Chapter 1 above. Christiane Rochefort's *Quand tu vas chez les femmes* ('When you go to the women's house') (Paris: Grasset, 1972), referred to in the Introduction, also touches on the mother–child relation. The analyst's thesis, for example, is comically entitled 'Oedipus in a Matriarchal Society' (p. 38), and the whip – the object–phallus which 'loaded my ego with extra meaning' (p. 43) – used on him during his visits to the women, is brandished by two female prostitutes.

38. Chantal Chawaf, *L'Intérieur des heures* (Paris: des femmes, 1987).

39. Emma Santos, *La Malcastrée* (Paris: Editions des femmes, 1976; first published Paris: Editions Maspéro, 1973).

40. See, for example, Santos' description of the 'language-machine' which turns the children's games with words back on themselves: 'The machine destroys the child. We become adult. We pay attention to what we say .... They cut everything from all children' (p. 83).

41. Jeanne Hyvrard, *Mère la mort* (Paris: Editions de minuit, 1976).

42. See also p. 62.

43. Chantal Chawaf, *Elwina, le roman fée* (Paris: Flammarion, 1985).

44. Chantal Chawaf, *Le Soleil et la terre* (Paris: Jean Jacques Pauvert, 1977).

Chapter 3 Theories of sexual difference

1. Sigmund Freud, 'Three Essays on the Theory of Sexuality' (1905), in *On Sexuality*, The Pelican Freud Library vol. 7, (Harmondsworth: Penguin, 1977) pp. 45–169.
2. The responses of the French feminist theorists and writers presented here do not represent the whole of French feminist thinking on this issue. In their editorial statement in the first issue of the feminist review *Questions feministes* ('Feminist questions'), the editorial collective wrote: 'We believe there is no such thing as a direct relationship to the body; to say that there is, is not subversive, because it denies the existence and the power of social forces – the very forces that oppress us, oppress our bodies' (1977). See Claire Duchen, *Feminism in France: From May '68 to Mitterrand*, (London: Routledge, 1986) p. 41. The section 'Women's Difference' in Claire Duchen's translated collection, *French Connections: Voices From the Women's Movement in France* (London: Hutchinson, 1987) pp. 55–77, offers English readers an extract from the work of sociologist Colette Guillaumin, who criticises Annie Leclerc for what she perceives as Leclerc's failure to take into account the role of economics and social conditioning in the creation of the 'virtues' she believes are intrinsic. Guillamin argues that there is nothing liberatory in women's claiming for ourselves the 'qualities' men have always allowed us and then appropriated for their own ends (see pp. 65–77). Christine Delphy's essay 'Protofeminism and Antifeminism', translated in Toril Moi's reader *French Feminist Thought* (Oxford: Blackwell, 1987) pp. 80–109, similarly attacks Annie Leclerc as representative of a position valuing biologically-derived differences at the expense of material, social and political action. Outlining Leclerc's task in *Parole de femme* as 'the recovery by women of a positive image of their biological selves; and the production of a theory of oppression', Delphy criticises Leclerc's argument for its dependance on a 'biologism' that is 'the exact mirror image of sexist ideology'. Leclerc 'never relates these values to the material and social structure', Delphy stresses, and thus implies that what must change is 'not the reality of women's lives' but our 'subjective evaluation of this reality'.
3. Julia Kristeva, *About Chinese Women* (1974), translated by Anita Barrows (London: Marion Boyars, 1977). The title refers to Kristeva's visit to China during the Spring of 1974, and the text is a compilation of her thoughts and reactions. An extract from *About Chinese Women* is translated in *The Kristeva Reader*, Toril Moi (ed.) (Oxford: Blackwell, 1986) pp. 138–59, by Séan Hand. All quotations are taken from this translation.
4. Julia Kristeva, 'A New Type of Intellectual: The Dissident' (1977), in *The Kristeva Reader*, Toril Moi (ed.) (Oxford: Blackwell, 1986) pp. 292–300,

translated by Séan Hand. All quotations are taken from this translation except where otherwise indicated.

5. The quote is from the transcript of a conversation with Kristeva at the ICA (*Desire*, ICA documents, p. 25). (See *The Kristeva Reader*, p. 9.)

6. The reference is from 'Women's Time' (1979), *The Kristeva Reader*, p. 196.

7. The quote is from an article in the *Nouvelle Revue de Psychanalyse* ('The New Review of Psychoanalysis') (1979), quoted in *The Kristeva Reader*, p. 11.

8. This point can be compared with that made by Annie Leclerc in *Parole de femme*, see Chapters 1 and 2 above.

9. Julia Kristeva, 'Women's Time' (1979), in *The Kristeva Reader*, pp. 187–213, translated by Alice Jardine and Harry Blake. All quotations are taken from this translation.

10. Luce Irigaray, 'This Sex Which Is Not One', in *This Sex Which Is Not One* (1977), translated by Catherine Porter (Cornell University Press, 1985) pp. 23–33. All quotations are taken from this translation.

11. Luce Irigaray, 'Sexual Difference', in *French Feminist Thought*, Toril Moi (ed.) (Oxford: Blackwell, 1987) pp. 118–30, translated by Séan Hand. Quotations are taken from this translation.

12. Luce Irigaray, 'Questions', in *This Sex Which Is Not One*, pp. 119–69. Quotations are taken from this translation.

13. Luce Irigaray, 'Volume-Fluidity', in *Speculum of the Other Woman* (1974), translated by Gillian C. Gill (Cornell University Press, 1985) pp. 227–40. Quotations are taken from this translation.

14. Luce Irigaray, 'The Power of Discourse and the Subordination of the Feminine', in *This Sex Which Is Not One*, pp. 68–85. Quotations are taken from this translation.

15. My emphasis.

16. Hélène Cixous, 'Sorties', in *The Newly Born Woman*, translated by Betsy Wing (University of Minnesota Press and Manchester University Press, 1986) pp. 63–132. All quotations are taken from this translation.

17. Hélène Cixous, 'Extreme Fidelity', in *Writing Differences*, Susan Sellers (ed.) (Milton Keynes: Open University Press, and New York: St. Martin's Press, 1988) pp. 9–36.

18. See 'Extreme Fidelity', p. 17.

19. Hélène Cixous, *Le Livre de Promethea* (Paris: Gallimard, 1983).

20. Hélène Cixous, *Vivre l'orange* (Paris: Editions des femmes, 1979).

21. Hélène Cixous, *L'Histoire terrible mais inachevée de Norodom Sihanouk roi du Cambodge* (Paris: Théâtre du Soleil, 1985).

22. Hélène Cixous, *L'Indiade ou l'Inde de leurs rêves* (Paris: Théâtre du Soleil, 1988).

23. See, for example, *Vivre l'orange*.

24. Interestingly a number of the male writers Cixous refers to as practitioners of an *écriture féminine*, such as Jean Genet and James Joyce, are also cited by Julia Kristeva in her work on the revolutionary potential

of poetic language. Cixous' reading of Kleist's *Penthesileia* in 'Sorties' (see note 16) gives a good illustration of how she perceives Kleist's feminine creation as offering an 'ascent towards a new history' (pp. 112–22).

25. Eugénie Lemoine-Luccioni, *Partage des femmes* (Paris: Editions du Seuil, 1976).

26. For an interesting discussion of Lemoine-Luccioni's insistence on the dangers of a feminism seeking sexual *equality* and her belief that women must claim our difference 'as-not-all' see Alice Jardine, *Gynesis* (Cornell University Press, 1985) pp. 169–71.

27. Annie Ernaux, *La Femme gelée* (Paris: Gallimard, 1981).

28. See the Preface, above.

29. Marie Cardinal, *Autrement Dit*, with Annie Leclerc (Paris: Editions Grasset, 1977). See also Chapter 1 above.

30. See p. 52.

31. See Chapters 4 and 5 below.

32. Benoîte Groult, *Ainsi soit-elle* (Paris: Editions Grasset, 1975). See also Chapter 1.

33. Chantal Chawaf, *Le Soleil et la terre* (Paris: Editions Pauvert, 1977). See also Chapters 1 and 2 above.

34. Michèle Perrein, *La Chineuse* (Paris: Editions Julliard, 1970). The title has a number of possible meanings in French and might be translated as 'the (feminine) worker' 'the (feminine) mocker' or 'the (feminine) beggar/hunter'. The verb *chiner* also means to mottle or cloud and there is a play on the Chinese connection: *La Chine* (China)/*La Chinoise* (the Chinese woman).

35. Marguerite Duras and Xavière Gauthier, *Les Parleuses* (Paris: Editions de Minuit, 1974). See also Chapter 1 above.

36. See Chapter 4 below.

37. Michèle Montrelay, *L'Ombre et le nom: sur la féminité* (Paris: Editions de Minuit, 1977).

38. See above.

39. See Chapter 4 below.

40. Madeleine Chapsal, *Une femme en exil* (Paris: Editions Grasset, 1978).

41. Julia Kristeva, 'Talking About *Polylogue*', with Françoise van Rossum-Guyon, in *French Feminist Thought*, Toril Moi (ed.) (Oxford: Basil Blackwell, 1987) p. 111–17, translated by Séan Hand. Quotations are taken from this translation.

Chapter 4 A woman's language?

1. See, for example, Dale Spender's *Man Made Language*, (London: Routledge and Kegan Paul, 1980). Readers of French might also consult Marina Yaguello's *Les Mots et les femmes* ('Words and Women') (Paris:

Payot, 1978) for an interesting example of French feminist work on language paralleling Anglo–American concerns.

2. Jacques Lacan, 'Le Séminaire XX' (1972–3), in *Encore*, (Paris: Seuil, 1975) p. 160. The translation is taken from Juliet Mitchell and Jacqueline Rose, *Feminine Sexuality: Jacques Lacan and the Ecole Freudienne*, (London: Macmillan, 1982) p. 50.

3. Julia Kristeva, *Revolution in Poetic Language* (1974), translated by Margaret Waller (Columbia University Press, 1984).

4. Julia Kristeva, *Desire in Language: A Semiotic Approach to Literature and Art* (1977, 1979), translated by Thomas Gora, Alice Jardine and Leon S. Roudiez (Columbia University Press, 1980, and Oxford: Blackwell, 1981).

5. Julia Kristeva, 'How Does One Speak to Literature?', in *Desire in Language*, pp. 92–123.

6. Ibid., p. 93.

7. See Chapter 2 above.

8. Julia Kristeva, 'From One Identity to Another', in *Desire in Language*, pp. 124–47.

9. Ibid., p. 136.

10. *Revolution in Poetic Language*, p. 67.

11. *The Kristeva Reader*, Toril Moi (ed.) (Oxford: Basil Blackwell, 1986) p. 28.

12. *Desire in Language*, p. 139.

13. 'The Ethics of Linguistics', in *Desire in Language*, pp. 23–35; p. 23.

14. *Revolution in Poetic Language*, p. 153.

15. *The Kristeva Reader*, p. 33.

16. See the Introduction, above.

17. *Revolution in Poetic Language*, p. 97.

18. Julia Kristeva, 'Word, Dialogue, and Novel', in *Desire in Language*, pp. 64–91. Quotations are taken from this translation.

19. See note 13 above. Quotations are taken from this translation except where indicated.

20. *Desire in Language*, p. 31.

21. See note 8 above.

22. *Desire in Language*, p. 142.

23. Ibid., p. 142.

24. Julia Kristeva, 'The Father, Love, and Banishment', in Ibid., pp. 148–58.

25. Ibid., p. 157.

26. Julia Kristeva, 'The Novel as Polylogue', in Ibid., pp. 159–209.

27. Ibid., p. 163.

28. Ibid., p. 159.

29. Ibid., p. 165.

30. Ibid., p. 166.

31. Ibid., p. 137.

32. *The Kristeva Reader*, p. 150.

33. *Desire in Language*, p. 146.
34. *The Kristeva Reader*, p. 36.
35. See 'Genotext and Phenotext', in *Revolution in Poetic Language*, pp. 86–9.
36. See 'How Does One Speak to Literature?', in *Desire in Language*, pp. 92–123. Quotations are taken from this translation unless indicated.
37. *Desire in Language*, p. 107.
38. Julia Kristeva, *Histoires d'armour* (Paris: Denoël, 1983). An extract from this volume is translated in *The Kristeva Reader* as 'Freud and Love: Treatment and Its Discontents', by Léon S. Roudiez, pp. 240–71.
39. Julia Kristeva, 'Motherhood According to Giovanni Bellini', in *Desire in Language*, pp. 237–70. Quotations are taken from this translation unless indicated.
40. See *The Kristeva Reader*, p. 177.
41. Julia Kristeva, 'Stabat Mater', in *The Kristeva Reader*, pp. 160–86, translated by Léon S. Roudiez. Quotations are taken from this translation.
42. See *Revolution in Poetic Language*, p. 83.
43. Julia Kristeva, 'The True-Real', in *The Kristeva Reader*, pp. 214–37, translated by Séan Hand. Quotations are taken from this translation.
44. See also Chapter 1 above.
45. See also Kristeva's discussion in the Introduction above. Kristeva's insistence might also be compared with that of Luce Irigaray – in *Le Corps-à-corps avec la mère* and *Amante marine* – that the murder of the mother is the founding act of Western society, and that to 'think of the mother' is thus to challenge patriarchal culture.
46. Julia Kristeva, 'A New Type of Intellectual: The Dissident', in *The Kristeva Reader*, pp. 292–300, translated by Séan Hand. Quotations are taken from this translation.
47. Julia Kristeva, 'Talking about *Polylogue*', with Françoise van Rossum-Guyon, in *French Feminist Thought: A Reader*, Toril Moil (ed.) (Oxford: Basil Blackwell, 1987) pp. 110–17, translated by Séan Hand. Quotations are taken from this translation except where indicated.
48. See note 13 above.
49. A parallel might again be drawn with the work of Jacques Lacan, for whom the aim of language should be the *breaking* of the tie between 'other' and 'Other' – the transposition of 'object' (of desire) onto (a fantasy of) 'truth'.
50. Luce Irigaray, 'Sexual Difference', in *French Feminist Thought*, pp. 118–30, translated by Séan Hand. Quotations are taken from this translation.
51. Luce Irigaray, 'Questions', in *This Sex Which Is Not One* (1977), translated by Catherine Porter (Cornell University Press, 1985) pp. 119-69. Quotations are taken from this translation.
52. See also Chapter 3 above.
53. Luce Irigaray, 'The "Mechanics" of Fluids', in *This Sex Which Is Not One*, pp. 106–18. Quotations are taken from this translation.

54. 'When Our Lips Speak Together', in *This Sex Which Is Not One*, pp. 205–18. Quotations are taken from this translation.
55. The links with Hélène Cixous' account of gender economies in terms of 'gift' and 'debt' are interesting here. (See the Introduction above.)
56. See note 51 above. Quotations are taken from this translation except where indicated.
57. 'The Power of Discourse and the Subordination of the Feminine', in *This Sex Which Is Not One*, p. 80.
58. Hélène Cixous, 'Sorties', in *The Newly Born Woman* (1975), with Catherine Clément, translated by Betsy Wing (University of Minnesota Press and Manchester University Press, 1986) pp. 63–132. Quotations are taken from this translation except where indicated.
59. Hélène Cixous and Catherine Clément, 'Exchange', in *The Newly Born Woman*, pp. 135–146. Quotations are taken from this translation.
60. *The Newly Born Woman*, p. 150.
61. The reference is to Jacques Derrida with whose work Cixous' theory has strong links. (See Chapter 1 above.)
62. Michèle Le Doeuff, 'Women and Philosophy', in *French Feminist Thought* pp. 181–209, translated by Debbie Pope. Quotations are taken from this translation.
63. Catherine Clément. *Miroirs du sujet* (Paris: Union Générale d'Editions, 1975).
64. Michèle Montrelay, *L'Ombre et le nom: sur la féminité* (Paris: Editions de Minuit, 1977). Quotations here are taken from the opening essay in the collection 'Sur "Le Ravissement de Lol V. Stein"', pp. 9–23.
65. 'Parole de femme: sur le transfert de l'hystérique', pp. 27–39. The quotation is taken from this essay.
66. 'Textes à l'infini', pp. 151–59. Quotations are taken from this essay except as indicated.
67. 'Recherches sur la féminité', pp. 69, 64. This essay is translated into English in *French Feminist Thought* as 'Inquiry into Femininity', by Parveen Adams, pp. 227–49.
68. 'La Dernière Femme?', pp. 163–64. Quotations are taken from this essay.
69. Danièle Sallenave, *Conversations conjugales* (Paris: POL, 1987).
70. Marguerite Duras and Xavière Gauthier, *Les Parleuses* (Paris: Editions de Minuit, 1974). In her preface to the volume, Xavière Gauthier stresses that the conversations are unedited as a result of their refusal to give the text 'the sort of rectitude of thought which obeys Cartesian logic' (p. 7).
71. Xavière Gauthier stresses the importance of listening to our desire (p. 64), since this is what propels us 'towards the other' (Duras, p. 182).
72. Both writers stress that the problem for women is that language codifies reality in ways which have been determined by men (see for example p. 20). They argue that writing has the power to break with this law, but suggest that such a revolution must come – not from challenging

language on its own terms since this will merely 'repeat what is going on outside' – but by 'listening to what is working inside' (p. 64).

73. I am indebted to Elizabeth Fallaize for commenting that Duras' more recent work does not altogether follow the pattern outlined in *Les Parleuses*.

74. Monique Wittig, 'The Mark of Gender', in *The Poetics of Gender*, Nancy K. Miller (ed.) (New York: Columbia University Press, 1986) pp. 63–73. Quotations are taken from this essay.

75. Monique Wittig, *Le Corps Lesbien* (Paris: Editions de Minuit, 1973).

76. 'j/e passe de ton bord, j/e fais éclater les petites unités de m/on m/oi, j/e suis menacée'.

Chapter 5 Towards an *écriture féminine*

1. See Jacques Derrida, *La Dissémination* (Paris: Seuil, 1972) especially 'La Pharmacie de Platon'.

2. Compare, for example, Luce Irigaray's insistence that this desire is the *self*-projection of *men's* fear and hence need to appropriate the terrifying – because threatening – knowledge that the origin is in (the body of) woman, see the Introduction above.

3. See Jacques Derrida, *Of Grammatology* (1967), translated by Gayatri Chakravorty Spivak (Baltimore: Johns Hopkins University Press, 1977) and *Marges de la philosophie* (Paris: Minuit, 1972).

4. Writing – *écriture* – is feminine in French.

5. Marguerite Duras and Xavière Gauthier, *Les Parleuses* (Paris: Minuit, 1974).

6. Duras and Gauthier also stress the need for the reader to interpret the text in their own way (p. 195).

7. Annie Leclerc, *Parole de femme* (Paris: Grasset, 1974).

8. In *Parole de femme*, Leclerc argues that it will be the inscription of a specifically female jouissance – in which 'I' is no longer 'seeking to define myself' but is searching instead 'to abolish what makes me say I' (p. 132) – that will initiate a change in the present hierarchical structure.

9. See also Chapter 4 above.

10. See Michèle Montrelay, *L'Ombre et le nom* (Paris: Minuit, 1977).

11. See Montrelay's argument that the writing of Marguerite Duras, instead of seeking to (im)pose the (lost) object, alows its 'absence to resound' (p. 54), Chapter 4 above.

12. In his reading of the German philosopher Hegel, in *Writing and Difference*, translated by Alan Bass (London: Routledge and Kegan Paul, 1978) Derrida concentrates on the metaphors Hegel uses to show how these disrupt the logic of Hegel's argument, and turn the argument on its head.

13. Luce Irigaray, 'Plato's *Hystera*', in *Speculum of the Other Woman* (1974), translated by Gillian C. Gill (New York: Cornell University Press, 1985) pp. 243–364. The quotations are from this translation.

14. Luce Irigaray, 'The Power of Discourse and the Subordination of the Feminine', *This Sex Which Is Not One* (1977), translated by Catherine Porter (New York: Cornell University Press, 1985) pp. 68–85. The quotations are from this translation.

15. Luce Irigaray, 'The Looking Glass, from the Other Side', in *This Sex Which Is Not One*, pp. 9–22. The quotations are from this translation.

16. Luce Irigaray, 'La Mystérique', in *Speculum of the Other Woman*, pp. 191–202. The quotations are from this translation.

17. Hélène Cixous, *The Newly Born Woman* (1975), with Catherine Clément, translated by Betsy Wing (University of Minnesota Press, 1986). Quotations are taken from 'Sorties', pp. 63–132, except as indicated.

18. Hélène Cixous, 'La Venue à l'écriture' (1976), collected in *Entre l'écriture* (Paris: des femmes, 1986). A translation of this collection is currently in preparation with Harvard University Press by Deborah Carpenter, Sarah Cornell and Susan Sellers. Quotations are taken from a manuscript translation of 'La Venue à l'écriture' by Deborah Carpenter as 'Her Arrival in Writing' though references are to the published French text.

19. Cixous' emphasis here is directed particularly against the work of Jacques Lacan.

20. 'Sorties', p. 94.

21. Hélène Cixous, 'Conversations', in *Writing Differences*, Susan Sellers (ed.) (Milton Keynes: Open University Press; and New York: St. Martin's Press, 1988).

22. 'La Venue à l'écriture', p. 68.

23. Ibid., p. 62.

24. Ibid., p. 49.

25. Ibid., p. 50. The writings of Hélène Cixous and Luce Irigaray, for whom the possibility of a feminine writing is to be given impetus by women's expression of our differences, can therefore be contrasted with Julia Kristeva's notion of a 'language revolution' in which – whilst women's exploration of our sex-role and relation to otherness may provide important parallels for the new writing – the major changes occur as a consequence of the semiotic forces re-casting the subject's relation to the symbolic function. Although Kristeva's concept of poetic writing as the attempt to 'break the code, to shatter language, to find . . . a discourse closer to the body and emotions, to the unnameable repressed by the social contract' (*The Kristeva Reader*), p. 200) has strong links with the work of Hélène Cixous and Luce Irigaray, Kristeva nevertheless stresses that any distinctive features of a specifically woman's writing are more likely to be the product of women's marginalised position than of our sexual-symbolic differences. (See Chapter 4 above.)

26. 'La Venue à l'écriture', p. 68

27. Cixous' reference to male writers as exponents of an *écriture féminine* has puzzled Anglo–American critics, as has Kristeva's reading of male writers in her work on the revolutionary potential of poetic language. It is important for both writers that, because of the way women have been positioned by patriarchy, women have been prevented from writing authentically, and that it is therefore not surprising that there are more examples of exceptional men writing 'as women' than women. (See also Chapter 3 above.)
28. 'La Venue à l'écriture', p. 48.
29. For a further dicussion of Hélène Cixous' thoughts on this point see *Writing Differences*, pp. 149–54.
30. See my discussion in 'Biting the Teacher's Apple: Opening Doors for Women in Higher Education', in *Teaching Women: Feminism and English Studies*, Ann Thompson and Helen Wilcox (eds) (Manchester University Press, 1989) pp. 30–32.
31. Cixous' discovery and early work on Clarice Lispector is documented in the French–English bilingual text *Vivre l'orange/To Live the Orange* (Paris: des femmes, 1979); English text translated by Hélène Cixous, Sarah Cornell and Ann Liddle.
32. See my discussion in 'Writing Woman: Hélène Cixous' Political "Sexts"', in *Women's Studies International Forum Special Issue on Political Fiction*, Candida Lacey (ed.) (Oxford, New York, Toronto, Sydney and Frankfurt: Pergamon Press, 1986) pp. 443–7.
33. See Cixous' reading of Lispector's work in 'Extreme Fidelity', translated by Ann Liddle and Susan Sellers, in *Writing Differences*, pp. 9–36.
34. 'La Venue à l'écriture', p. 56. For a more detailed account of Cixous' use of the unconscious in her writing see *Delighting the Heart: A Notebook by Women Writers*, Susan Sellers (ed.) (London: The Women's Press, 1989) pp. 18, 69, 98.
35. See note 31 above.
36. *Vivre l'orange*, p. 76.
37. 'La Venue à l'écriture', p. 33.
38. See 'Conversations', pp. 147–148.
39. Hélène Cixous' project can be compared with the work of the twentieth century German philosopher Martin Heidegger, whose writings she frequently refers to in her Paris seminar. Heidegger has argued that the object created by our conceptual system in the West must be freed from its subservient and imprisoned position before man – as subject – can become liberated. Heidegger advocates listening, and a careful and patient attention to the process of 'being', as well as the acquisition of a knowledge which does not seek to impose itself on the world. A useful introduction to Heidegger's work for the English reader is *Poetry, Language, Thought*, translated by Albert Hofstadter (New York: Harper and Row, 1975).
40. Hélène Cixous' *Angst* (1977), translated by Jo Levy (London: John Calder and New York: Riverrun Press, 1985) discussed above, also

exemplifies a feminine writing. The exploration of the relations between self and others (see p. 70), the author's avowed aim to create an other 'scene' in which love, and not the law, will predominate (pp. 99–100), and the various means used to achieve this aim (for example the author's exploration of her [woman's] sex [pp. 180–81]) can fruitfully be compared with Cixous' discussion of feminine writing.

41. Hélène Cixous, *Le Livre de Promethea* (Paris: Gallimard, 1983). A translation of this text into English is currently in preparation by Betsy Wing for Harvard University Press. A translated extract from *Le Livre de Promethea*, together with a detailed reading, is given by Sarah Cornell in her essay 'Hélène Cixous' *Le Livre de Promethea*: Paradise Refound', *Writing Differences*, pp. 127–40.

42. Christiane Rochefort, *C'est bizarre l'écriture* (Paris: Grasset, 1970).

43. Christiane Rochefort, *Les Petits Enfants du siècle* (Paris: Grasset, 1961).

44. Marie Cardinal, *Autrement dit*, with Annie Leclerc (Paris: Grasset, 1977).

45. Cardinal does however believe texts are differently interpreted depending on whether they are written by men or women (p. 82). She also argues that women's writing often shows evidence of similar stylistic features which, she suggests, are most likely the product of the writers' attempts to prove themselves equal to men (p. 82).

46. Jeanne Hyvrard, *Mère la mort* (Paris: Minuit, 1976).

47. Chantal Chawaf, *Elwina, le roman fée* (Paris: Flammarion, 1985).

48. Chantal Chawaf, *Le Soleil et la terre* (Paris: Pauvert, 1977).

49. See for example, *Elwina, le roman fée*, pp. 84–5.

50. Ibid., p. 64.

51. Chantal Chawaf, *L'Intérieur des heures* (Paris: des femmes, 1987).

52. 'Objects, their colours, their volumes spoke amongst themselves. Like humans. She listened to the boxes, the cushions, the table-cloths, the covers, the furniture reply to a ray of light or refuse the darkening of the sky or sing, at night, under the agonising light of the lamps' (p. 36; see also p. 186).

53. See for example, the constant change of subject from *tu* (you) to *fils-foetus* (foetus-son) to *elle* (she) to *vous* (you plural) on pages 274–5.

54. Marugerite Duras, *The Lover* (1984), translated by Barbara Bray (London: Flamingo, 1986).

55. 'When you let the body alone, to seek and find and take what it likes . . . then everything is right', *The Lover*, p. 47.

56. See, for example: 'from the moment that writing is not all things merged . . . . From the moment that it is not, each time, all things confounded through a single inexpressible essence, writing is nothing but advertisement', *The Lover*, p. 12.

57. Monique Wittig, *Les Guérillères* (Paris: Minuit, 1969).

58. Geneviève Serreau, *Un enfer très convenable* (Paris: Gallimard, 1981).

59. Marie Redonnet, *Rose Mélie Rose* (Paris: Minuit, 1987).
60. Michèle Ramond, *Vous* (Paris: des femmes, 1988).
62. A number of the words are the author's own invention:
'C'est dans l'attente, l'espiement, la trape, l'amour, la traque, qu'il pousse l'arbre
dans la transe qu'il se transfigure l'objet
dans le traïssement de ma bouche et de mon oeil'.

62. See Claire Etcherelli's *Elise ou la vraie vie* ('Elise or Real Life') (Paris: Denoël, 1967) for an example of French women's writing which does not share the concerns of an *écriture féminine*. Etcherelli's graphic depiction of the material oppression of women's, the factory workers' and the immigrants' lives echoes the themes and mode of presentation of much Anglo-American feminist fiction.

63. Angela Carter, *The Passion of New Eve* (1977) (London: Virago, 1982).

64. Marge Piercy, *Woman on the Edge of Time* (1976) (London: The Women's Press, 1979).

65. See, as an example, Gayatri Chakravorty Spivak's argument, in 'French Feminism in an International Frame', *Yale French Studies*, vol. 62, 1981, that 'even if one knows how to undo identities, one does not necessarily escape the historical determination of sexism' (p. 169). Janet Todd, in her *Feminist Literary History* (Cambridge: Polity Press, 1988) similarly argues that the (self) preoccupations of French feminism obscure not only history but the material power relations which language reflects (p. 71).

66. See the forthcoming Harvester volume, *The Body and the Text*, on the implications of *études féminines* (feminine studies) for reading, writing and education.

67. See, as an example, Terry Eagleton's criticism of Julia Kristeva in his *Literary Criticism: An Introduction* (Oxford: Blackwell, 1983): 'she pays too little attention to the political *content* of a text' (p. 190). See also Ann Rosalind Jones' essay 'Writing the Body: Toward An Understanding of *Écriture Féminine*', in *Feminist Literary Theory: A Reader*, Mary Eagleton (ed.) (Oxford: Blackwell, 1986) pp. 228–31.

68. There are signs that such a marriage is beginning to take plae. See, for example, Naomi Schor's 'Reading Double: Sand's Difference', in *The Poetics of Gender*, Nancy Miller (ed.) (New York: Columbia University Press, 1986) pp. 248–69 (especially her insistence that 'a new articulation must be elaborated to take into account the place of history in the play of difference', p. 267). American feminist Adrienne Rich, in her *Of Woman Born: Motherhood as Experience and Institution* (1976) (London: Virago, 1977) argues for a re-valuing of our physical selves as a 'resource' rather than a 'destiny', as well as a place for the corporeal in understanding.

69. I am referring to such experiments as the controversial attempt to implant test-tube embryos in men, and the direct cloning of female eggs. Patricia Spallone's *Beyond Conception: The New Politics of Reproduction*,

(Basingstoke: Macmillan, 1989) provides a helpful introduction to the general area of reproductive engineering for non-specialist readers.

70. See Annie Leclerc's criticism, in *Parole de femme*, of the dangers of substituting a new master in place of the old inherent in Anglo–American feminist insistence on equality (p. 38).

Bibliography

References

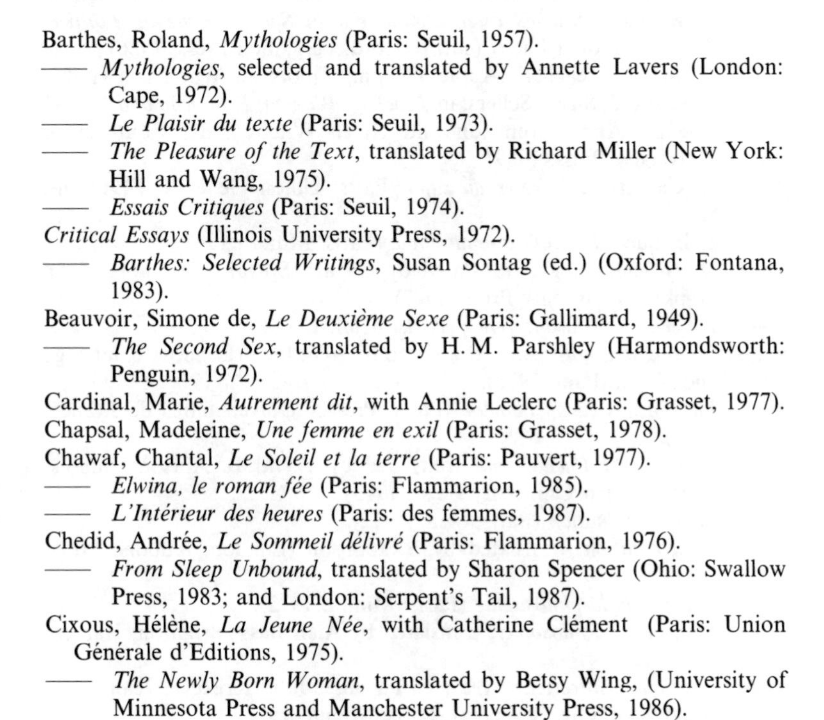

Barthes, Roland, *Mythologies* (Paris: Seuil, 1957).

—— *Mythologies*, selected and translated by Annette Lavers (London: Cape, 1972).

—— *Le Plaisir du texte* (Paris: Seuil, 1973).

—— *The Pleasure of the Text*, translated by Richard Miller (New York: Hill and Wang, 1975).

—— *Essais Critiques* (Paris: Seuil, 1974).

Critical Essays (Illinois University Press, 1972).

—— *Barthes: Selected Writings*, Susan Sontag (ed.) (Oxford: Fontana, 1983).

Beauvoir, Simone de, *Le Deuxième Sexe* (Paris: Gallimard, 1949).

—— *The Second Sex*, translated by H.M. Parshley (Harmondsworth: Penguin, 1972).

Cardinal, Marie, *Autrement dit*, with Annie Leclerc (Paris: Grasset, 1977).

Chapsal, Madeleine, *Une femme en exil* (Paris: Grasset, 1978).

Chawaf, Chantal, *Le Soleil et la terre* (Paris: Pauvert, 1977).

—— *Elwina, le roman fée* (Paris: Flammarion, 1985).

—— *L'Intérieur des heures* (Paris: des femmes, 1987).

Chedid, Andrée, *Le Sommeil délivré* (Paris: Flammarion, 1976).

—— *From Sleep Unbound*, translated by Sharon Spencer (Ohio: Swallow Press, 1983; and London: Serpent's Tail, 1987).

Cixous, Hélène, *La Jeune Née*, with Catherine Clément (Paris: Union Générale d'Editions, 1975).

—— *The Newly Born Woman*, translated by Betsy Wing, (University of Minnesota Press and Manchester University Press, 1986).

—— *La Venue à l'écriture*, with Catherine Clément and Madeleine Gagnon, (Paris: Union Générale d'Editions, 1977).

—— *Angst* (Paris: des femmes, 1977).

—— *Angst* translated by Jo Levy (London: John Calder; and New York: Riverrun Press, 1985).

—— *Vivre l'orange/To Live the Orange*, English text translated by Sarah Cornell, Ann Liddle and Hélène Cixous (Paris: des femmes, 1979).

—— *Le Livre de Promethea* (Paris: Gallimard, 1983).
—— *L'Histoire terrible mais inachevée de Norodom Sihanouk roi du Cambodge* (Paris: Théâtre du Soleil, 1985).
—— *Entre l'écriture* (Paris: des femmes, 1986).
—— *l'Indiade ou l'Inde de leurs rêves* (Paris: Théâtre du Soleil, 1988).
—— 'Conversations' and 'Extreme Fidelity', in *Writing Differences*, Susan Sellers (ed.) (Milton Keynes: Open University Press; and New York: St. Martin's Press, 1988).
—— 'The Double World of Writing', 'Listening to the Truth' and 'Writing as a Second Heart' in *Delighting the Heart: A Notebook by Women Writers*, Susan Sellers (ed.) (London: The Women's Press, 1989).
—— 'Writing Woman: Hélène Cixous' Political "Sexts"', Susan Sellers, in *Women's Studies International Forum Special Issue on Political Fiction* Candida Lacey (ed.) (Oxford: Pergamon Press, 1986).
—— 'Biting the Teacher's Apple: Opening Doors for Women in Higher Education', Susan Sellers, in *Teaching Women: Feminism and English Studies*, Ann Thompson and Helen Wilcox (eds) (Manchester University Press, 1989).
Clément, Catherine, *Miroirs du sujet* (Paris: Union Générale d'Editions, 1975).
Derrida, Jacques, *De la Grammatologie* (Paris: Minuit, 1967).
—— *Of Grammatology*, translated by Gayatri Spivak (Baltimore: John Hopkins University Press, 1977).
—— *L'Ecriture et la différence* (Paris: Seuil, 1967).
—— *Writing and Difference*, translated by Alan Bass (London: Routledge and Kegan Paul, 1978).
—— *La Voix et le phénomène* (Paris: Presses Universitaires de France, 1967).
—— *Speech and Phenomena*, translated by David B. Allison (Illinois: Northwestern University Press, 1973).
—— *La Dissémination* (Paris: Seuil, 1972).
—— *Dissemination*, translated by B. Johnson (London: Athlone Press, 1981).
—— *Marges de la philosophie* (Paris: Minuit, 1972).
—— *Margins of Philosophy*, translated by Alan Bass (Brighton: Harvester, 1982).
—— *Positions* (Entretiens avec Henri Ronse, Julia Kristeva, Jean-Louis Houdebine, Guy Scarpeta) (Paris: Minuit, 1972).
Duchen, Claire, *Feminism in France: From May '68 to François Mitterand* (London: Routledge and Kegan Paul, 1986).
—— *French Connections: Voices from the Women's Movement in France* (London: Hutchinson, 1987).
Duras, Marguerite, *Les Parleuses*, with Xavière Gauthier (Paris: Minuit, 1974).
—— *L'Amant* (Paris: Minuit, 1984).

—— *The Lover*, translated by Barbara Fray (London: Flamingo, 1986).
Ernaux, Annie, *Le Femme gelée* (Paris: Gallimard, 1981).
Foucault, Michel, *Les Mots et les choses: une archéologie des sciences humaines* (Paris: Gallimard, 1966).
—— *The Order of Things: An Archaeology of the Human Sciences* (London: Tavistock, 1974).
—— *L'Archéologie du Savoir* (Paris: Bibliotheque des Sciences Humaines, 1969).
—— *The Archaeology of Knowledge* (London: Tavistock, 1972).
Freud, Sigmund, *The Interpretation of Dreams*, *Introductory Lectures on Psychoanalysis* and *Three Essays on the Theory of Sexuality* in *The Standard Edition of the Complete Psychological Works of Sigmund Freud*, edited by James Strachey in 24 voluems (London: Hogarth, 1953–74).
Gauthier, Xavière, *Les Parleuses*, with Marguerite Duras (Paris: Minuit, 1974).
Groult, Benoîte, *Ainsi Soit-Elle* (Paris: Grasset, 1975).
Hegel, Georg, *The Phenomenology of Spirit* (1807), translated by A.V. Miller, (Oxford University Press, 1979).
Hyvrard, Jeanne, *Mère la mort* (Paris: Minuit, 1976).
Irigaray, Luce, *Spèculum de l'autre femme* (Paris: Minuit, 1974).
—— *Speculum of the Other Woman*, translated by Gillian C. Gill (New York: Cornell University Press, 1985).
—— *Ce Sexe qui n'en est pas un* (Paris: Minuit, 1977).
—— *This Sex Which Is Not One*, translated by Catherine Porter (New York: Cornell University Press, 1985).
Jardine, Alice, *Gynesis* (New York: Cornell University Press, 1985).
Kristeva, Julia, *La Révolution du langage poétique* (Paris: Seuil, 1974).
—— *Revolution in Poetic Language*, translated by Margaret Waller, (Columbia University Press, 1984).
—— *Des Chinoises* (Paris: des femmes, 1974).
—— *About Chinese Women*, translated by Anita Barrows, (London: Marion Boyars, 1977).
—— *Desire in Language: A Semiotic Approach to Literature and Art*, translated by Thomas Gora, Alice Jardine and Leon S. Roudiez, (Columbia University Press, 1980; and Oxford: Blackwell, 1981).
—— *Histoires d'amour* (Paris: Denoël, 1983).
—— *The Kristeva Reader*, Toril Moi (ed.) (Oxford: Blackwell, 1986).
Lacan, Jacques, *Ecrits* (2 vols) (Paris: Seuil, 1966 and 1971).
—— *Ecrits: A Selection*, translated by Alan Sheridan (London: Tavistock, 1977).
—— 'Le Seminaire XX', in *Encore* (Paris: Seuil, 1975).
—— *Feminine Sexuality: Jacques Lacan and the Ecole Freudienne*, by Juliet Mitchell and Jacqueline Rose (eds) and translated by Jacqueline Rose (Basingstoke: Macmillan, 1982).
Leclerc, Annie, *Parole de femme* (Paris: Grasset, 1974).
Lemoine-Luccioni, Eugénie, *Partage des femmes* (Paris: Seuil, 1976).

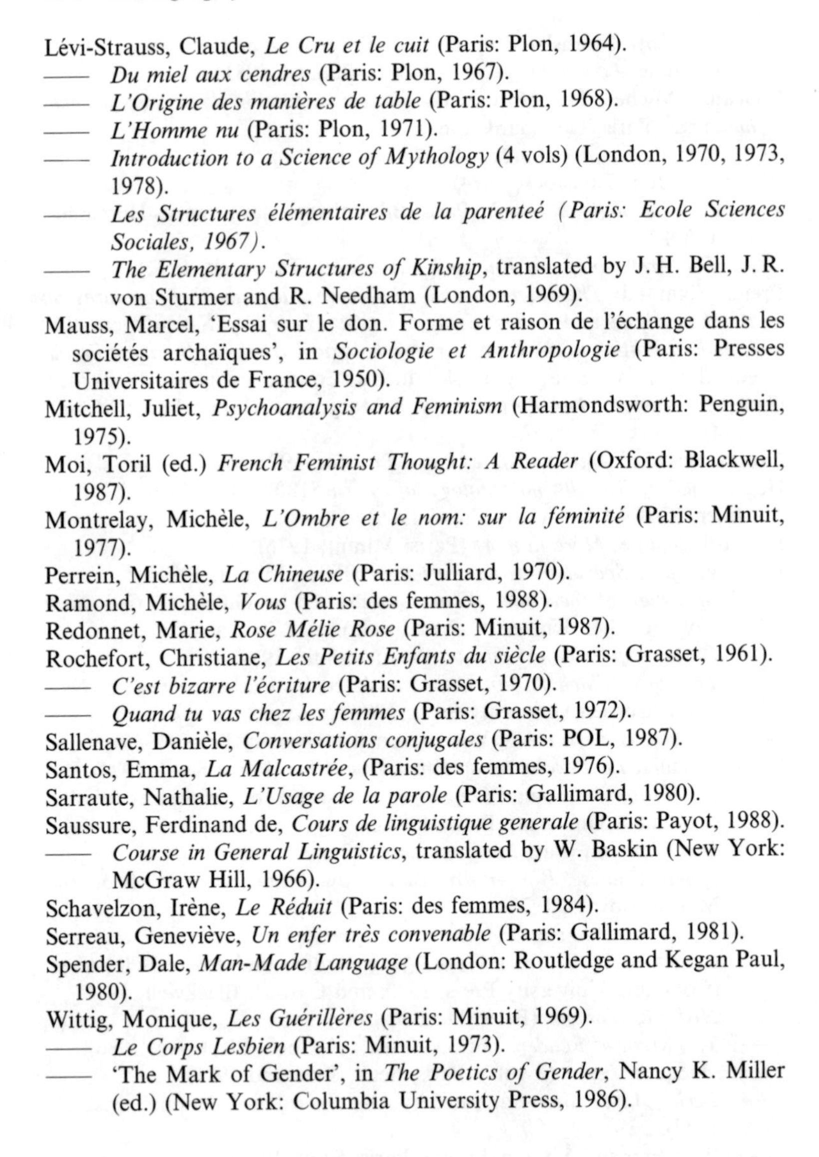

Lévi-Strauss, Claude, *Le Cru et le cuit* (Paris: Plon, 1964).
—— *Du miel aux cendres* (Paris: Plon, 1967).
—— *L'Origine des manières de table* (Paris: Plon, 1968).
—— *L'Homme nu* (Paris: Plon, 1971).
—— *Introduction to a Science of Mythology* (4 vols) (London, 1970, 1973, 1978).
—— *Les Structures élémentaires de la parenteé (Paris: Ecole Sciences Sociales, 1967).*
—— *The Elementary Structures of Kinship*, translated by J.H. Bell, J.R. von Sturmer and R. Needham (London, 1969).
Mauss, Marcel, 'Essai sur le don. Forme et raison de l'échange dans les sociétés archaïques', in *Sociologie et Anthropologie* (Paris: Presses Universitaires de France, 1950).
Mitchell, Juliet, *Psychoanalysis and Feminism* (Harmondsworth: Penguin, 1975).
Moi, Toril (ed.) *French Feminist Thought: A Reader* (Oxford: Blackwell, 1987).
Montrelay, Michèle, *L'Ombre et le nom: sur la féminité* (Paris: Minuit, 1977).
Perrein, Michèle, *La Chineuse* (Paris: Julliard, 1970).
Ramond, Michèle, *Vous* (Paris: des femmes, 1988).
Redonnet, Marie, *Rose Mélie Rose* (Paris: Minuit, 1987).
Rochefort, Christiane, *Les Petits Enfants du siècle* (Paris: Grasset, 1961).
—— *C'est bizarre l'écriture* (Paris: Grasset, 1970).
—— *Quand tu vas chez les femmes* (Paris: Grasset, 1972).
Sallenave, Danièle, *Conversations conjugales* (Paris: POL, 1987).
Santos, Emma, *La Malcastrée*, (Paris: des femmes, 1976).
Sarraute, Nathalie, *L'Usage de la parole* (Paris: Gallimard, 1980).
Saussure, Ferdinand de, *Cours de linguistique generale* (Paris: Payot, 1988).
—— *Course in General Linguistics*, translated by W. Baskin (New York: McGraw Hill, 1966).
Schavelzon, Irène, *Le Réduit* (Paris: des femmes, 1984).
Serreau, Geneviève, *Un enfer très convenable* (Paris: Gallimard, 1981).
Spender, Dale, *Man-Made Language* (London: Routledge and Kegan Paul, 1980).
Wittig, Monique, *Les Guérillères* (Paris: Minuit, 1969).
—— *Le Corps Lesbien* (Paris: Minuit, 1973).
—— 'The Mark of Gender', in *The Poetics of Gender*, Nancy K. Miller (ed.) (New York: Columbia University Press, 1986).

Recommended Further Reading

In order to save space I have not repeated here those suggestions for further reading included in the Notes.

Theory

Althusser, Louis, 'Ideology and the State', in *Lenin and Philosophy and Other Essays* translated by Ben Brewster, (London, 1971).
Atack, Margaret and Phil Powrie (eds), *Contemporary French Fiction by Women: Perspectives* (Manchester University Press, 1990).
Belsey, Catherine, *Critical Practice* (London: Methuen, 1980).
Bowie, Malcolm, 'Jacques Lacan', in *Structuralism and Since: From Lévi-Strauss to Derrida*, John Sturrock (ed.) (Oxford University Press, 1979).
Coward, Rosalind, *Female Desire: Women's Sexuality Today* (London: Paladin, 1984).
Eagleton, Terry, *Literary Theory: An Introduction* (Oxford: Blackwell, 1983).
Frosh, Stephen, *The Politics of Psychoanalysis: An Introduction to Freudian and Post-Freudian Theory* (Basingstoke: Macmillan, 1987).
Gallop, Jane, *Feminism and Psychoanalysis: The Daughter's Seduction* (Basingstoke: Macmillan, 1982).
Gauthier, Xavière, *Suurealisme et sexualité (Paris: Gallimard, 1971).*
Green, Gayle and Coppélia Kahn (eds), *Making A Difference: Feminist Literary Criticism* (London: Methuen, 1985).
Grosz, Elizabeth, *Sexual Subversions* (Sydney: Allen and Unwin, 1990).
Herrmann, Claudine, *Les Voleuses de langue* (Paris: des femmes, 1976).
Humm, Maggie, *Feminist Criticism: Women as Contemporary Critics* (Brighton: Harvester, 1986).
Jardine, Alice and Anne Menke, 'Exploding the Issue: "French" "Women" "Writers" and "The Canon" – Fourteen Interviews', in *Yale French Studies 75* (Yale University, 1988).
Jeffers, Ann and David Robey (eds), *Modern Literary Theory: A Comparative Introduction* (London: Batsford, 1982).
Jouve, Nicole Ward , *White Woman Speaks With Forked Tongue*: *Criticism as Autobiography* (London: Routledge, 1990).
Marini, Marcelle, *Territoires du féminin*, with Marguerite Duras (Paris: Minuit, 1977).
Marks, Elaine and Isabelle de Courtivron (eds), *New French Feminisms* (Brighton: Harvester, 1981).
Moi, Toril, *Sexual/Textual Politics: Feminist Literary Theory* (London: Methuen, 1985).
Norris, Christopher, *Deconstruction: Theory and Practice* (London: Methuen, 1982).
Ruthven, K.K., *Feminist Literary Studies: An Introduction* (University of Cambridge Press, 1984).
Selden, Raman, *Contemporary Literary Theory* (Brighton: Harvester, 1985).
Sperber, Dan, 'Claude Lévi-Strauss', in *Structuralism and Since: From Lévi-Strauss to Derrida*, John Sturrock (ed.), (Oxford University Press, 1979).
Sturrock, John, 'Roland Barthes', in *Structuralism and Since: From Lévi-Strauss to Derrida*, John Sturrock (ed.) (Oxford University Press, 1979).

Tristan, Anne, *Histories d'Amour: Le Cabinet de Barbe-Bleue* (Paris: Calmann Lévy, 1979).

Weedon, Chris, *Feminist Practice and Poststructuralist Theory* (Oxford: Blackwell, 1987).

White, Hayden, 'Michel Foucault', in *Structuralism and Since: From Lévi-Strauss to Derrida*, John Sturrock (ed.) (Oxford University Press, 1979).

Whitford, Margaret, 'Luce Irigaray's Critique of Rationality' in Morwenna Griffiths and Margaret Whitford (eds), *Feminist Perspectives in Philosophy* (London: Macmillan, 1988).

—— *Luce Irigaray*: *Philosophy in the Feminine* (London: Routledge, forthcoming).

Young, Robert (ed.), *Untying the Text: A Post-Structuralist Reader* (London: Routledge and Kegan Paul, 1981).

Texts

Boissard, Janine, *Une femme neuve* (Paris: Fayard, 1980).

Cardinal, Marie, *La Clé sur la porte* (Paris: Grasset, 1972).

—— *Les Mots pour le dire* (Paris: Grasset, 1975).

Chawaf, Chantal, *Blé de semences* (Paris: Mercure de France, 1976).

—— *Landes* (Paris: Stock, 1980).

Desanti, Dominique, *Le Chemin de père* (Paris: Grasset, 1981).

Duras, Marguerite, *Le Navire Night, Césarée, Les Mains négatives, Aurélia Steiner, Aurélia Steiner, Aurélia Steiner* (Paris: Mercure de France, 1979).

Etcherelli, Claire, *Elise ou la vraie vie* (Paris: Denoël, 1967).

Gauthier, Xavière, *Rose Saignée* (Paris: des femmes, 1974).

Hyvrard, Jeanne, *Auditions musicales certains soirs d'éte* (Paris: des femmes, 1984).

—— *La Baisure*, *Que se partagent encore les eaux* (Paris: des femmes, 1984).

—— *Canal de la Toussaint* (Paris: des femmes, 1985).

—— *La Pensée corps* (Paris: des femmes, 1989).

Jouve, Nicole Ward, Le *Spectre du gris* (Paris: des femmes, 1977).

—— *Shades of Grey* (London: Virago, 1981).

Lange, Monique, *Les Cabines de bain* (Paris: Gallimard, 1982).

Leclerc, Annie, *Hommes et femmes* (Paris: Grasset, 1985).

Sallenave, Danièle, *Le Voyage d'Amsterdam ou les règles de la conversation* (Paris: Flammarion, 1977).

Wittig, Monique, *Brouillon pour un dictionnaire des amantes*, with Zeig Sande (Paris: Grasset, 1976).

Index